hawkeye

RIO BRAVO

MATT FRACTION
WRITER

ISSUE #17

CHRIS ELIOPOULOS
WITH DAVID AJA (PP. 1 & 20)
ARTISTS

JORDIE BELLAIRE
COLOR ARTIST

DAVID AJA
COVER ART

ISSUE #12

FRANCESCO FRANCAVILLA
ARTIST/COLORS/COVER

ISSUES #13, #15, #19 & #21-22

DAVID AJA
ARTIST/COVER

MATT HOLLINGSWORTH
COLOR ARTIST

CHRIS ELIOPOULOS WITH DAVID AJA (#19)
LETTERERS

DEVIN LEWIS
ASSISTANT EDITOR

TOM BRENNAN
ASSOCIATE EDITOR

SANA AMANAT & STEPHEN WACKER
EDITORS

COLLECTION EDITOR: **JENNIFER GRÜNWALD** • ASSISTANT EDITOR: **SARAH BRUNSTAD**
ASSOCIATE MANAGING EDITOR: **ALEX STARBUCK** • EDITOR, SPECIAL PROJECTS: **MARK D. BEAZLEY**
SENIOR EDITOR, SPECIAL PROJECTS: **JEFF YOUNGQUIST** • SVP PRINT, SALES & MARKETING: **DAVID GABRIEL**

EDITOR IN CHIEF: **AXEL ALONSO** • CHIEF CREATIVE OFFICER: **JOE QUESADA**
PUBLISHER: **DAN BUCKLEY** • EXECUTIVE PRODUCER: **ALAN FINE**

WKEYE VOL. 4: RIO BRAVO. Contains material originally published in magazine form as HAWKEYE #12-13, #15, #17, #19 and #21-22. First printing 2015. ISBN# 978-0-7851-8531-4. Published by MARVEL ORLDWIDE, INC., a subsidiary of MARVEL ENTERTAINMENT, LLC. OFFICE OF PUBLICATION: 135 West 50th Street, New York, NY 10020. **Printed in the U.S.A.** ALAN FINE, President, rvel Entertainment; DAN BUCKLEY, President, TV, Publishing and Brand Management; JOE QUESADA, Chief Creative Officer; TOM BREVOORT, SVP of Publishing; DAVID BOGART, SVP of Operations & Procurement, blishing; C.B. CEBULSKI, VP of International Development & Brand Management; DAVID GABRIEL, SVP Print, Sales & Marketing; JIM O'KEEFE, VP of Operations & Logistics; DAN CARR, Executive Director of Publishing chnology; SUSAN CRESPI, Editorial Operations Manager; ALEX MORALES, Publishing Operations Manager; STAN LEE, Chairman Emeritus. For information regarding advertising in Marvel Comics or on Marvel.com, ase contact Jonathan Rheingold, VP of Custom Solutions & Ad Sales, at jrheingold@marvel.com. For Marvel subscription inquiries, please call 800-217-9158. **Manufactured between 6/10/2015 and 7/13/2015 by R. DONNELLEY, INC., SALEM, VA, USA.**

987654321

17

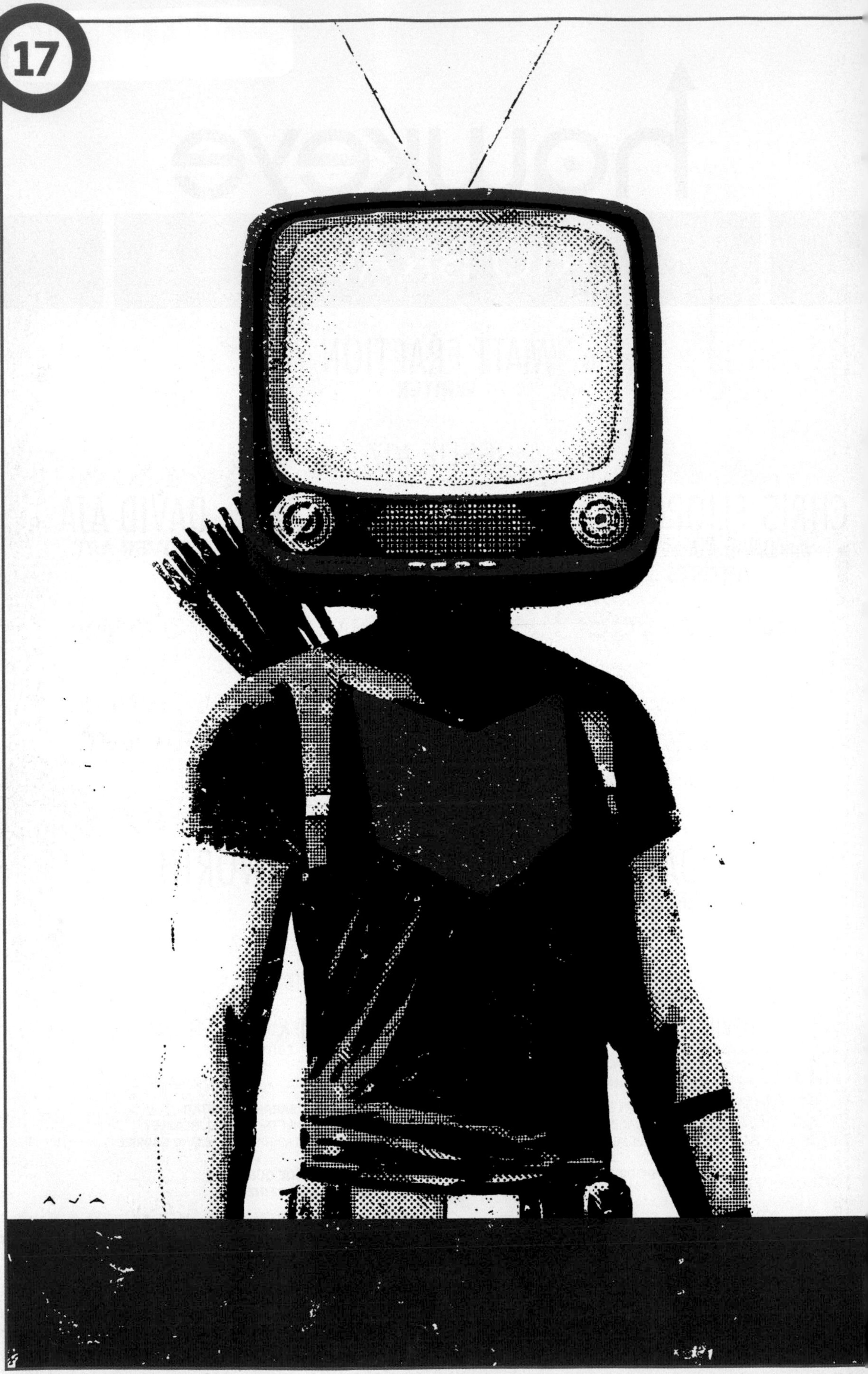

clint barton, a.k.a.

hawkeye

'twas in hawkeye #6, on the last page of the book,
clint watched christmas cartoons--no really, go look.
now it's your turn to see hawkguy's new winter friends,
and how they react when evil descends!
why are you still reading this improvised rhyme?
this is the greatest comic ever--stop wasting time!

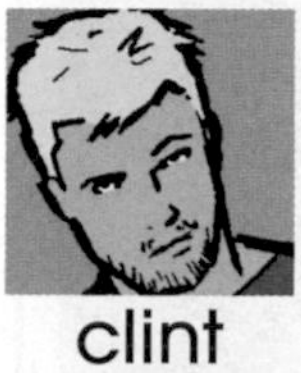

clint barton
(hawkeye)
avenger

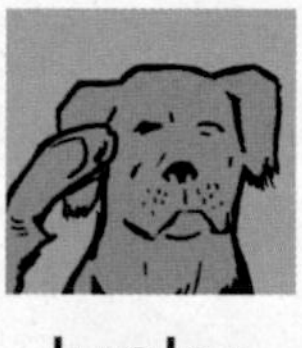

lucky
(pizza dog)

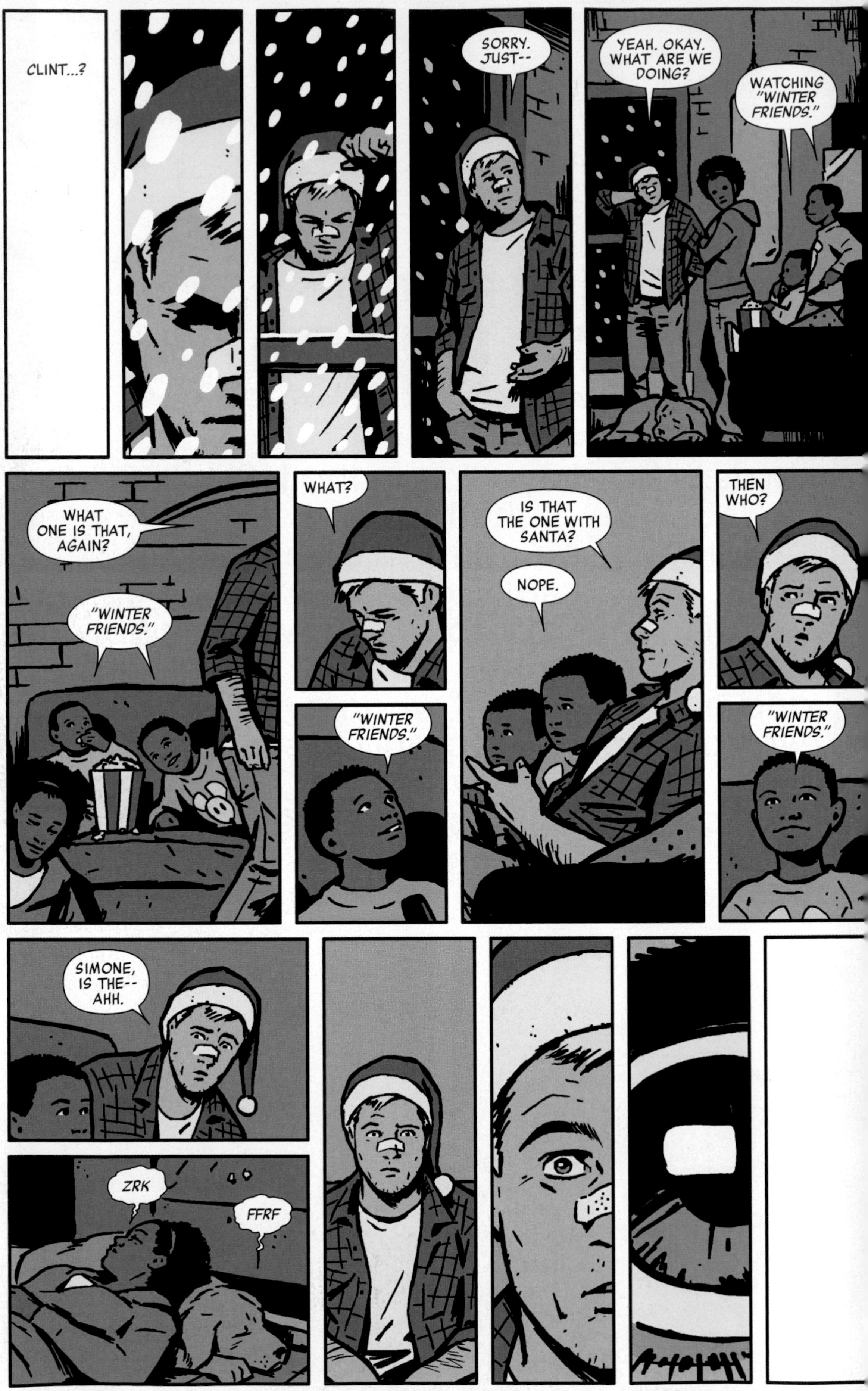
CLINT...?
SORRY. JUST--
YEAH. OKAY. WHAT ARE WE DOING?
WATCHING "WINTER FRIENDS."
WHAT ONE IS THAT, AGAIN?
"WINTER FRIENDS."
WHAT?
"WINTER FRIENDS."
IS THAT THE ONE WITH SANTA?
NOPE.
THEN WHO?
"WINTER FRIENDS."
SIMONE, IS THE-- AHH.
ZRK
FFRF

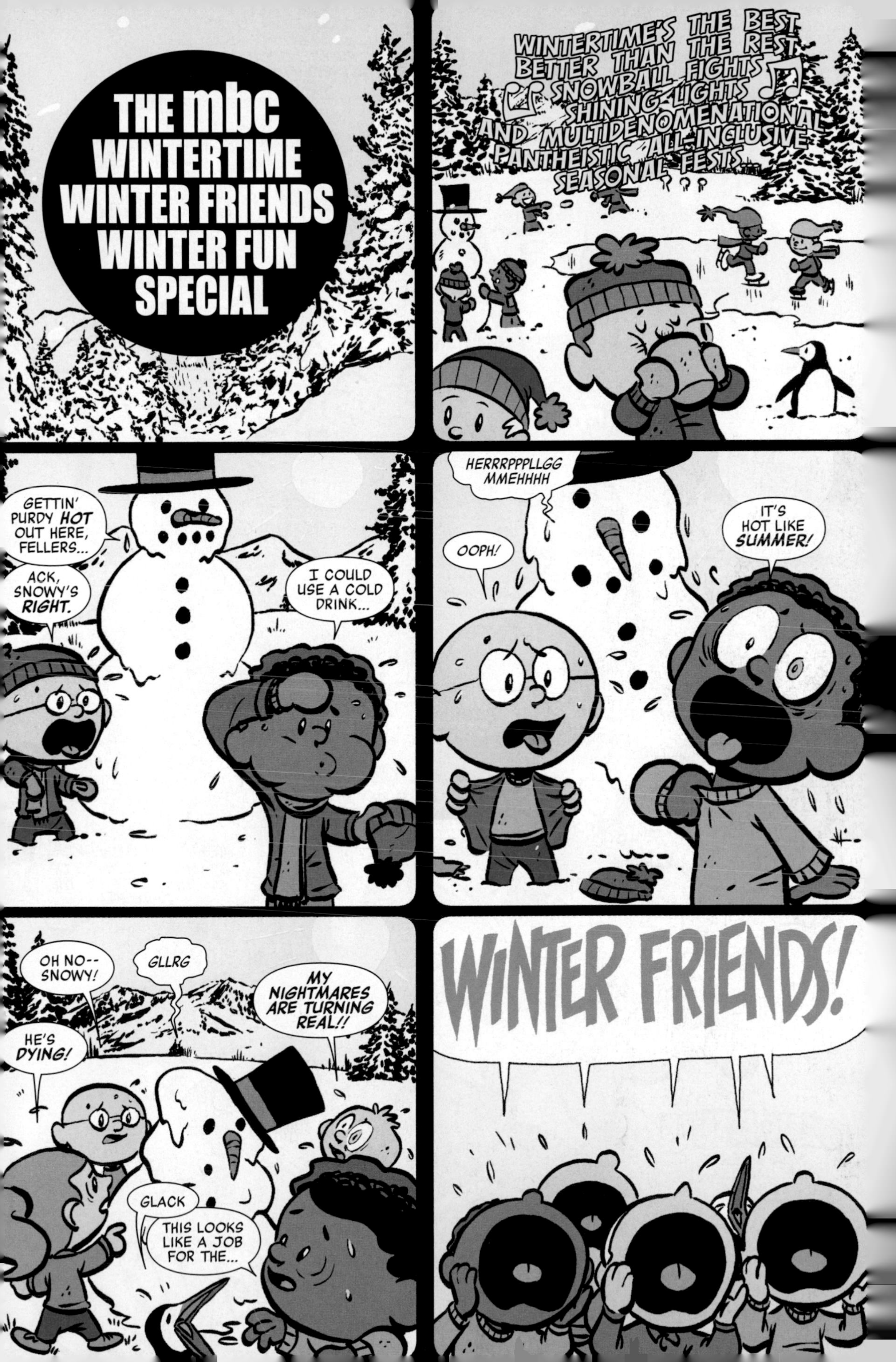
THE mbc WINTERTIME WINTER FRIENDS WINTER FUN SPECIAL
WINTERTIME'S THE BEST
BETTER THAN THE REST
SNOWBALL FIGHTS
SHINING LIGHTS
AND MULTIDENOMENATIONAL
PANTHEISTIC ALL-INCLUSIVE
SEASONAL FESTS...
GETTIN' PURDY HOT OUT HERE, FELLERS...
ACK, SNOWY'S RIGHT.
I COULD USE A COLD DRINK...
HERRRPPPLLGG MMEHHHH
OOPH!
IT'S HOT LIKE SUMMER!
OH NO-- SNOWY!
GLLRG
MY NIGHTMARES ARE TURNING REAL!!
HE'S DYING!
GLACK
THIS LOOKS LIKE A JOB FOR THE...
WINTER FRIENDS!

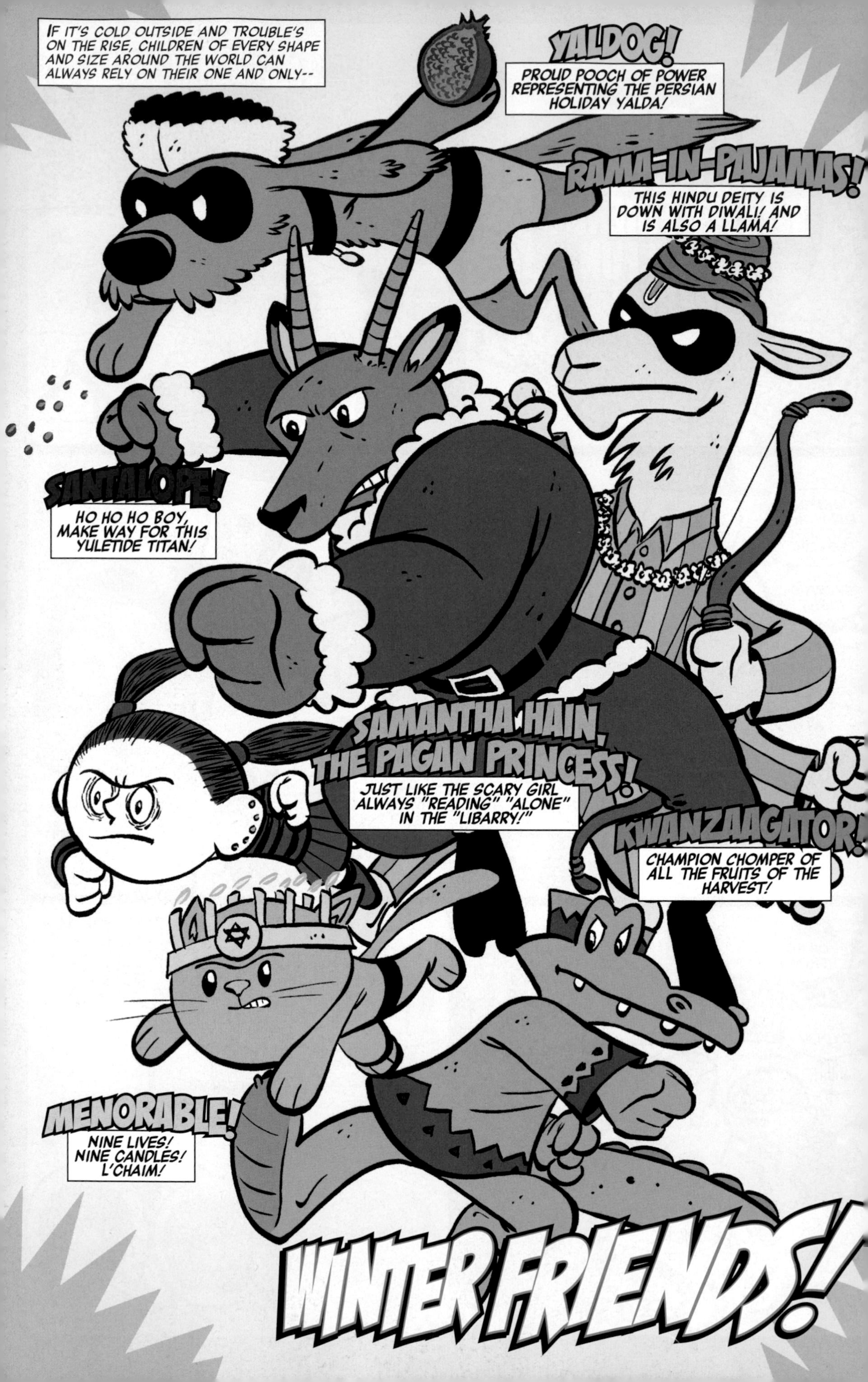
IF IT'S COLD OUTSIDE AND TROUBLE'S ON THE RISE, CHILDREN OF EVERY SHAPE AND SIZE AROUND THE WORLD CAN ALWAYS RELY ON THEIR ONE AND ONLY--
YALDOG!
PROUD POOCH OF POWER REPRESENTING THE PERSIAN HOLIDAY YALDA!
RAMA-IN-PAJAMAS!
THIS HINDU DEITY IS DOWN WITH DIWALI! AND IS ALSO A LLAMA!
SANTALOPE!
HO HO HO BOY, MAKE WAY FOR THIS YULETIDE TITAN!
SAMANTHA HAIN, THE PAGAN PRINCESS!
JUST LIKE THE SCARY GIRL ALWAYS "READING" "ALONE" IN THE "LIBARRY!"
KWANZAAGATOR!
CHAMPION CHOMPER OF ALL THE FRUITS OF THE HARVEST!
MENORABLE!
NINE LIVES! NINE CANDLES! L'CHAIM!
WINTER FRIENDS!

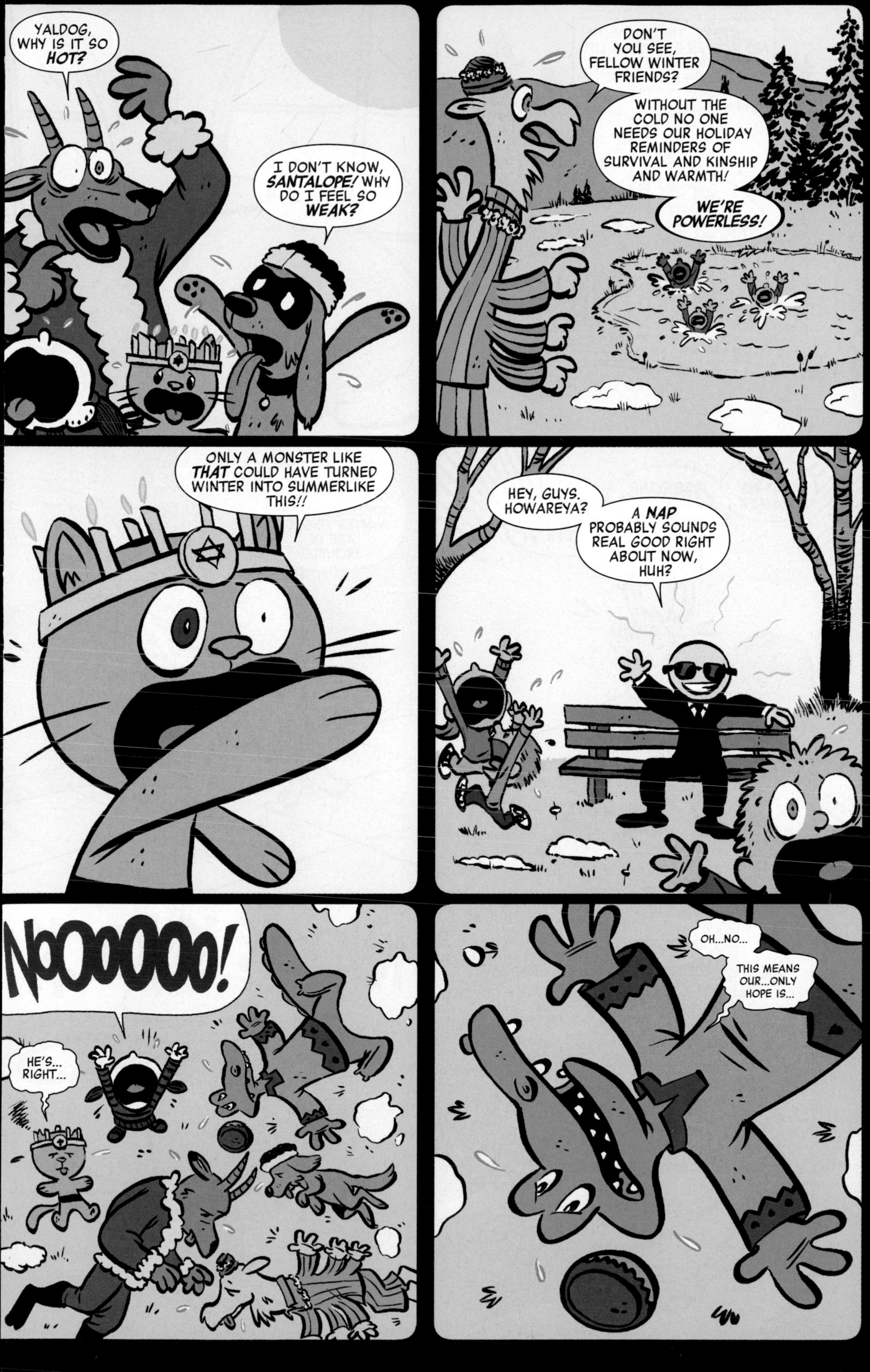
YALDOG, WHY IS IT SO HOT?
I DON'T KNOW, SANTALOPE! WHY DO I FEEL SO WEAK?
DON'T YOU SEE, FELLOW WINTER FRIENDS?
WITHOUT THE COLD NO ONE NEEDS OUR HOLIDAY REMINDERS OF SURVIVAL AND KINSHIP AND WARMTH!
WE'RE POWERLESS!
ONLY A MONSTER LIKE THAT COULD HAVE TURNED WINTER INTO SUMMERLIKE THIS!!
HEY, GUYS. HOWAREYA?
A NAP PROBABLY SOUNDS REAL GOOD RIGHT ABOUT NOW, HUH?
NOOOOOO!
HE'S... RIGHT...
OH...NO...
THIS MEANS OUR...ONLY HOPE IS...

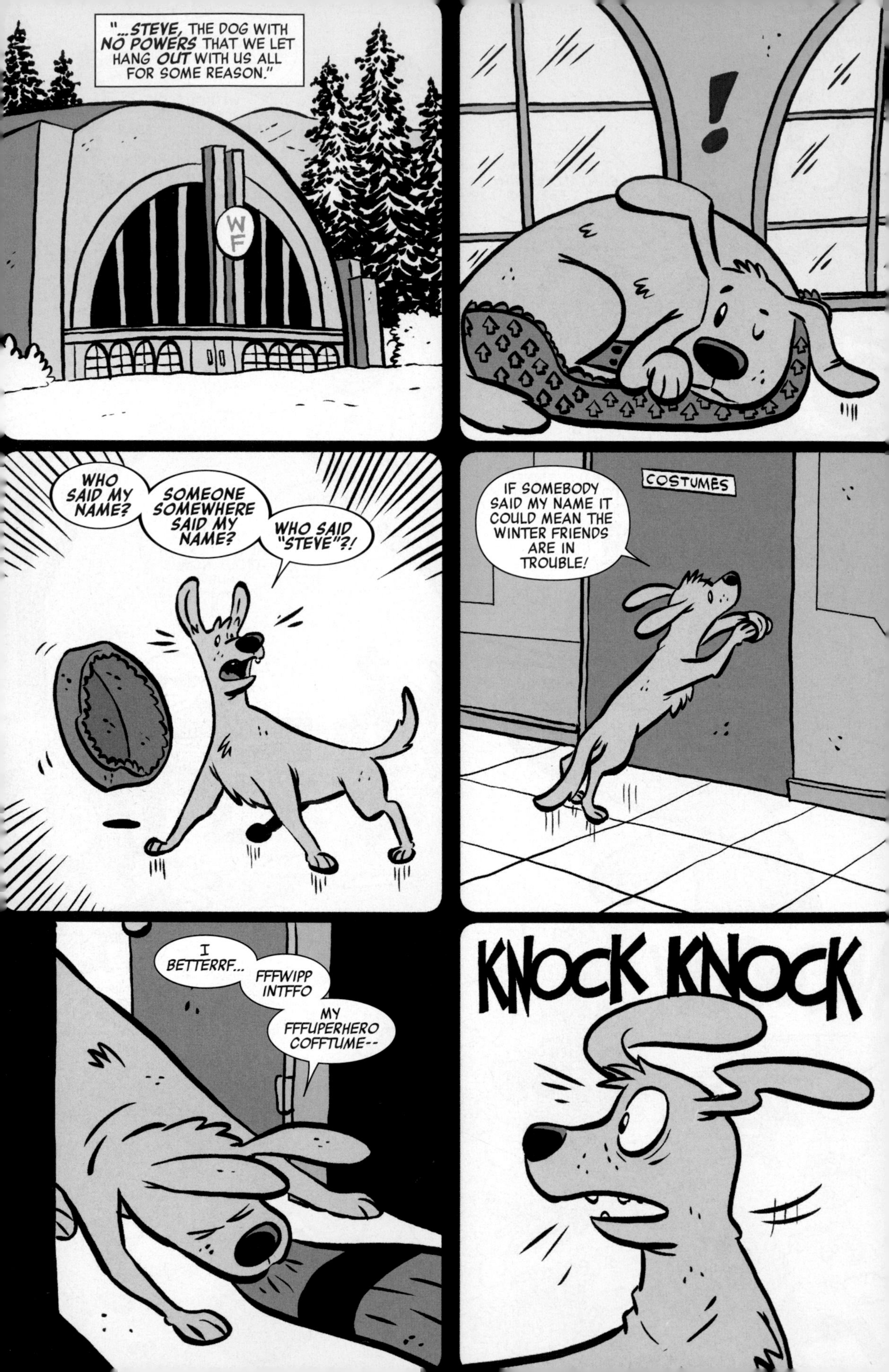
"...STEVE, THE DOG WITH NO POWERS THAT WE LET HANG OUT WITH US ALL FOR SOME REASON."
WF
!
WHO SAID MY NAME?
SOMEONE SOMEWHERE SAID MY NAME?
WHO SAID "STEVE"?!
COSTUMES
IF SOMEBODY SAID MY NAME IT COULD MEAN THE WINTER FRIENDS ARE IN TROUBLE!
I BETTERRF...
FFFWIPP INTFFO
MY FFFUPERHERO COFFTUME--
KNOCK KNOCK

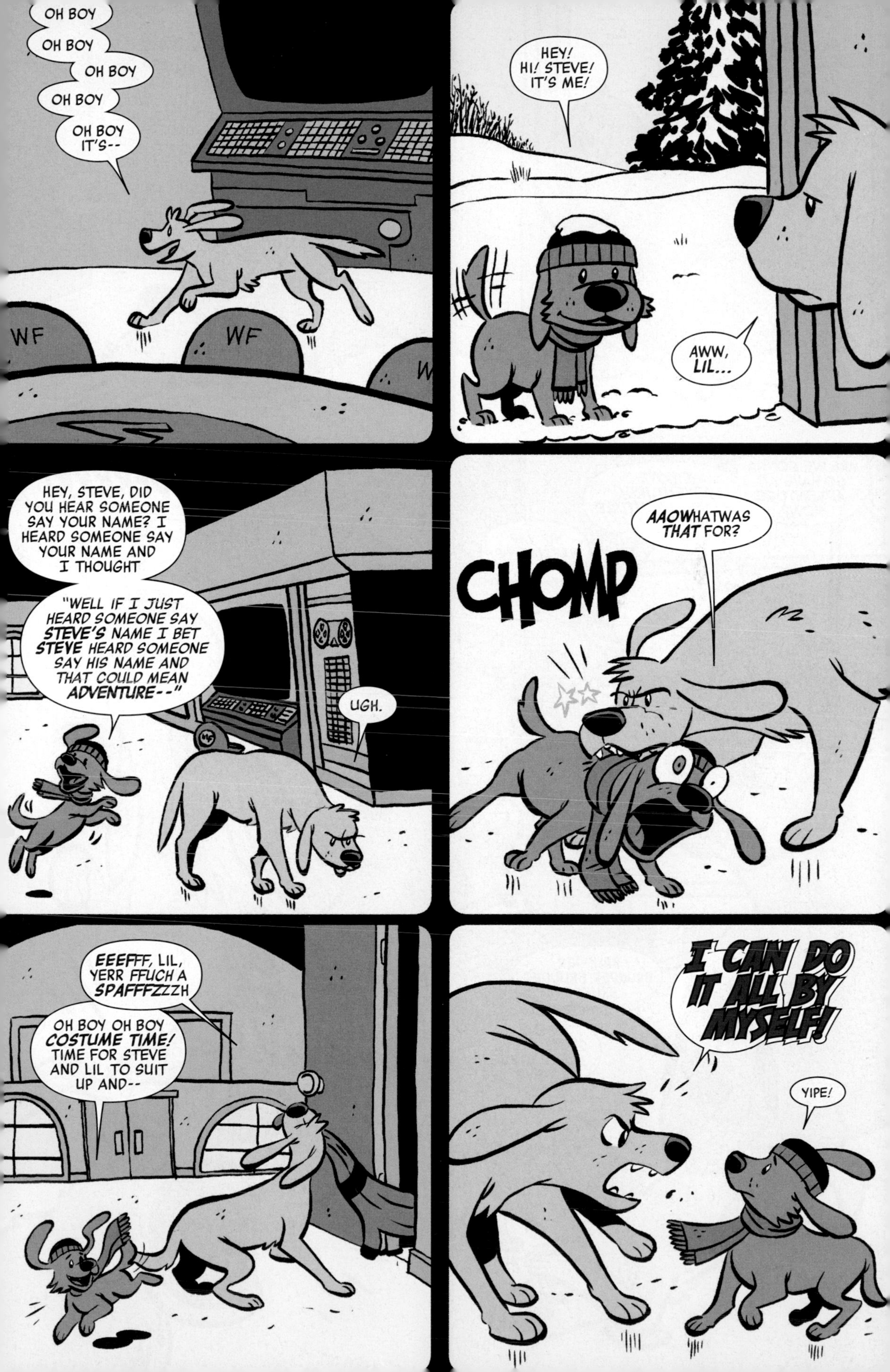
OH BOY
OH BOY
OH BOY
OH BOY
OH BOY IT'S--
HEY! HI! STEVE! IT'S ME!
AWW, LIL...
HEY, STEVE, DID YOU HEAR SOMEONE SAY YOUR NAME? I HEARD SOMEONE SAY YOUR NAME AND I THOUGHT
"WELL IF I JUST HEARD SOMEONE SAY STEVE'S NAME I BET STEVE HEARD SOMEONE SAY HIS NAME AND THAT COULD MEAN ADVENTURE--"
UGH.
CHOMP
AAOWHATWAS THAT FOR?
EEEFFF, LIL, YERR FFUCH A SPAFFFZZZH
OH BOY OH BOY COSTUME TIME! TIME FOR STEVE AND LIL TO SUIT UP AND--
I CAN DO IT ALL BY MYSELF!
YIPE!

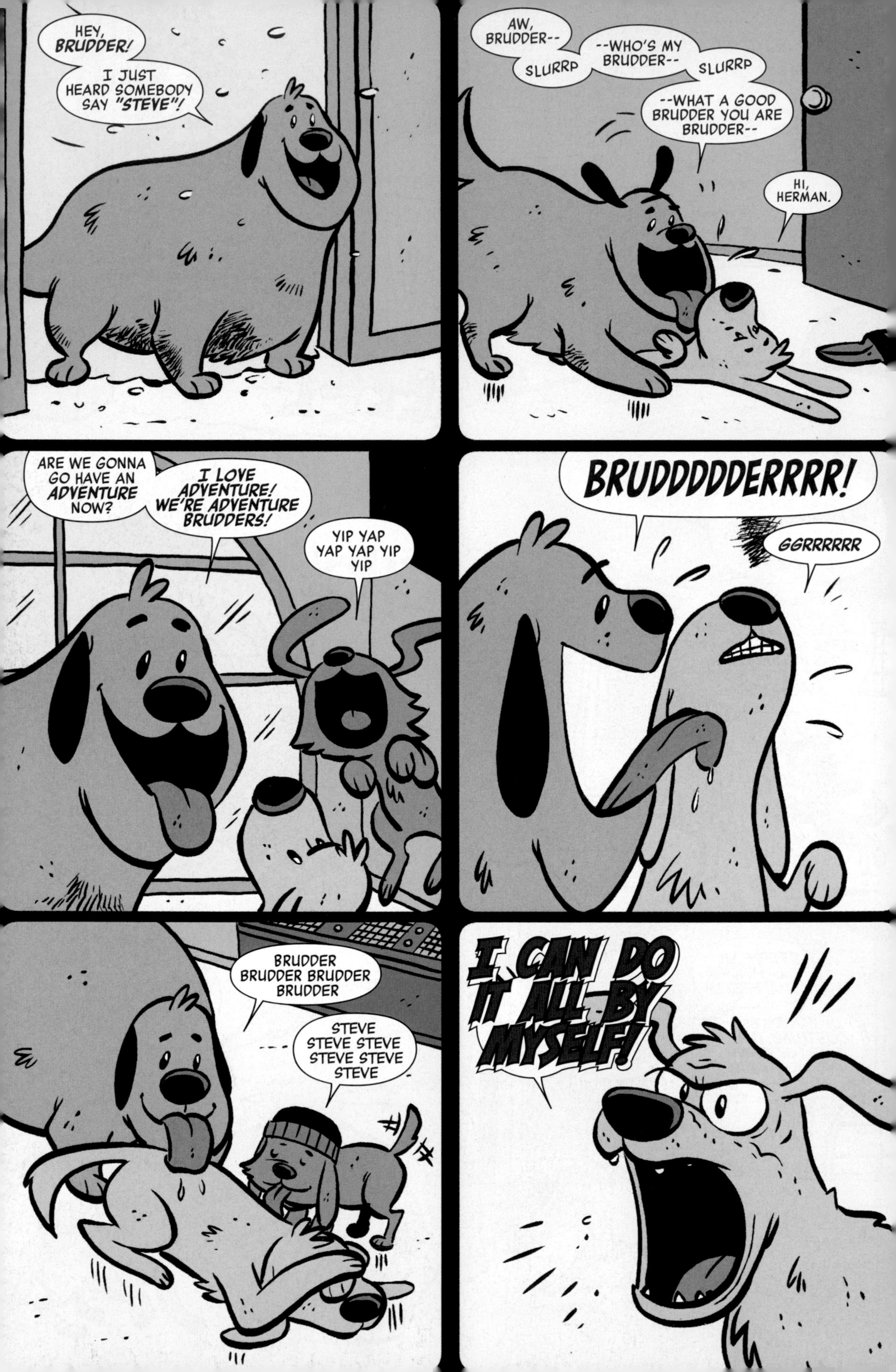
HEY, BRUDDER!
I JUST HEARD SOMEBODY SAY "STEVE"!
AW, BRUDDER--
SLURRP
--WHO'S MY BRUDDER--
SLURRP
--WHAT A GOOD BRUDDER YOU ARE BRUDDER--
HI, HERMAN.
ARE WE GONNA GO HAVE AN ADVENTURE NOW?
I LOVE ADVENTURE! WE'RE ADVENTURE BRUDDERS!
YIP YAP YAP YAP YIP YIP
BRUDDDDDERRRR!
GGRRRRRR
BRUDDER BRUDDER BRUDDER BRUDDER
STEVE STEVE STEVE STEVE STEVE STEVE
I CAN DO IT ALL BY MYSELF!

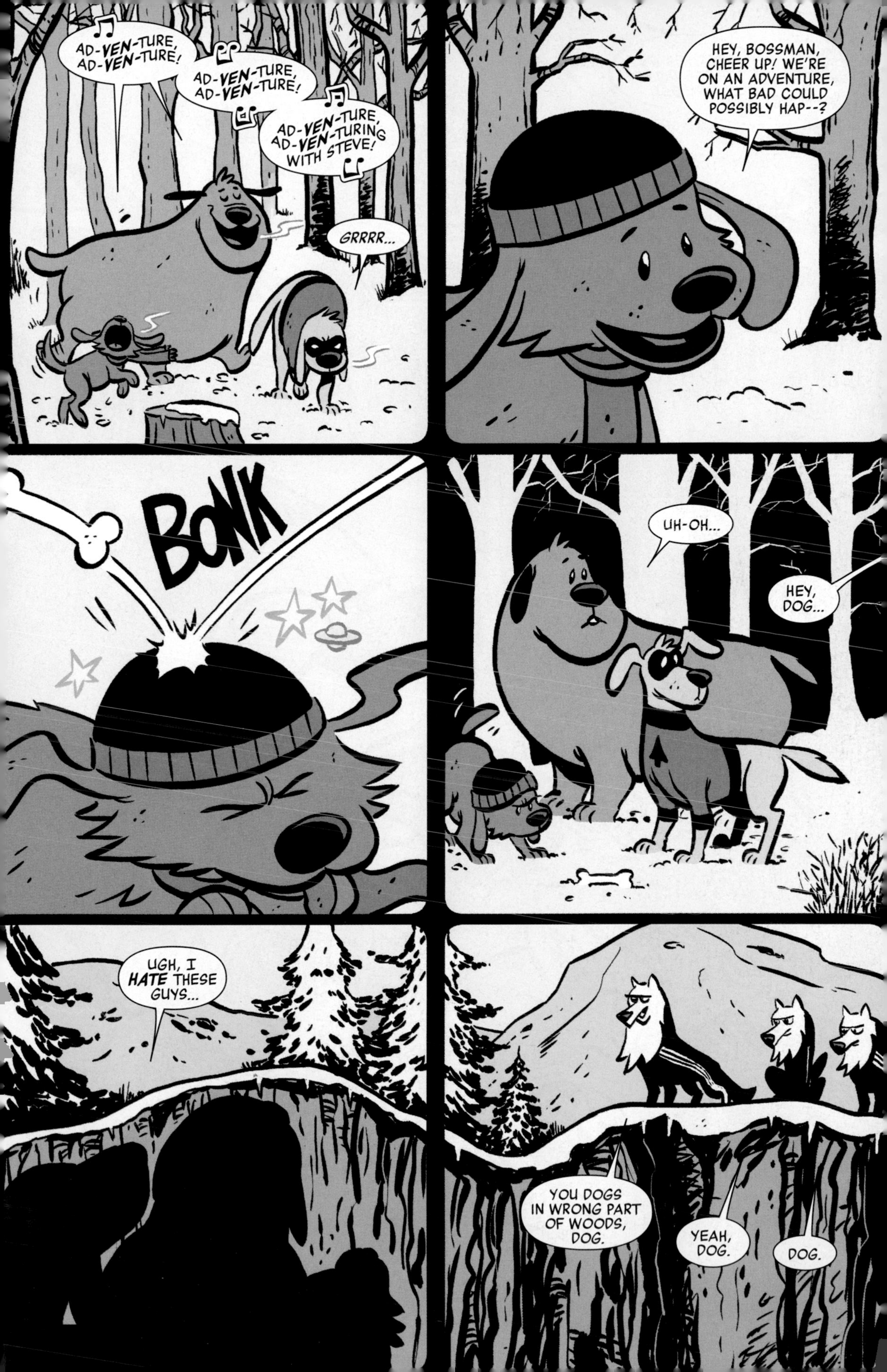
AD-VEN-TURE, AD-VEN-TURE!
AD-VEN-TURE, AD-VEN-TURE!
AD-VEN-TURE, AD-VEN-TURING WITH STEVE!
GRRRR...
HEY, BOSSMAN, CHEER UP! WE'RE ON AN ADVENTURE, WHAT BAD COULD POSSIBLY HAP--?
BONK
UH-OH...
HEY, DOG...
UGH, I HATE THESE GUYS...
YOU DOGS IN WRONG PART OF WOODS, DOG.
YEAH, DOG.
DOG.

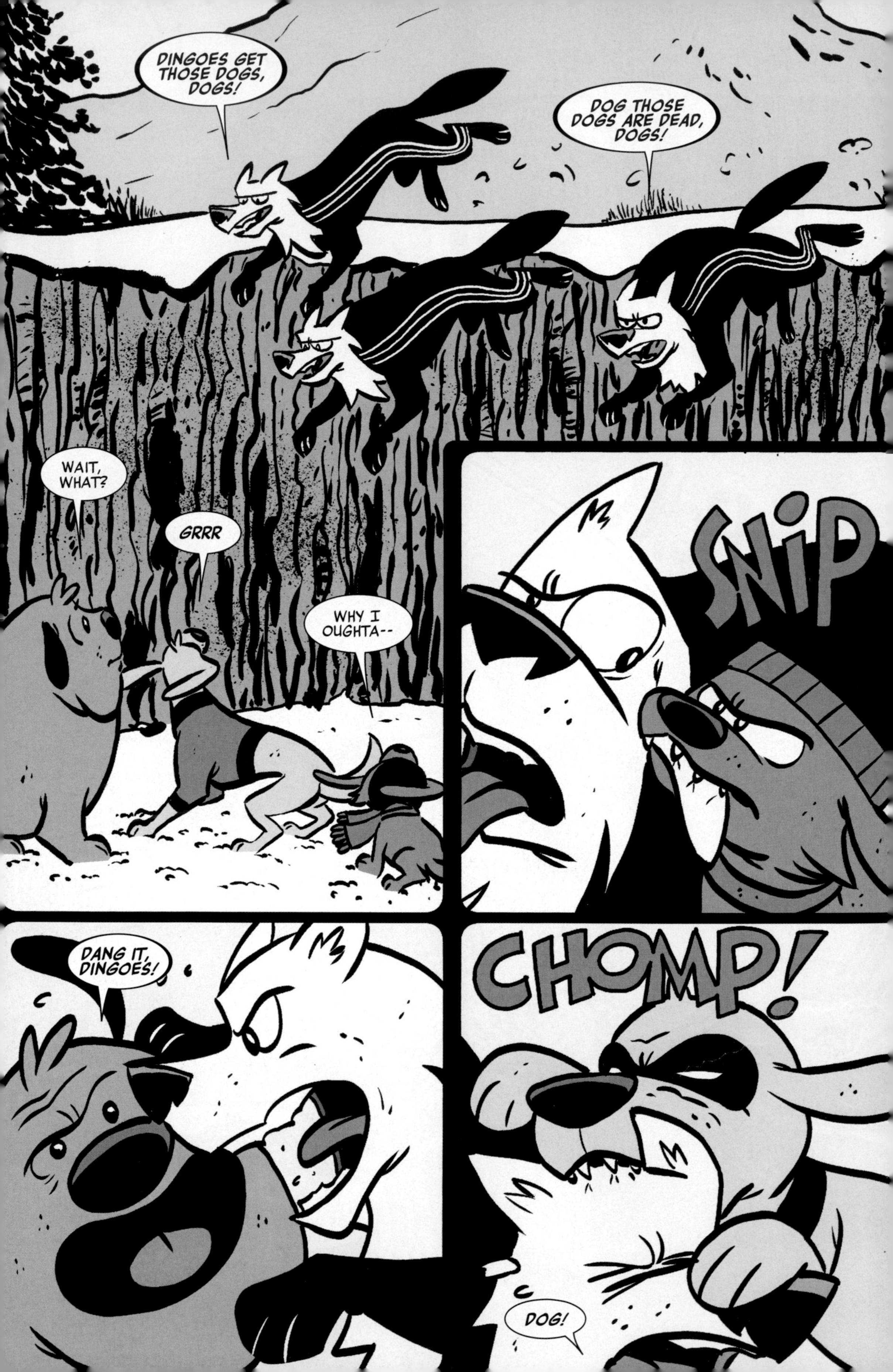
DINGOES GET THOSE DOGS, DOGS!
DOG THOSE DOGS ARE DEAD, DOGS!
WAIT, WHAT?
GRRR
WHY I OUGHTA--
SNIP
DANG IT, DINGOES!
CHOMP!
DOG!

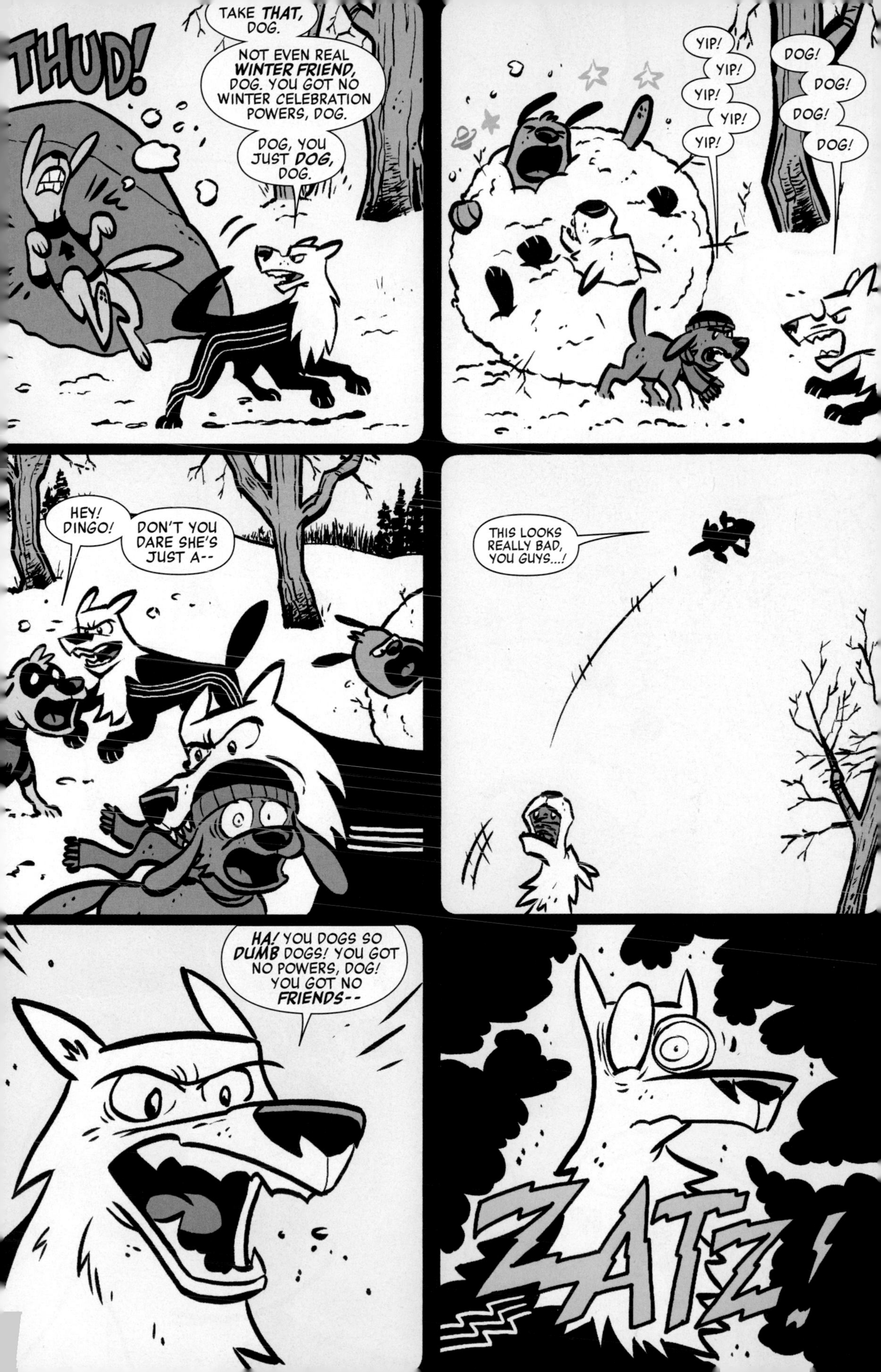
THUD!
TAKE **THAT**, DOG.
NOT EVEN REAL **WINTER FRIEND**, DOG. YOU GOT NO WINTER CELEBRATION POWERS, DOG.
DOG, YOU JUST **DOG**, DOG.
YIP! YIP! YIP! YIP! YIP!
DOG! DOG! DOG! DOG!
HEY! DINGO!
DON'T YOU DARE SHE'S JUST A--
THIS LOOKS REALLY BAD, YOU GUYS...!
HA! YOU DOGS SO **DUMB** DOGS! YOU GOT NO POWERS, DOG! YOU GOT NO **FRIENDS--**
ZATZ!

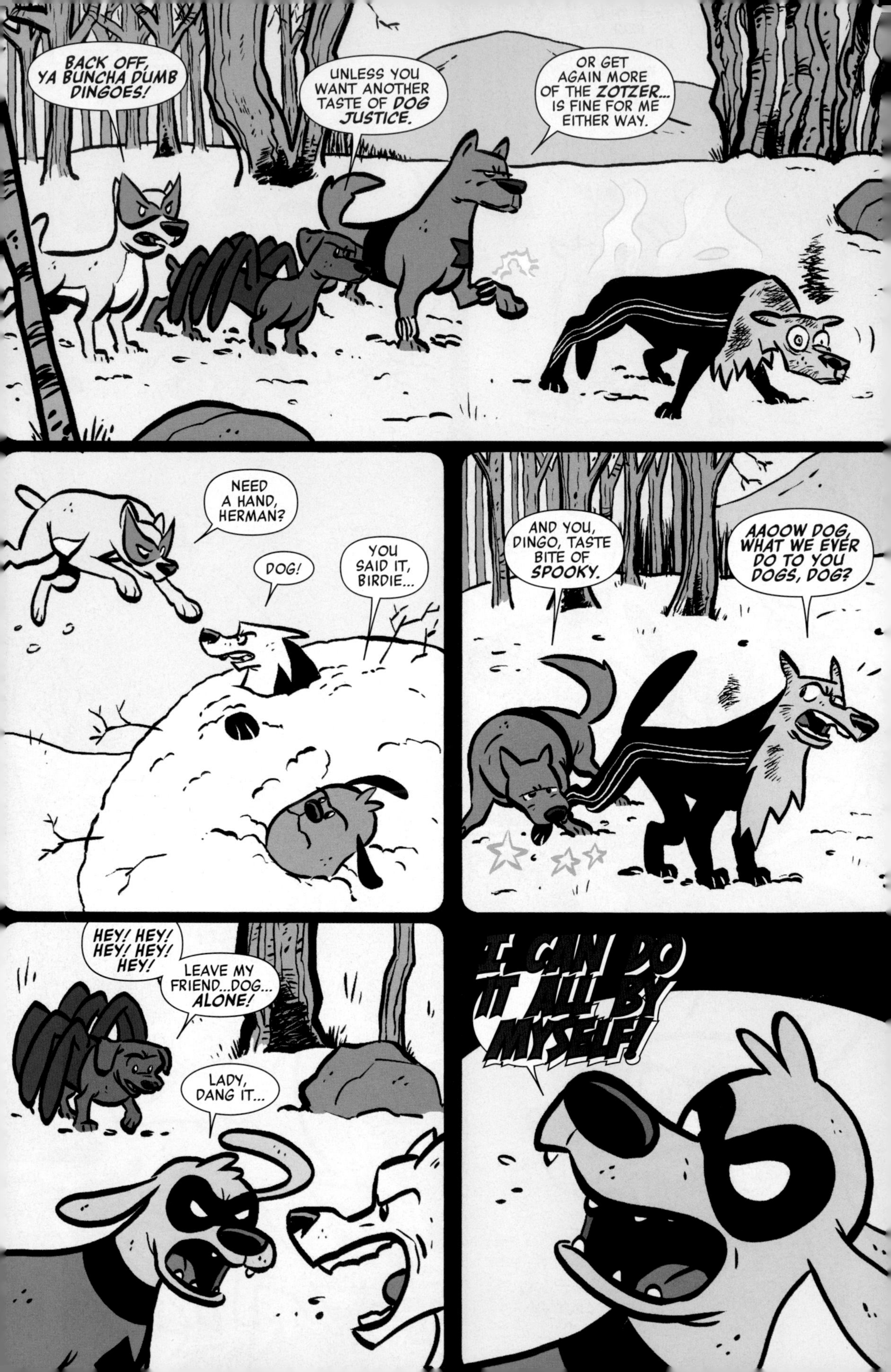
BACK OFF, YA BUNCHA DUMB DINGOES!
UNLESS YOU WANT ANOTHER TASTE OF DOG JUSTICE.
OR GET AGAIN MORE OF THE ZOTZER... IS FINE FOR ME EITHER WAY.
NEED A HAND, HERMAN?
DOG!
YOU SAID IT, BIRDIE...
AND YOU, DINGO, TASTE BITE OF SPOOKY.
AAOOW DOG, WHAT WE EVER DO TO YOU DOGS, DOG?
HEY! HEY! HEY! HEY! HEY!
LEAVE MY FRIEND...DOG... ALONE!
LADY, DANG IT...
I CAN DO IT ALL BY MYSELF!

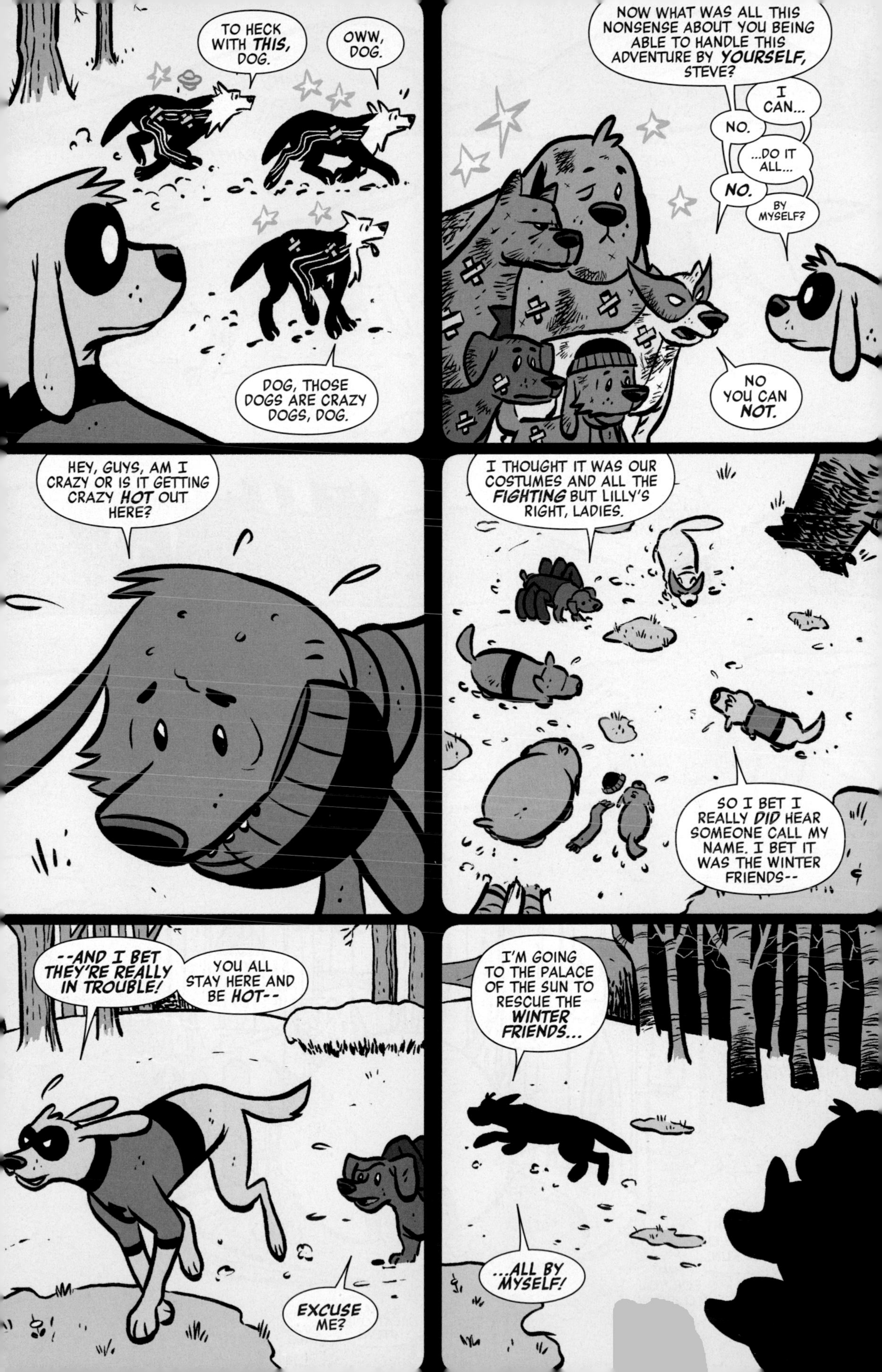

TO HECK WITH THIS, DOG.
OWW, DOG.
DOG, THOSE DOGS ARE CRAZY DOGS, DOG.
NOW WHAT WAS ALL THIS NONSENSE ABOUT YOU BEING ABLE TO HANDLE THIS ADVENTURE BY YOURSELF, STEVE?
I CAN...
NO.
...DO IT ALL...
NO.
BY MYSELF?
NO YOU CAN NOT.
HEY, GUYS, AM I CRAZY OR IS IT GETTING CRAZY HOT OUT HERE?
I THOUGHT IT WAS OUR COSTUMES AND ALL THE FIGHTING BUT LILLY'S RIGHT, LADIES.
SO I BET I REALLY DID HEAR SOMEONE CALL MY NAME. I BET IT WAS THE WINTER FRIENDS--
--AND I BET THEY'RE REALLY IN TROUBLE!
YOU ALL STAY HERE AND BE HOT--
EXCUSE ME?
I'M GOING TO THE PALACE OF THE SUN TO RESCUE THE WINTER FRIENDS...
...ALL BY MYSELF!

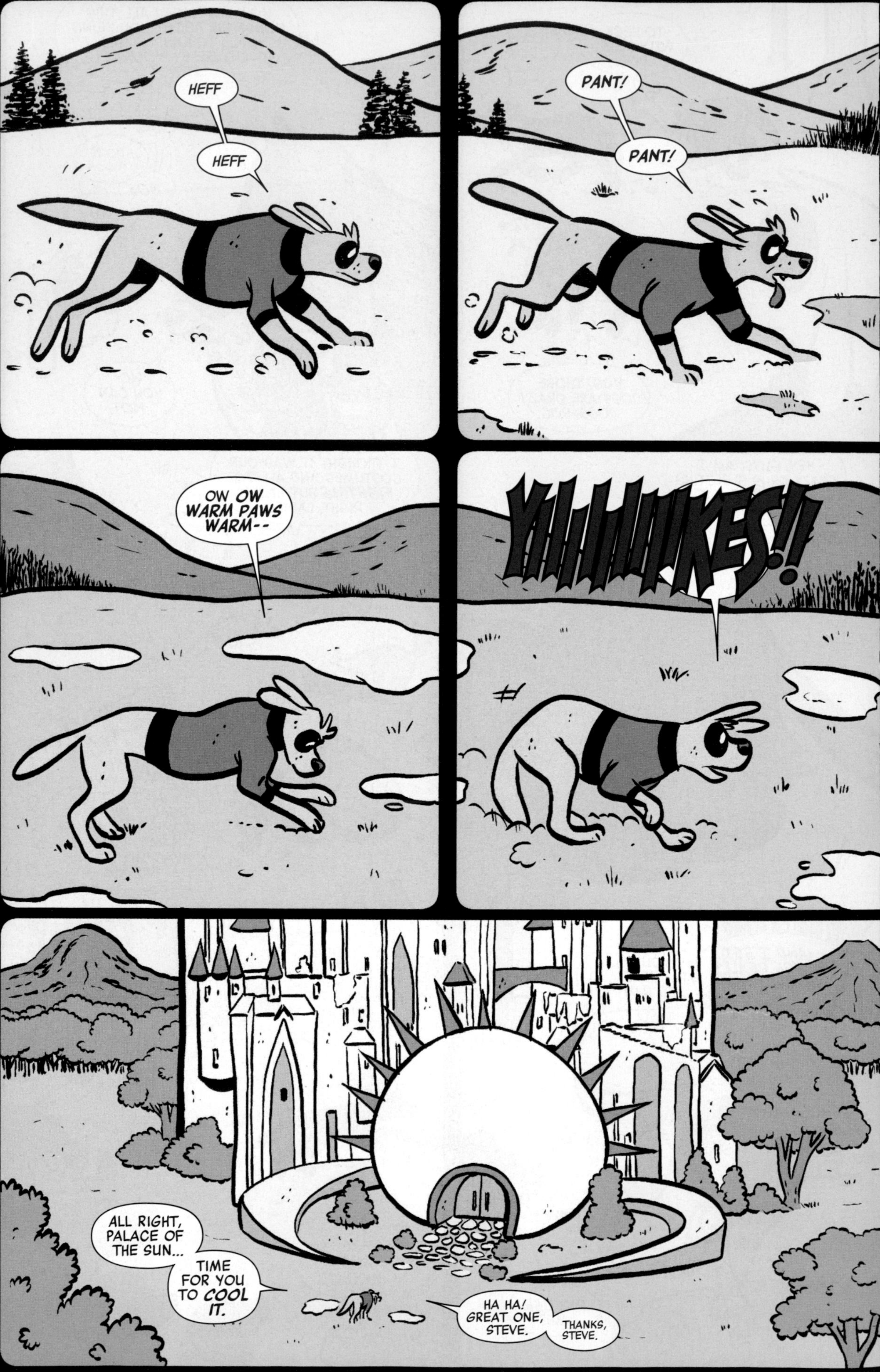
HEFF
HEFF
PANT!
PANT!
OW OW WARM PAWS WARM--
YIIIIIIIKES!!
ALL RIGHT, PALACE OF THE SUN...
TIME FOR YOU TO COOL IT.
HA HA! GREAT ONE, STEVE.
THANKS, STEVE.

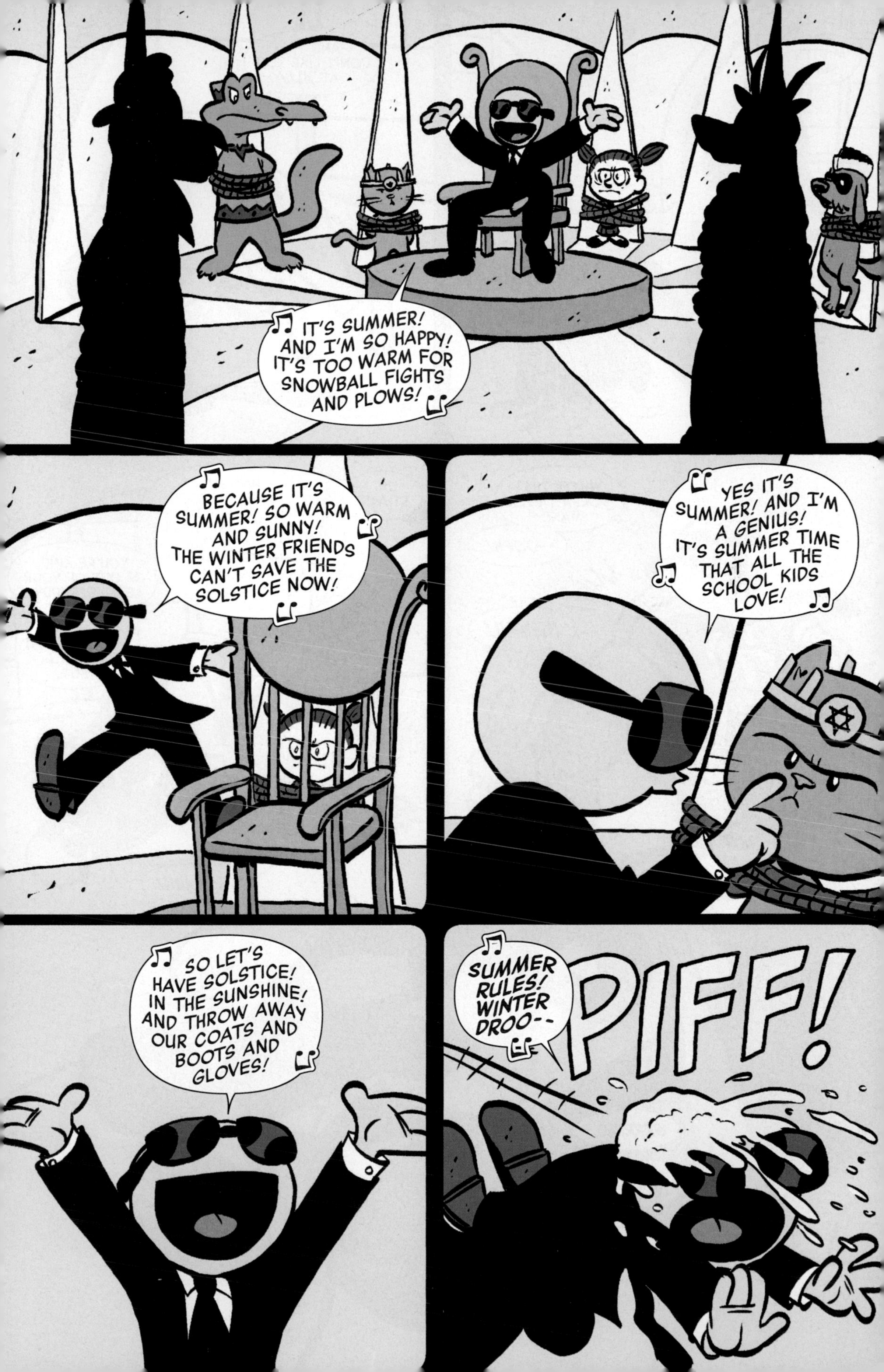
IT'S SUMMER! AND I'M SO HAPPY! IT'S TOO WARM FOR SNOWBALL FIGHTS AND PLOWS!
BECAUSE IT'S SUMMER! SO WARM AND SUNNY! THE WINTER FRIENDS CAN'T SAVE THE SOLSTICE NOW!
YES IT'S SUMMER! AND I'M A GENIUS! IT'S SUMMER TIME THAT ALL THE SCHOOL KIDS LOVE!
SO LET'S HAVE SOLSTICE! IN THE SUNSHINE! AND THROW AWAY OUR COATS AND BOOTS AND GLOVES!
SUMMER RULES! WINTER DROO--
PIFF!

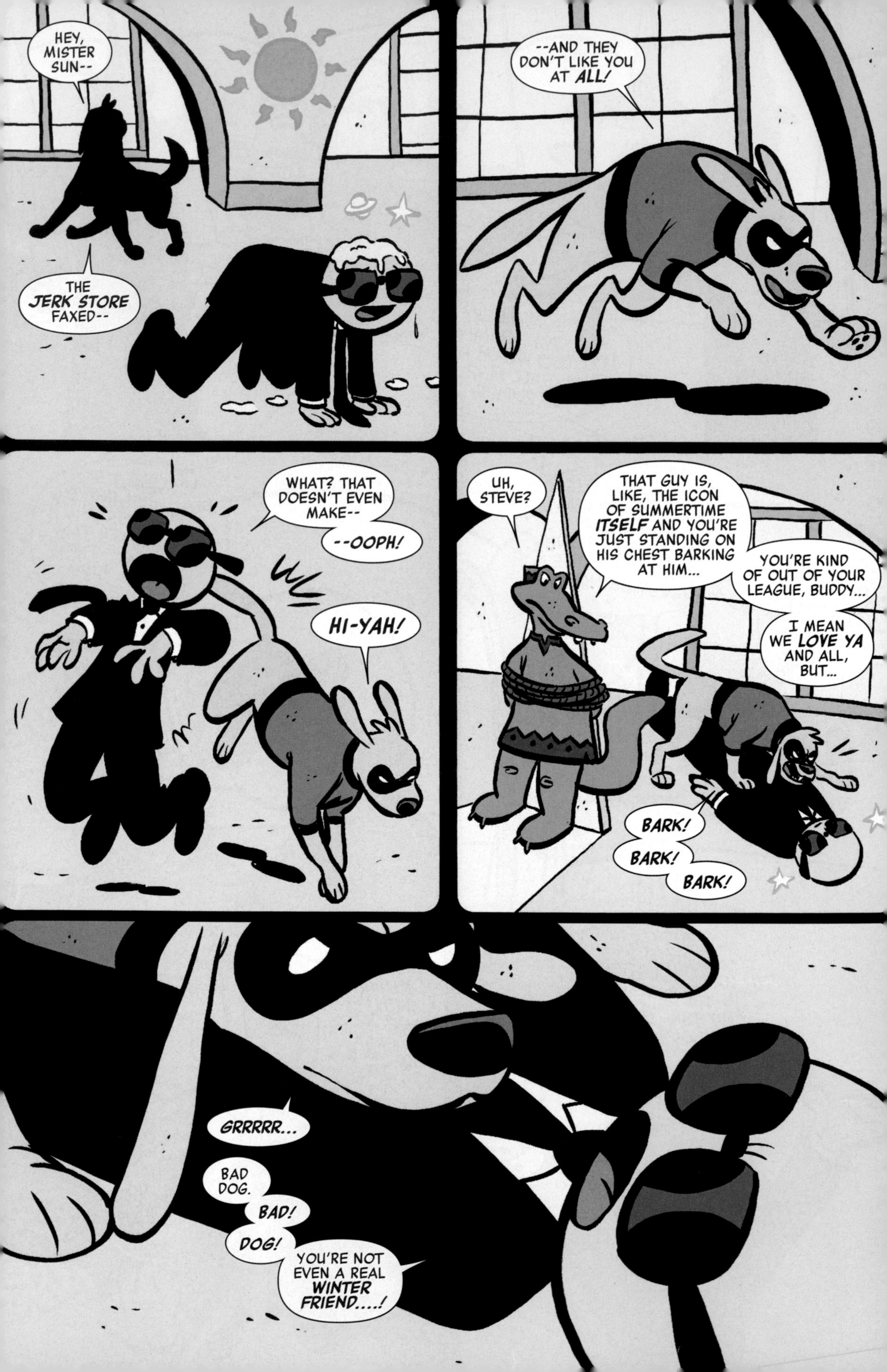

HEY, MISTER SUN--
THE JERK STORE FAXED--
--AND THEY DON'T LIKE YOU AT ALL!
WHAT? THAT DOESN'T EVEN MAKE--
--OOPH!
HI-YAH!
UH, STEVE?
THAT GUY IS, LIKE, THE ICON OF SUMMERTIME ITSELF AND YOU'RE JUST STANDING ON HIS CHEST BARKING AT HIM...
YOU'RE KIND OF OUT OF YOUR LEAGUE, BUDDY...
I MEAN WE LOVE YA AND ALL, BUT...
BARK!
BARK!
BARK!
GRRRRR...
BAD DOG.
BAD!
DOG!
YOU'RE NOT EVEN A REAL WINTER FRIEND....!

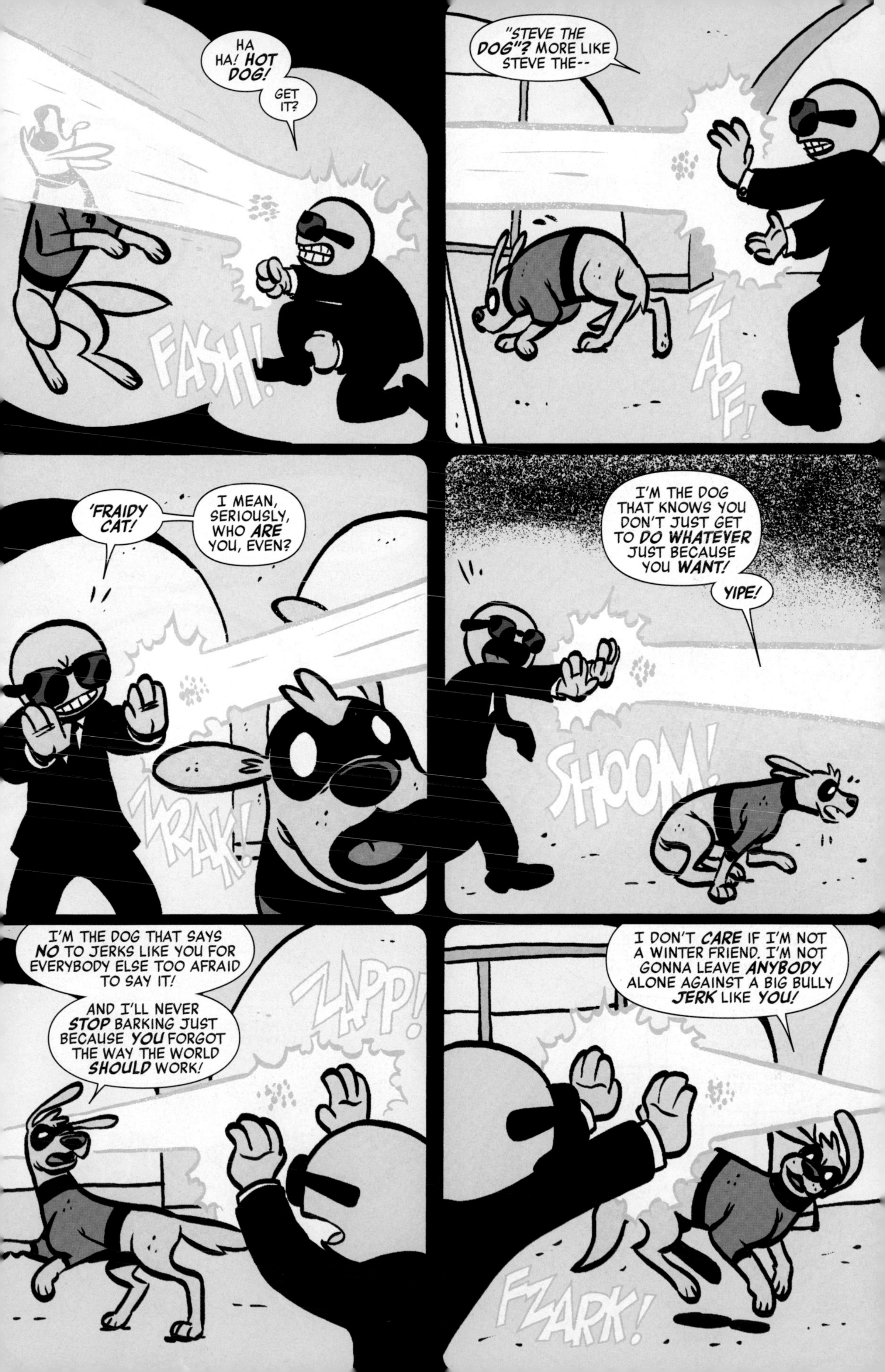
HA HA! HOT DOG!
GET IT?
FASH!
"STEVE THE DOG"? MORE LIKE STEVE THE--
ZAPF!
'FRAIDY CAT!
I MEAN, SERIOUSLY, WHO ARE YOU, EVEN?
MRAK!
I'M THE DOG THAT KNOWS YOU DON'T JUST GET TO DO WHATEVER JUST BECAUSE YOU WANT!
YIPE!
SHOOM!
I'M THE DOG THAT SAYS NO TO JERKS LIKE YOU FOR EVERYBODY ELSE TOO AFRAID TO SAY IT!
AND I'LL NEVER STOP BARKING JUST BECAUSE YOU FORGOT THE WAY THE WORLD SHOULD WORK!
ZAPP!
I DON'T CARE IF I'M NOT A WINTER FRIEND. I'M NOT GONNA LEAVE ANYBODY ALONE AGAINST A BIG BULLY JERK LIKE YOU!
FZARK!

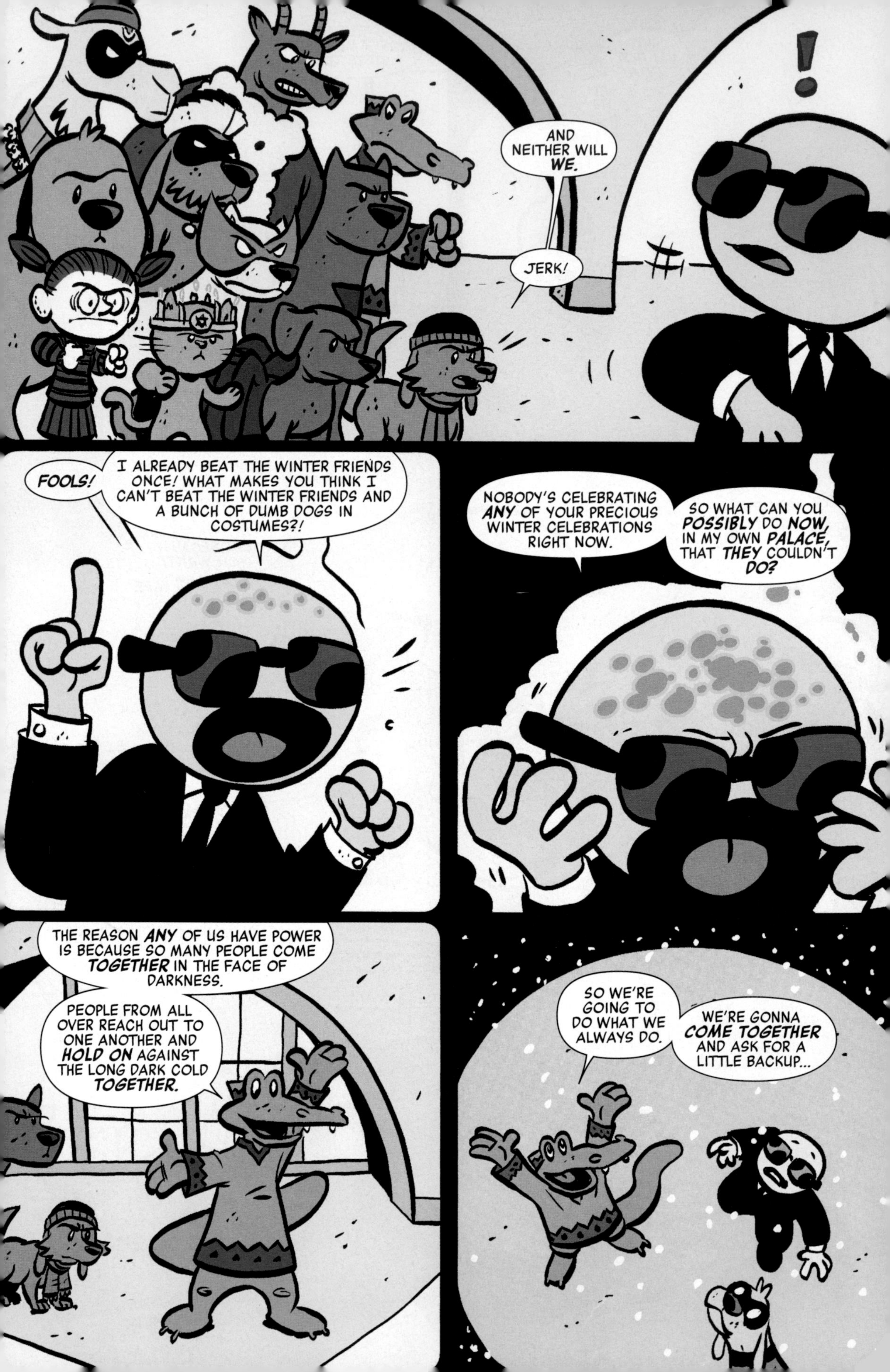
!
AND NEITHER WILL WE.
JERK!
FOOLS!
I ALREADY BEAT THE WINTER FRIENDS ONCE! WHAT MAKES YOU THINK I CAN'T BEAT THE WINTER FRIENDS AND A BUNCH OF DUMB DOGS IN COSTUMES?!
NOBODY'S CELEBRATING ANY OF YOUR PRECIOUS WINTER CELEBRATIONS RIGHT NOW.
SO WHAT CAN YOU POSSIBLY DO NOW, IN MY OWN PALACE, THAT THEY COULDN'T DO?
THE REASON ANY OF US HAVE POWER IS BECAUSE SO MANY PEOPLE COME TOGETHER IN THE FACE OF DARKNESS.
PEOPLE FROM ALL OVER REACH OUT TO ONE ANOTHER AND HOLD ON AGAINST THE LONG DARK COLD TOGETHER.
SO WE'RE GOING TO DO WHAT WE ALWAYS DO.
WE'RE GONNA COME TOGETHER AND ASK FOR A LITTLE BACKUP...

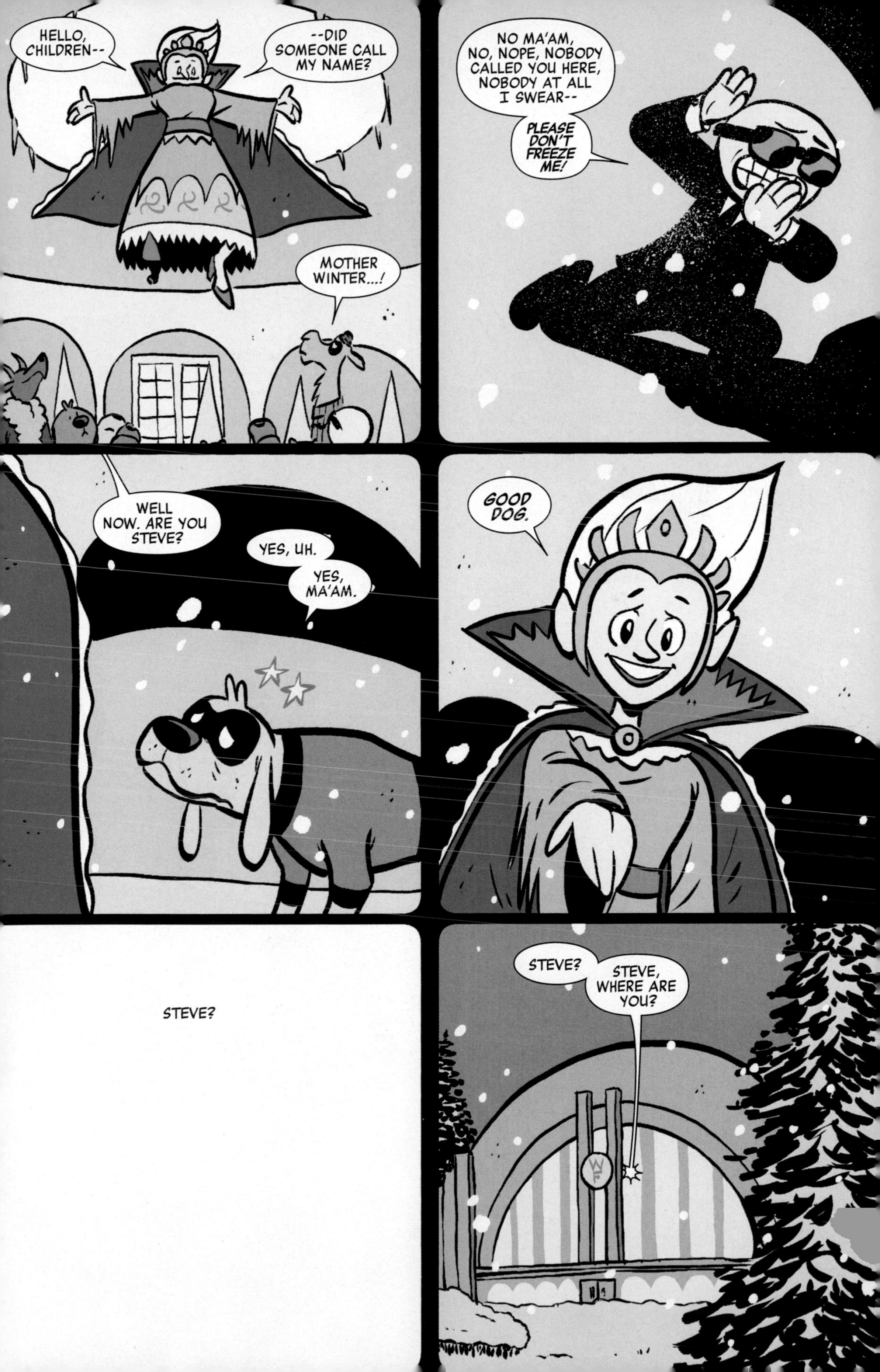
HELLO, CHILDREN--
--DID SOMEONE CALL MY NAME?
MOTHER WINTER...!
NO MA'AM, NO, NOPE, NOBODY CALLED YOU HERE, NOBODY AT ALL I SWEAR--
PLEASE DON'T FREEZE ME!
WELL NOW. ARE YOU STEVE?
YES, UH.
YES, MA'AM.
GOOD DOG.
STEVE?
STEVE?
STEVE, WHERE ARE YOU?

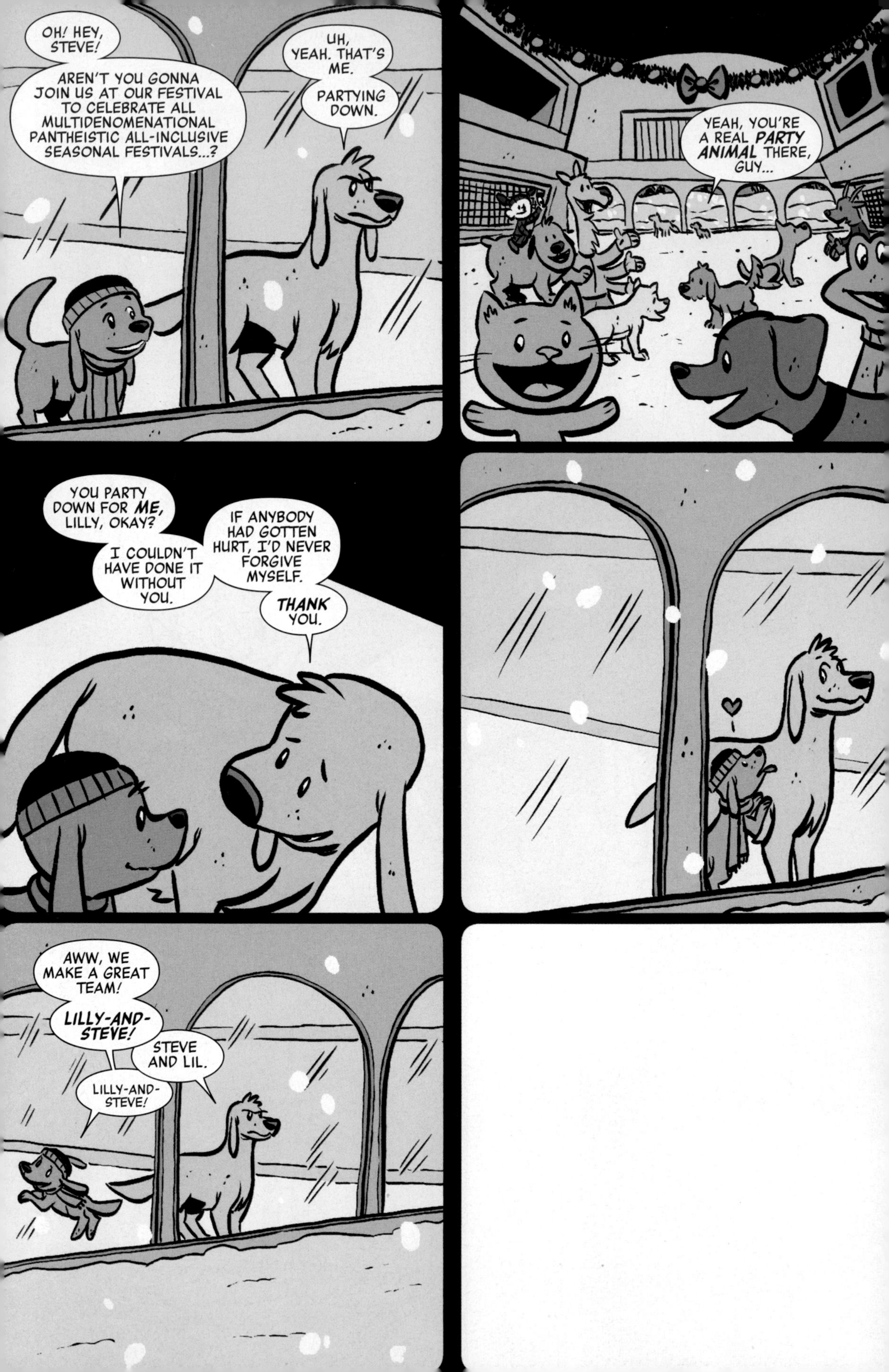
OH! HEY, STEVE!
AREN'T YOU GONNA JOIN US AT OUR FESTIVAL TO CELEBRATE ALL MULTIDENOMENATIONAL PANTHEISTIC ALL-INCLUSIVE SEASONAL FESTIVALS...?
UH, YEAH. THAT'S ME.
PARTYING DOWN.
YEAH, YOU'RE A REAL **PARTY ANIMAL** THERE, GUY...
YOU PARTY DOWN FOR *ME*, LILLY, OKAY?
I COULDN'T HAVE DONE IT WITHOUT YOU.
IF ANYBODY HAD GOTTEN HURT, I'D NEVER FORGIVE MYSELF.
THANK YOU.
AWW, WE MAKE A GREAT TEAM!
LILLY-AND-STEVE!
STEVE AND LIL.
LILLY-AND-STEVE!

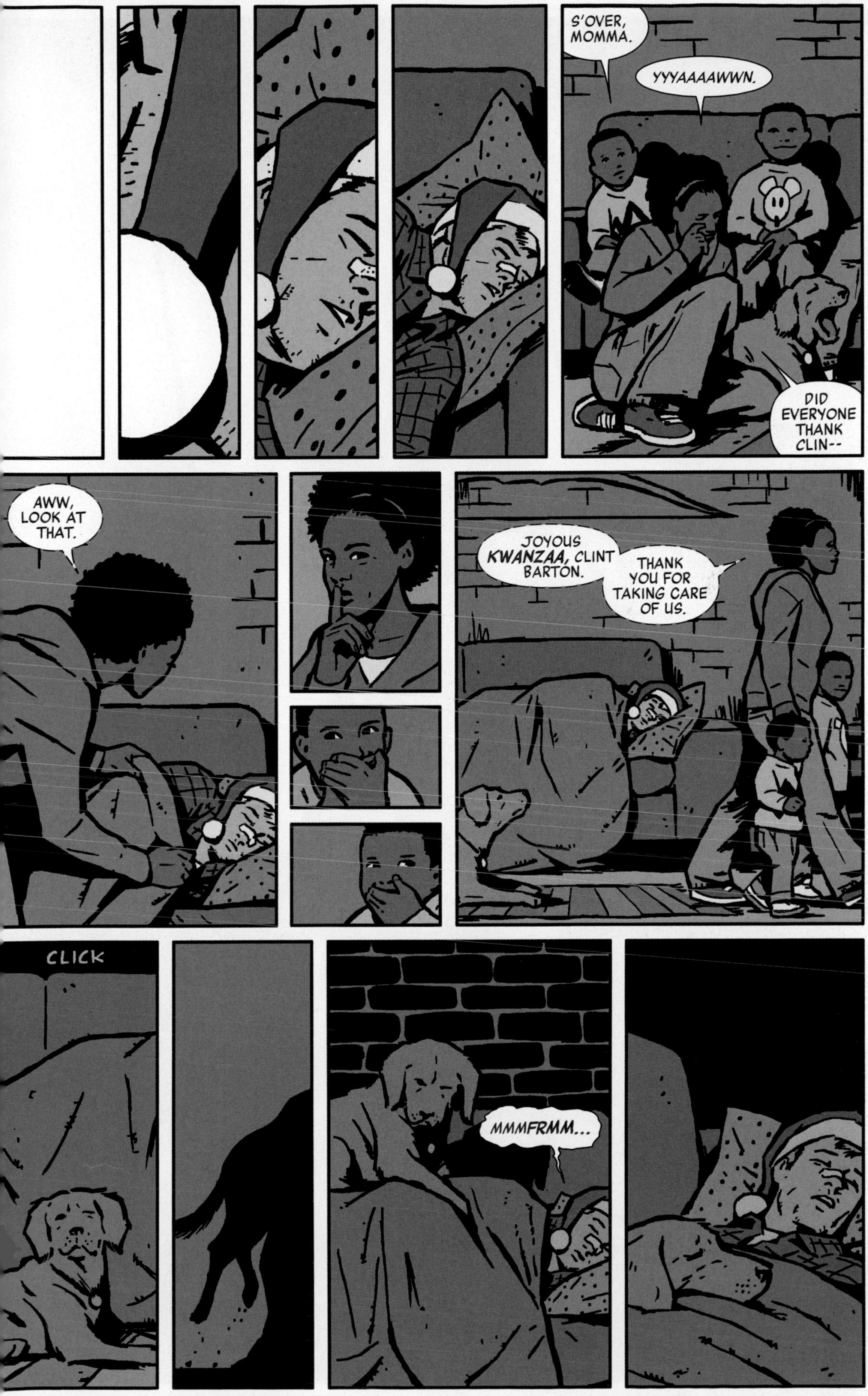
S'OVER, MOMMA.
YYYAAAAWWN.
DID EVERYONE THANK CLIN--
AWW, LOOK AT THAT.
JOYOUS KWANZAA, CLINT BARTON.
THANK YOU FOR TAKING CARE OF US.
CLICK
MMMFRMM...

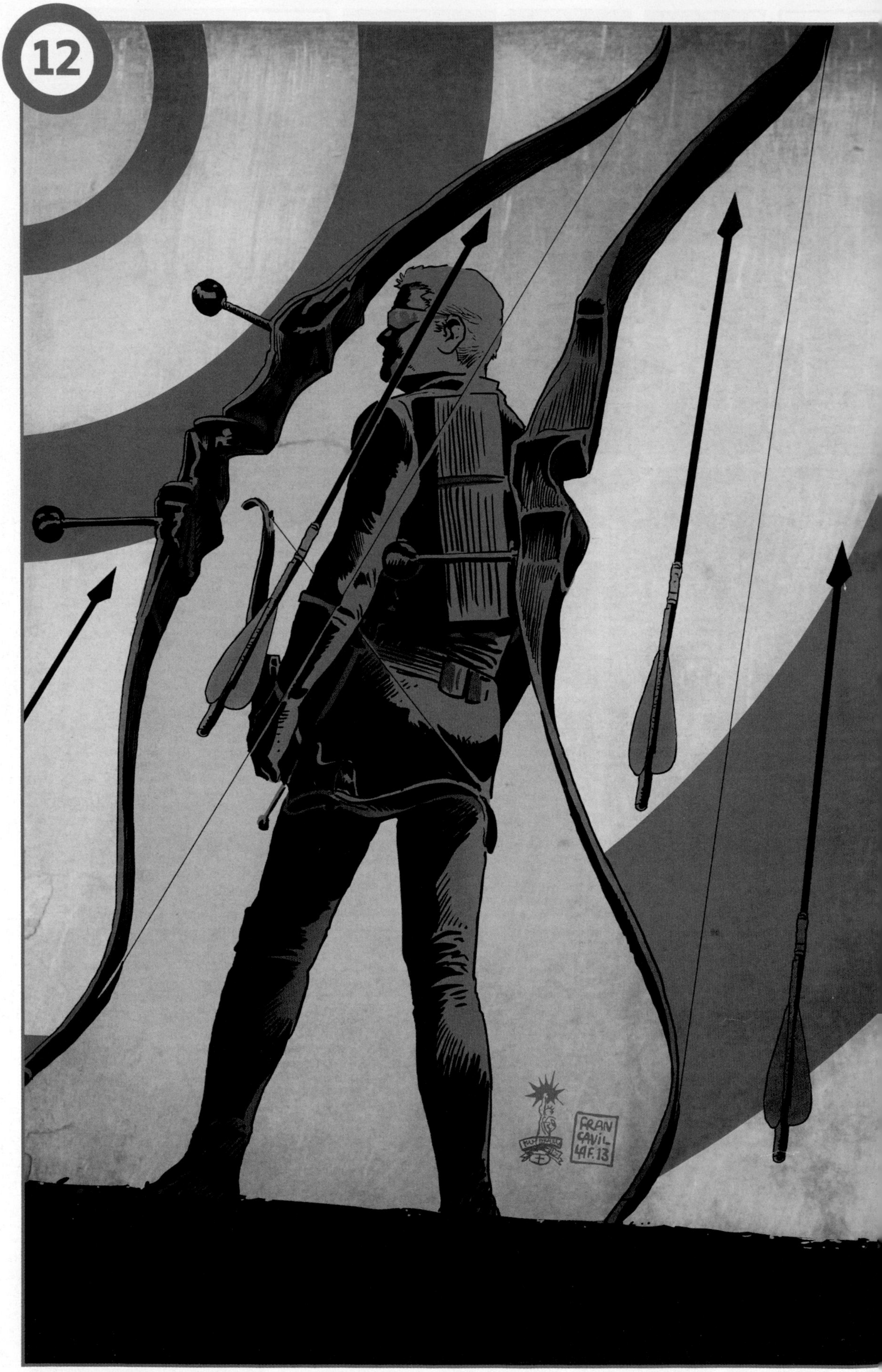
12
FRAN
CAVIL
LAF.13

barney barton,
the brother of

hawkeye

traded on his brother's name once upon a time.

long story short, he was a fake avenger and it worked out about as well as you'd think.

he's been a carnie, a crook, an f.b.i. agent, a victim and a villain.

when clint last saw him, he'd donated bone marrow to save his brother's eyesight.

also clint might have stolen a whole lot of money from him.

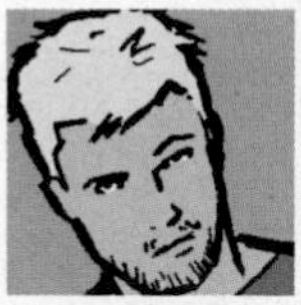

clint
barton
(hawkeye)

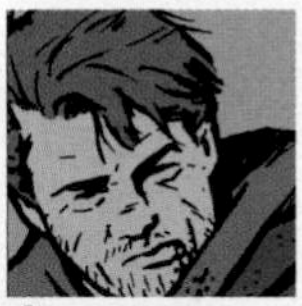

barney
barton
(trick shot)

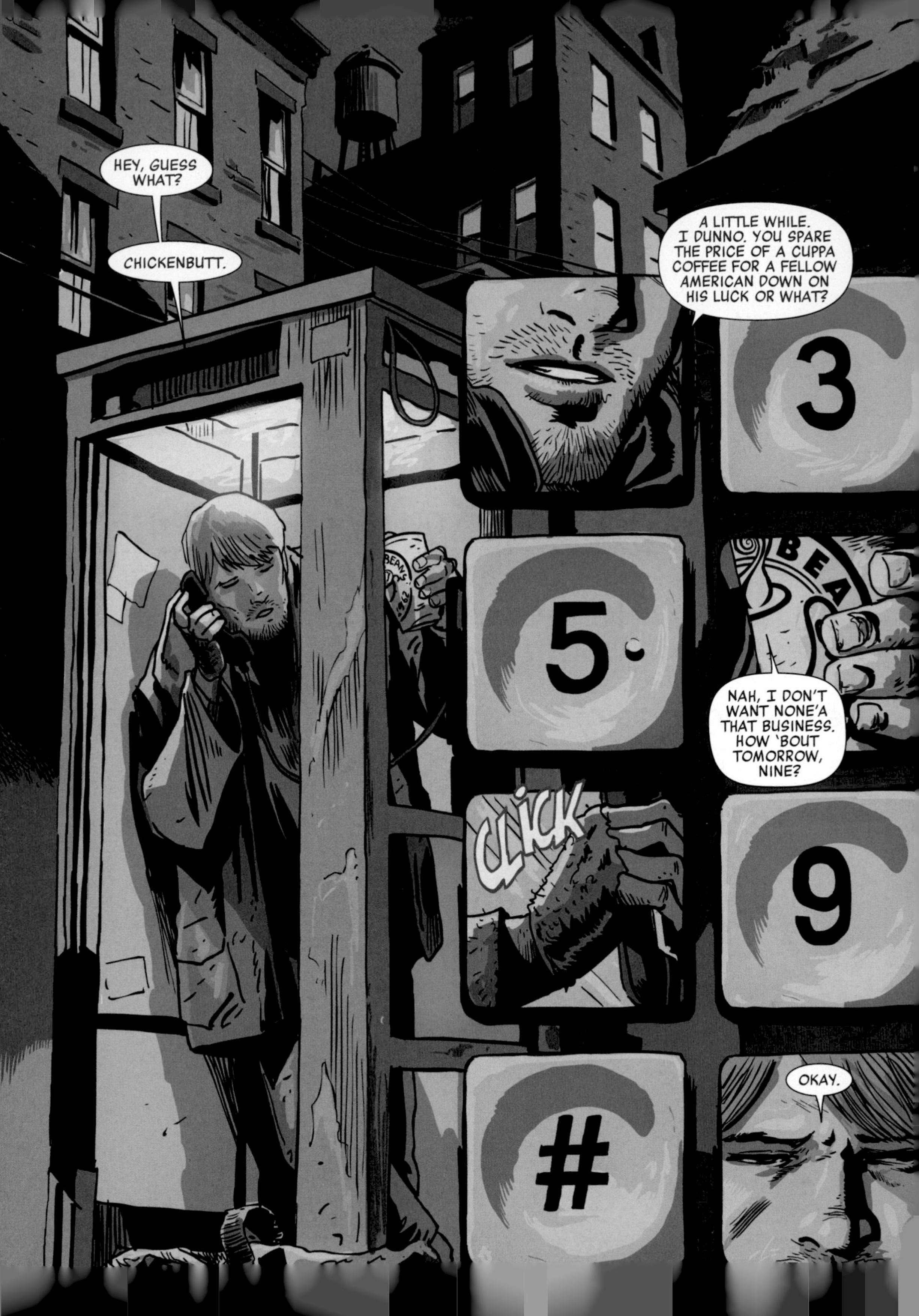
HEY, GUESS WHAT?
CHICKENBUTT.
A LITTLE WHILE. I DUNNO. YOU SPARE THE PRICE OF A CUPPA COFFEE FOR A FELLOW AMERICAN DOWN ON HIS LUCK OR WHAT?
3
5
NAH, I DON'T WANT NONE'A THAT BUSINESS. HOW 'BOUT TOMORROW, NINE?
CLICK
9
#
OKAY.

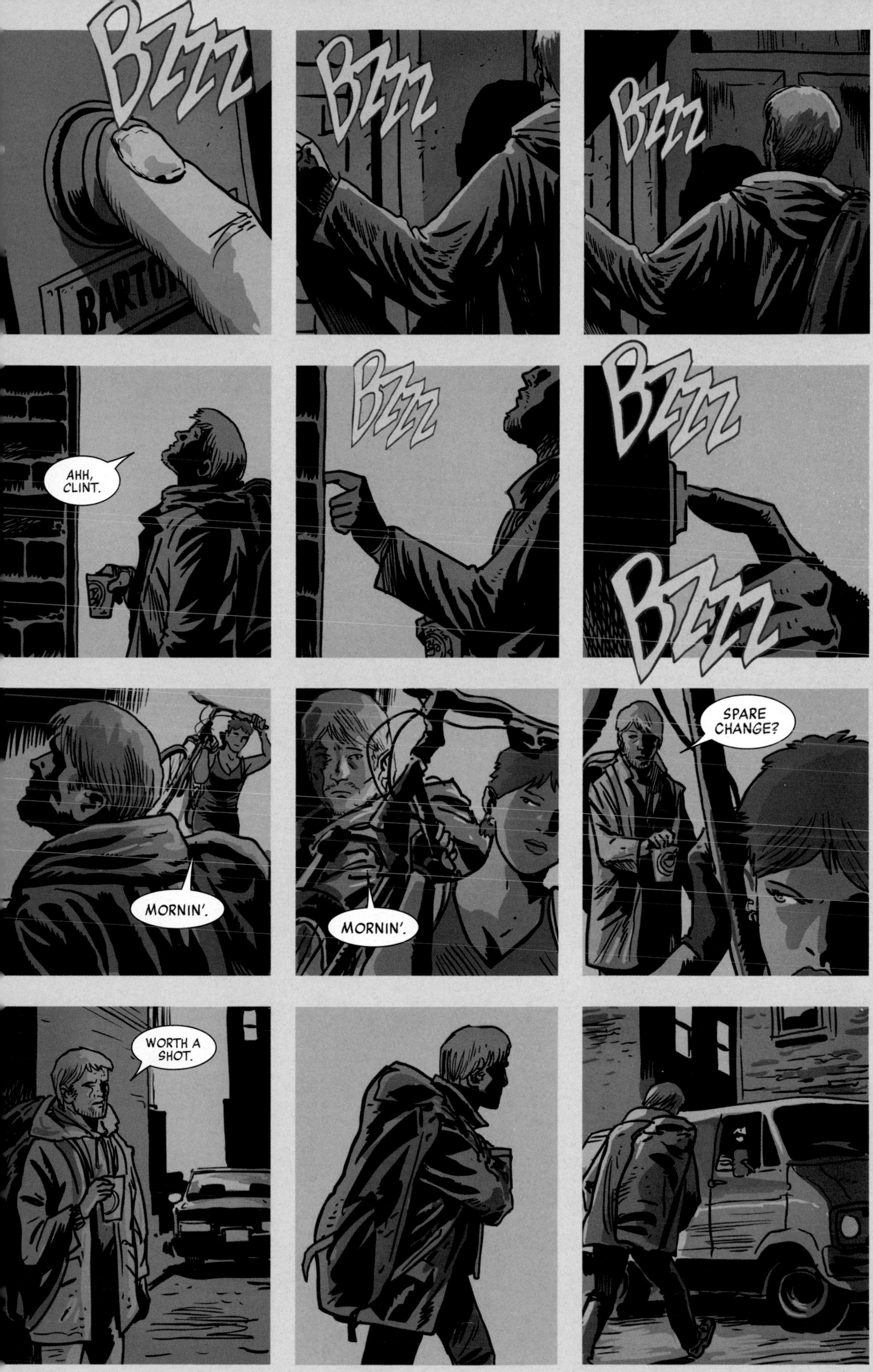
BZZZ
BARTON
BZZZ
BZZZ
AHH, CLINT.
BZZZ
BZZZ
BZZZ
MORNIN'.
MORNIN'.
SPARE CHANGE?
WORTH A SHOT.

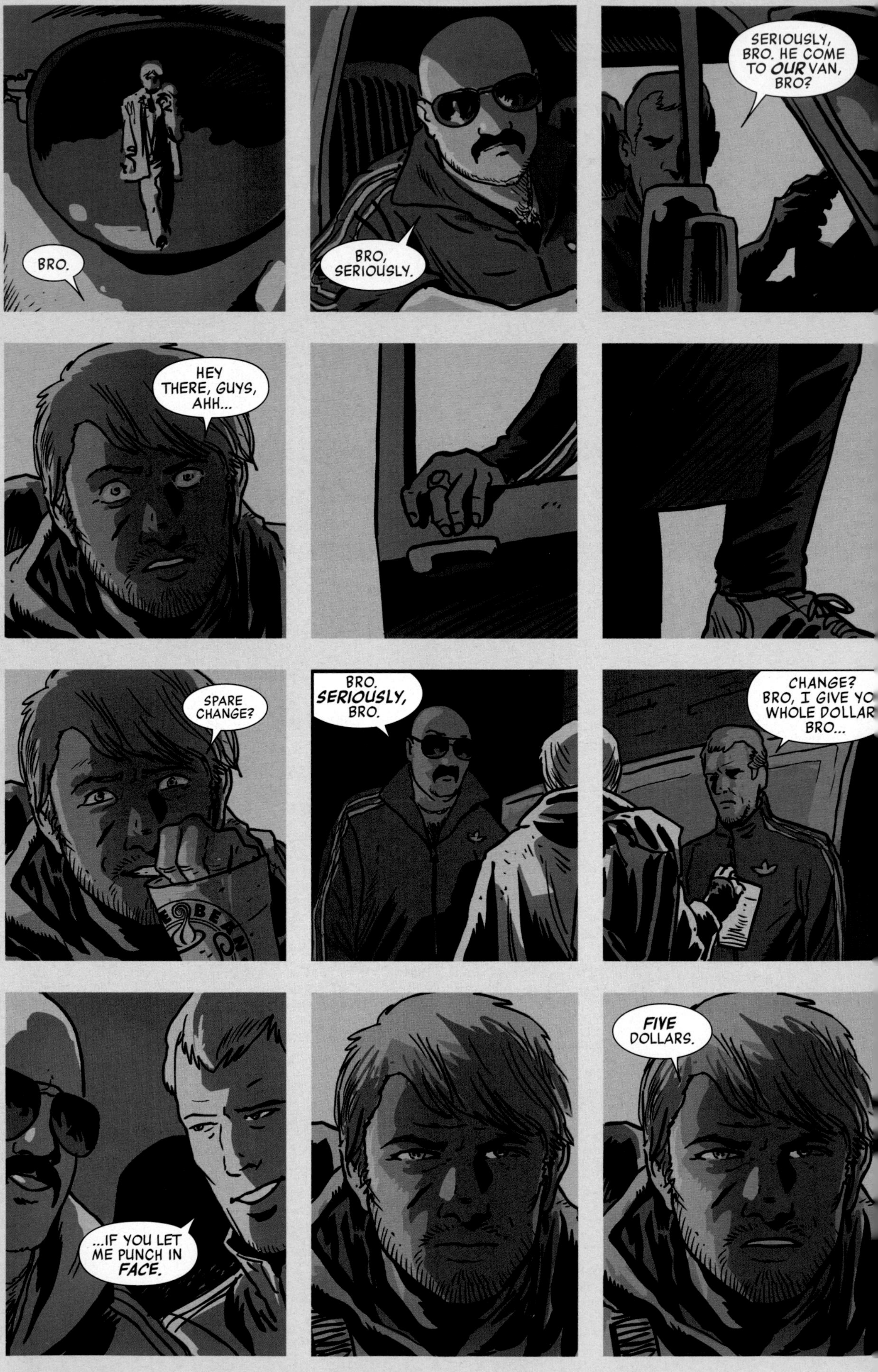

BRO.
BRO, SERIOUSLY.
SERIOUSLY, BRO. HE COME TO OUR VAN, BRO?
HEY THERE, GUYS, AHH...
SPARE CHANGE?
BRO. SERIOUSLY, BRO.
CHANGE? BRO, I GIVE YO WHOLE DOLLAR BRO...
...IF YOU LET ME PUNCH IN FACE.
FIVE DOLLARS.

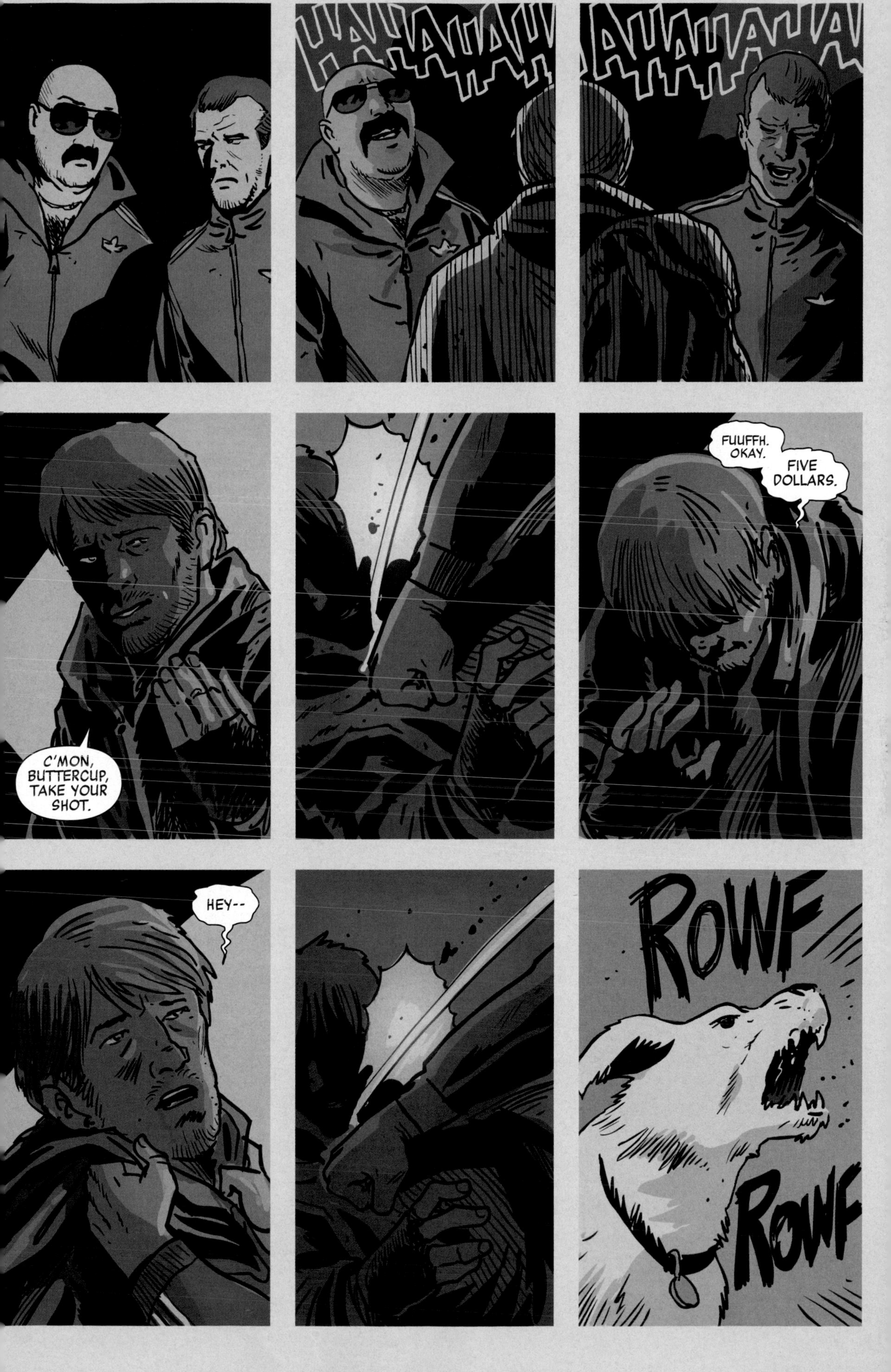
HAHAHAHAHAHAHAHA
C'MON, BUTTERCUP, TAKE YOUR SHOT.
FUUFFH. OKAY.
FIVE DOLLARS.
HEY--
ROWF
ROWF

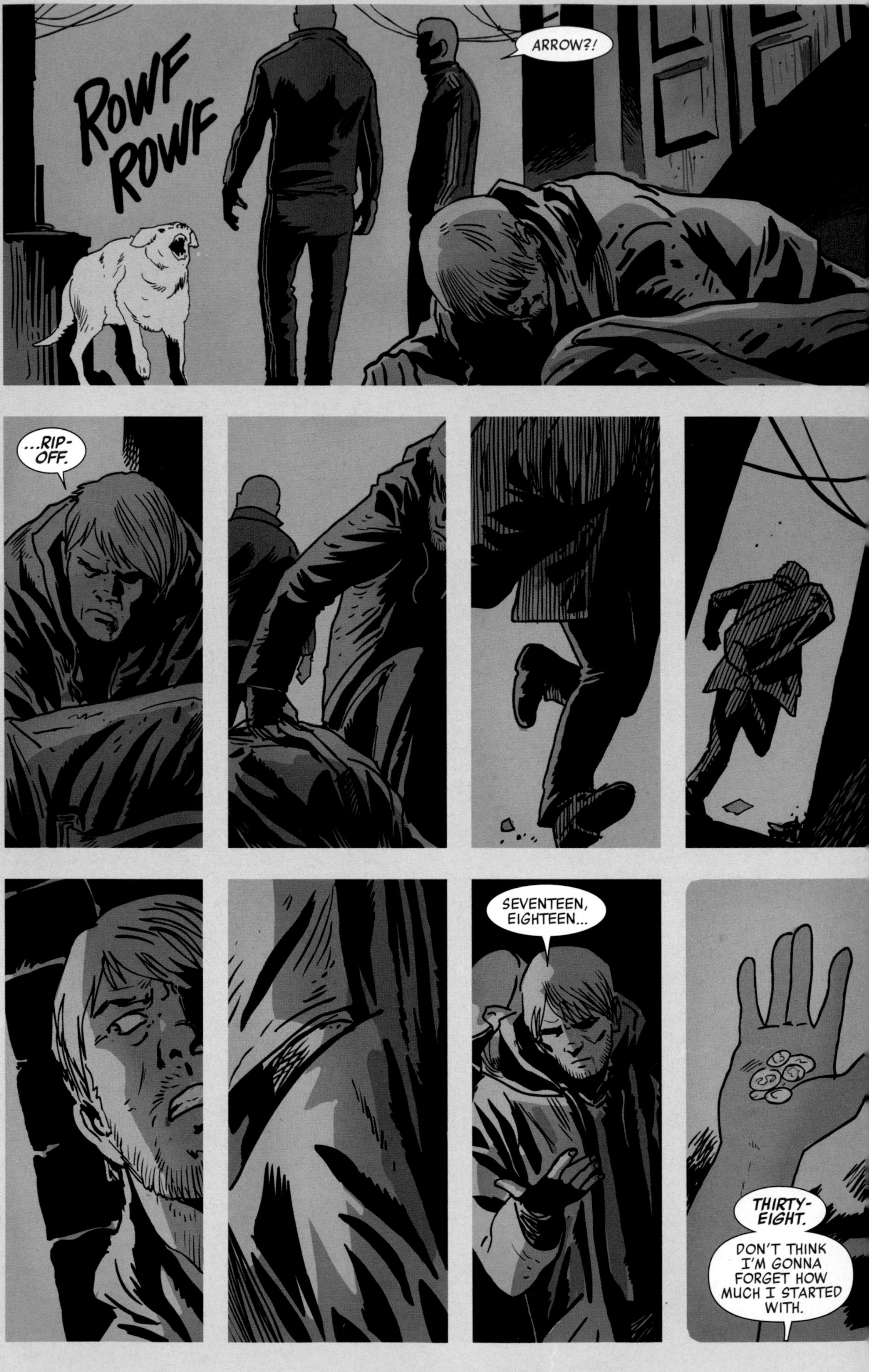
ROWF ROWF
ARROW?!
...RIP-OFF.
SEVENTEEN, EIGHTEEN...
THIRTY-EIGHT.
DON'T THINK I'M GONNA FORGET HOW MUCH I STARTED WITH.

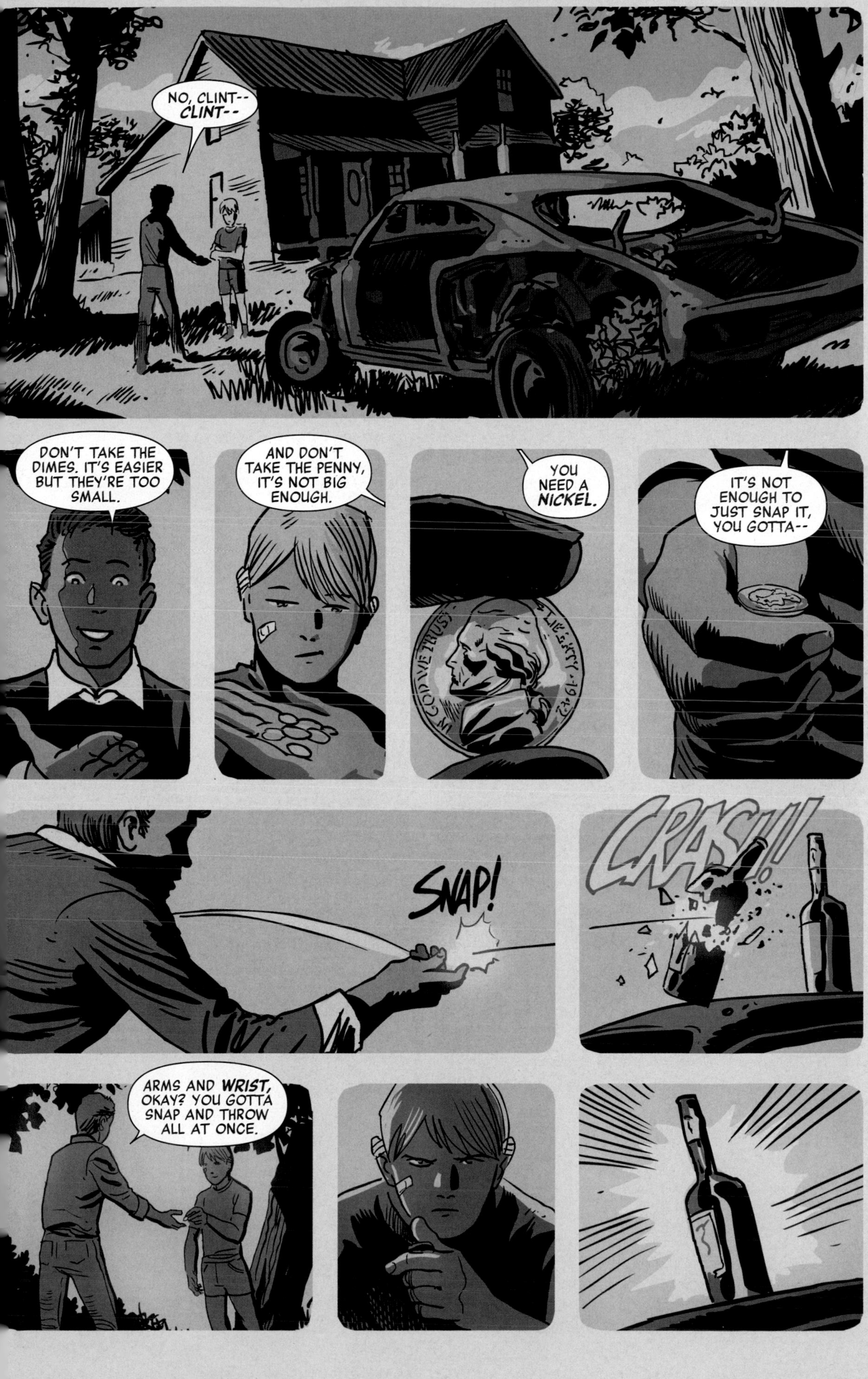
NO, CLINT--
CLINT--
DON'T TAKE THE DIMES. IT'S EASIER BUT THEY'RE TOO SMALL.
AND DON'T TAKE THE PENNY, IT'S NOT BIG ENOUGH.
YOU NEED A NICKEL.
IN GOD WE TRUST
LIBERTY
1942
IT'S NOT ENOUGH TO JUST SNAP IT, YOU GOTTA--
SNAP!
CRASH!!
ARMS AND WRIST, OKAY? YOU GOTTA SNAP AND THROW ALL AT ONCE.

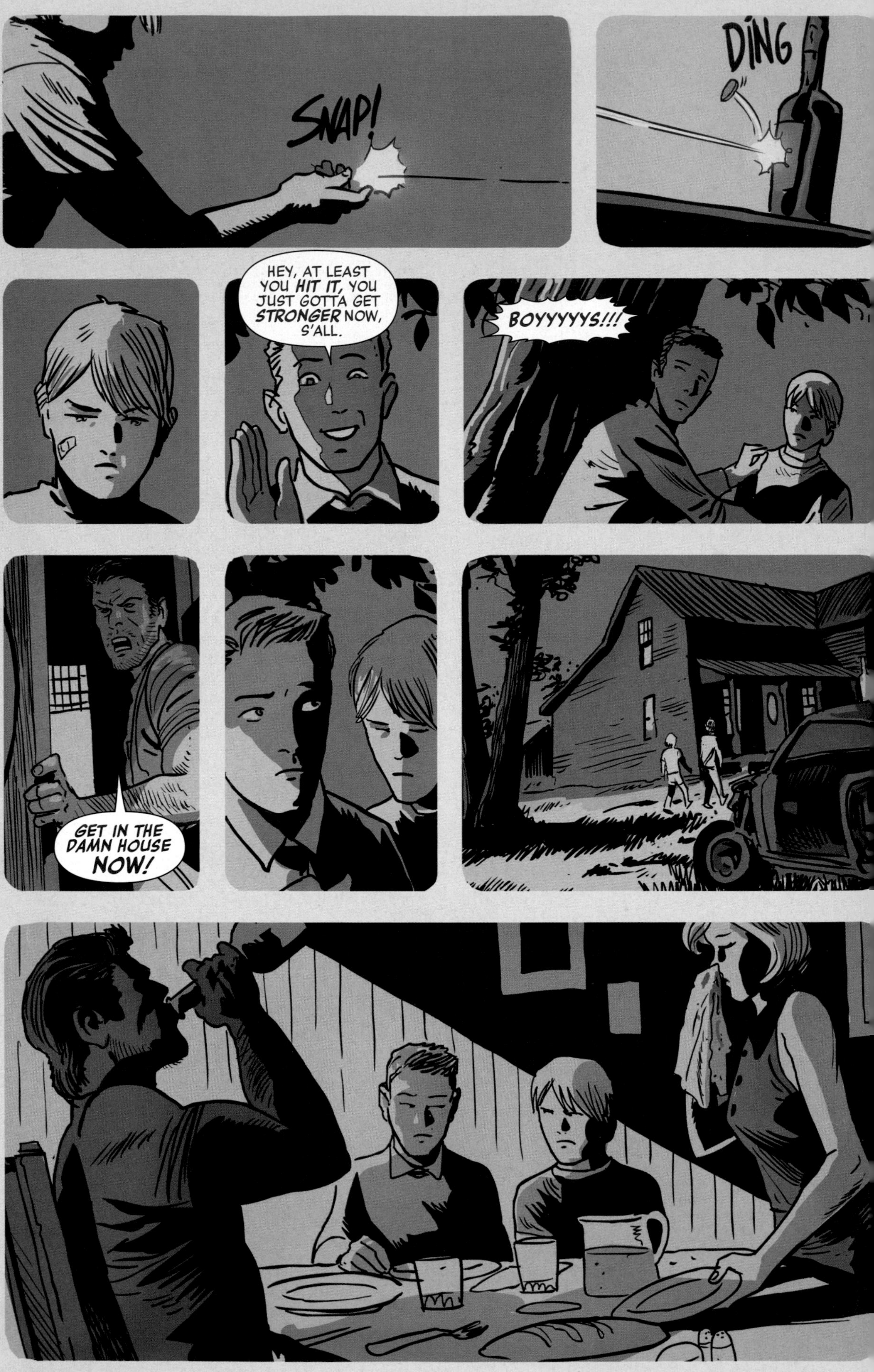
SNAP!
DING
HEY, AT LEAST YOU HIT IT, YOU JUST GOTTA GET STRONGER NOW, S'ALL.
BOYYYYYS!!!
GET IN THE DAMN HOUSE NOW!

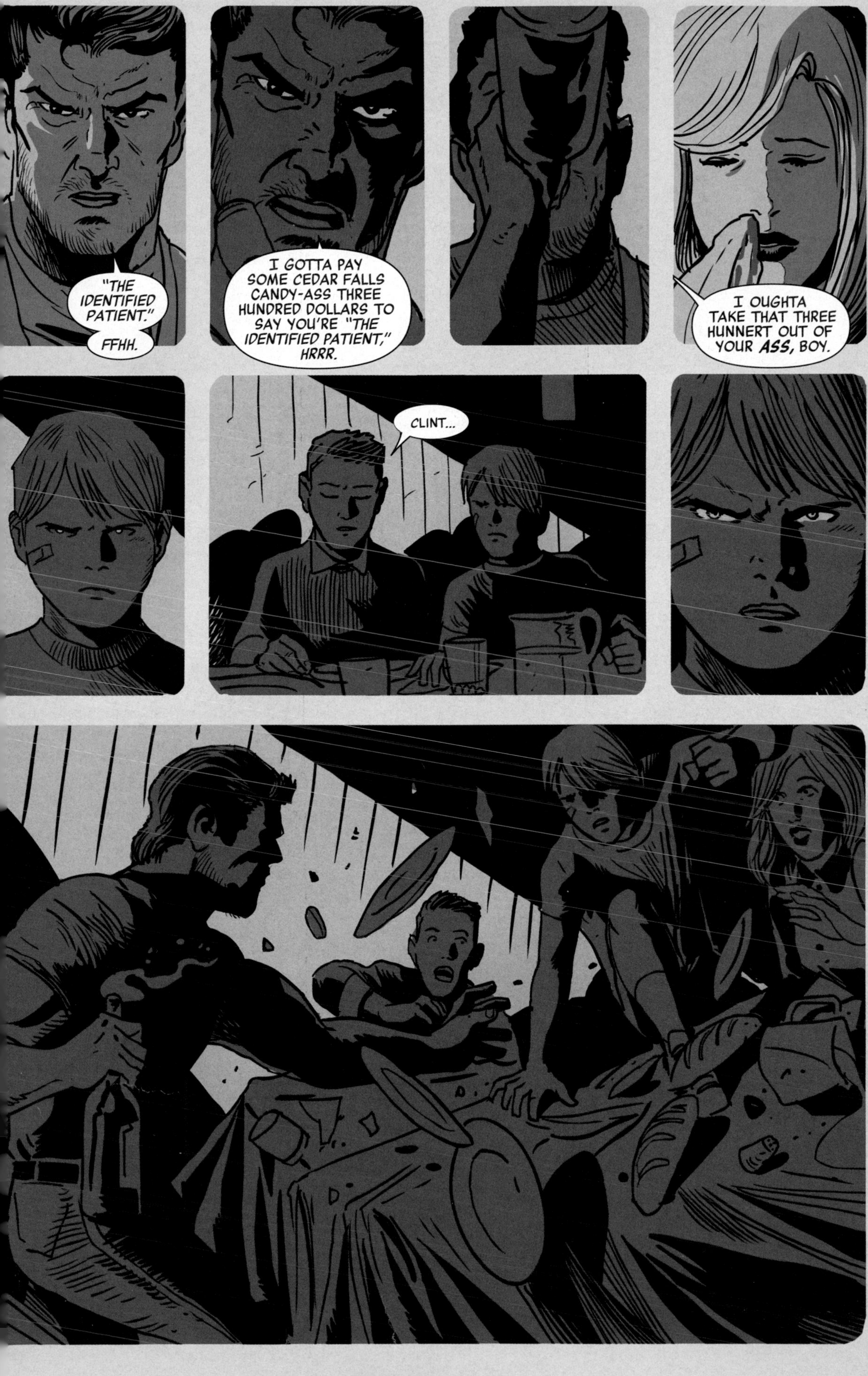
"THE IDENTIFIED PATIENT."
FFHH.
I GOTTA PAY SOME CEDAR FALLS CANDY-ASS THREE HUNDRED DOLLARS TO SAY YOU'RE "THE IDENTIFIED PATIENT," HRRR.
I OUGHTA TAKE THAT THREE HUNNERT OUT OF YOUR ASS, BOY.
CLINT...

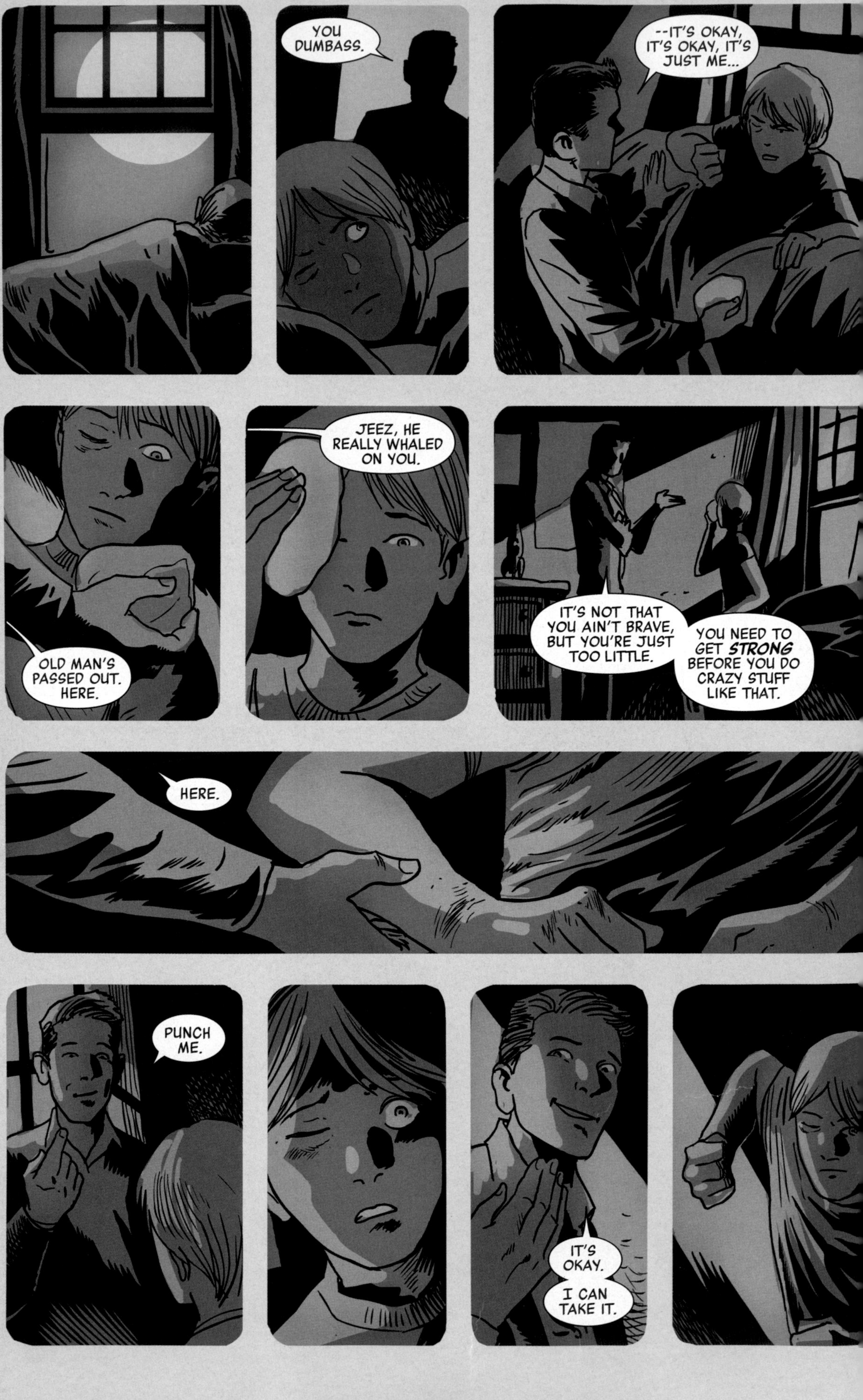
YOU DUMBASS.
--IT'S OKAY, IT'S OKAY, IT'S JUST ME...
OLD MAN'S PASSED OUT. HERE.
JEEZ, HE REALLY WHALED ON YOU.
IT'S NOT THAT YOU AIN'T BRAVE, BUT YOU'RE JUST TOO LITTLE.
YOU NEED TO GET STRONG BEFORE YOU DO CRAZY STUFF LIKE THAT.
HERE.
PUNCH ME.
IT'S OKAY.
I CAN TAKE IT.

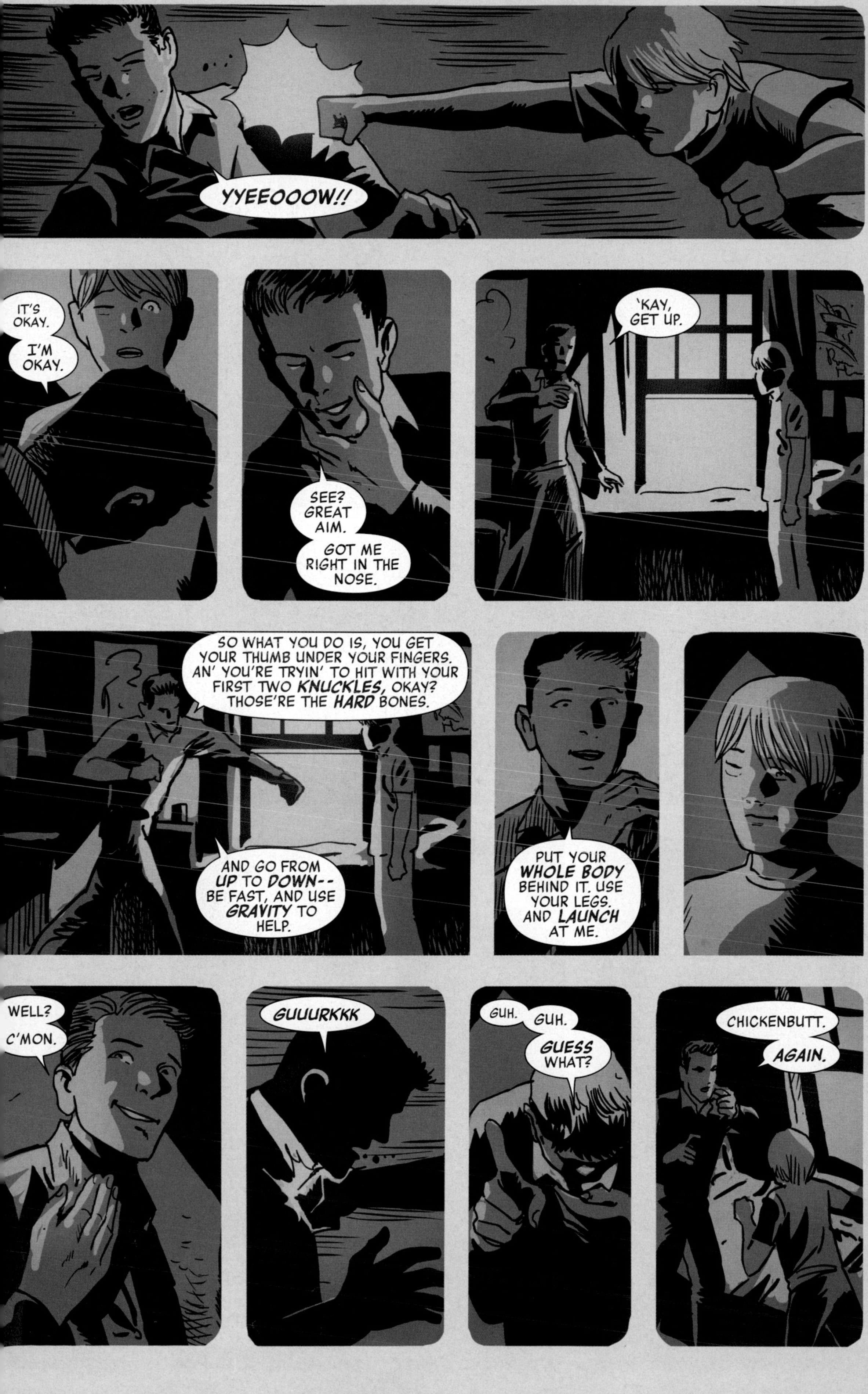
YYEEOOOW!!
IT'S OKAY.
I'M OKAY.
SEE? GREAT AIM.
GOT ME RIGHT IN THE NOSE.
'KAY, GET UP.
SO WHAT YOU DO IS, YOU GET YOUR THUMB UNDER YOUR FINGERS. AN' YOU'RE TRYIN' TO HIT WITH YOUR FIRST TWO KNUCKLES, OKAY? THOSE'RE THE HARD BONES.
AND GO FROM UP TO DOWN-- BE FAST, AND USE GRAVITY TO HELP.
PUT YOUR WHOLE BODY BEHIND IT. USE YOUR LEGS. AND LAUNCH AT ME.
WELL? C'MON.
GUUURKKK
GUH.
GUH.
GUESS WHAT?
CHICKENBUTT.
AGAIN.

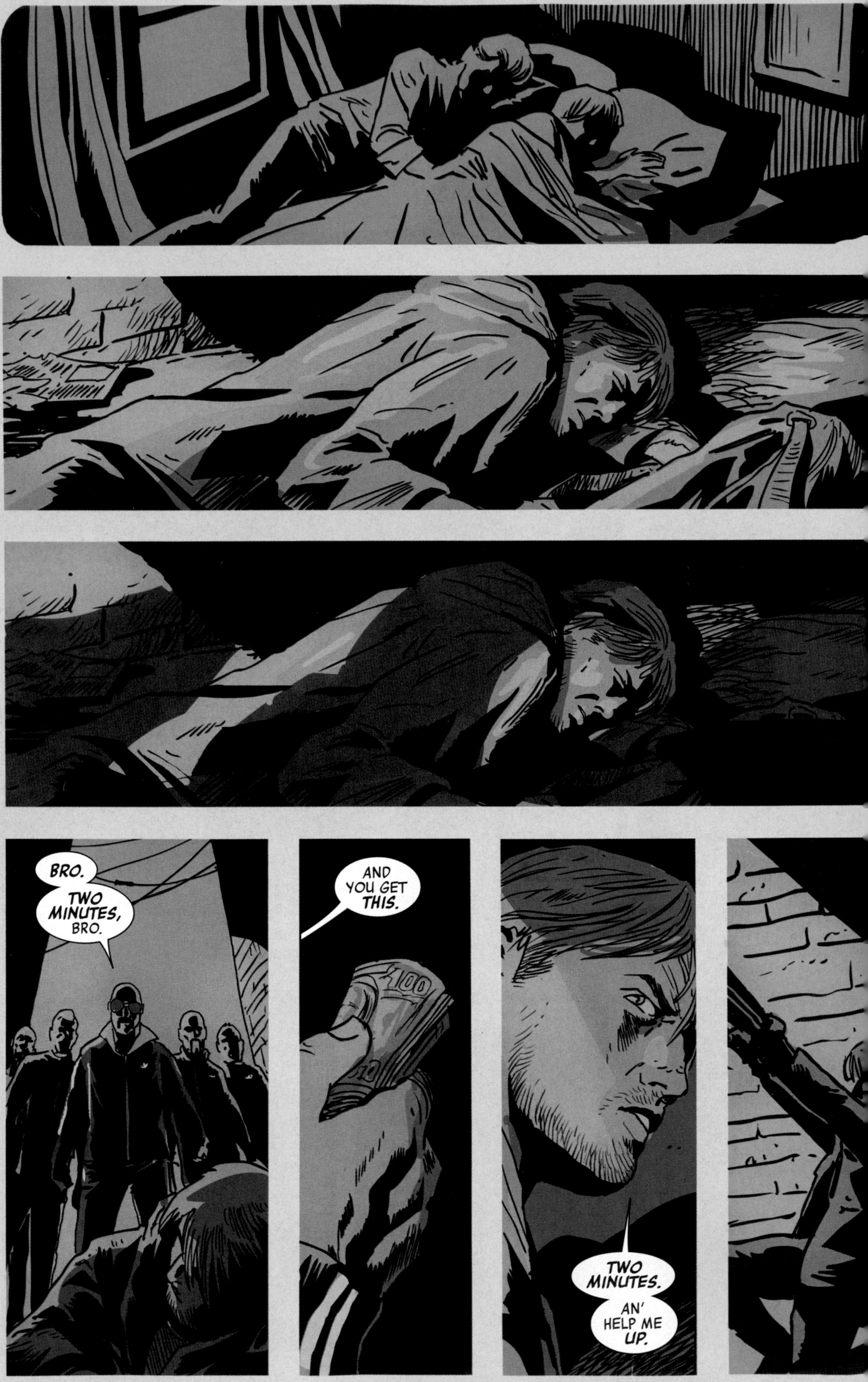
BRO.
TWO MINUTES, BRO.
AND YOU GET THIS.
TWO MINUTES.
AN' HELP ME UP.

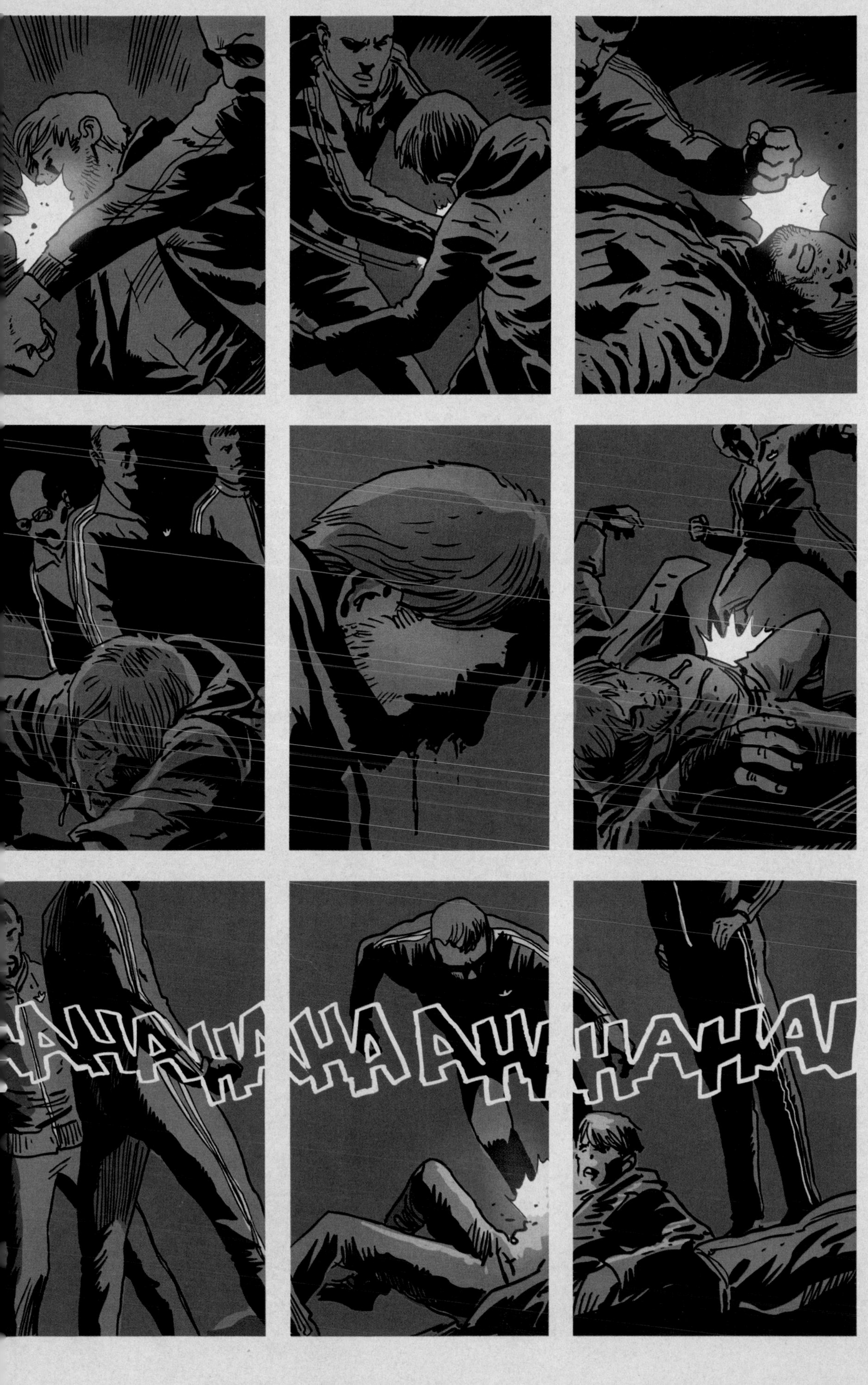
AHAHAHAHAHAHAHAHA

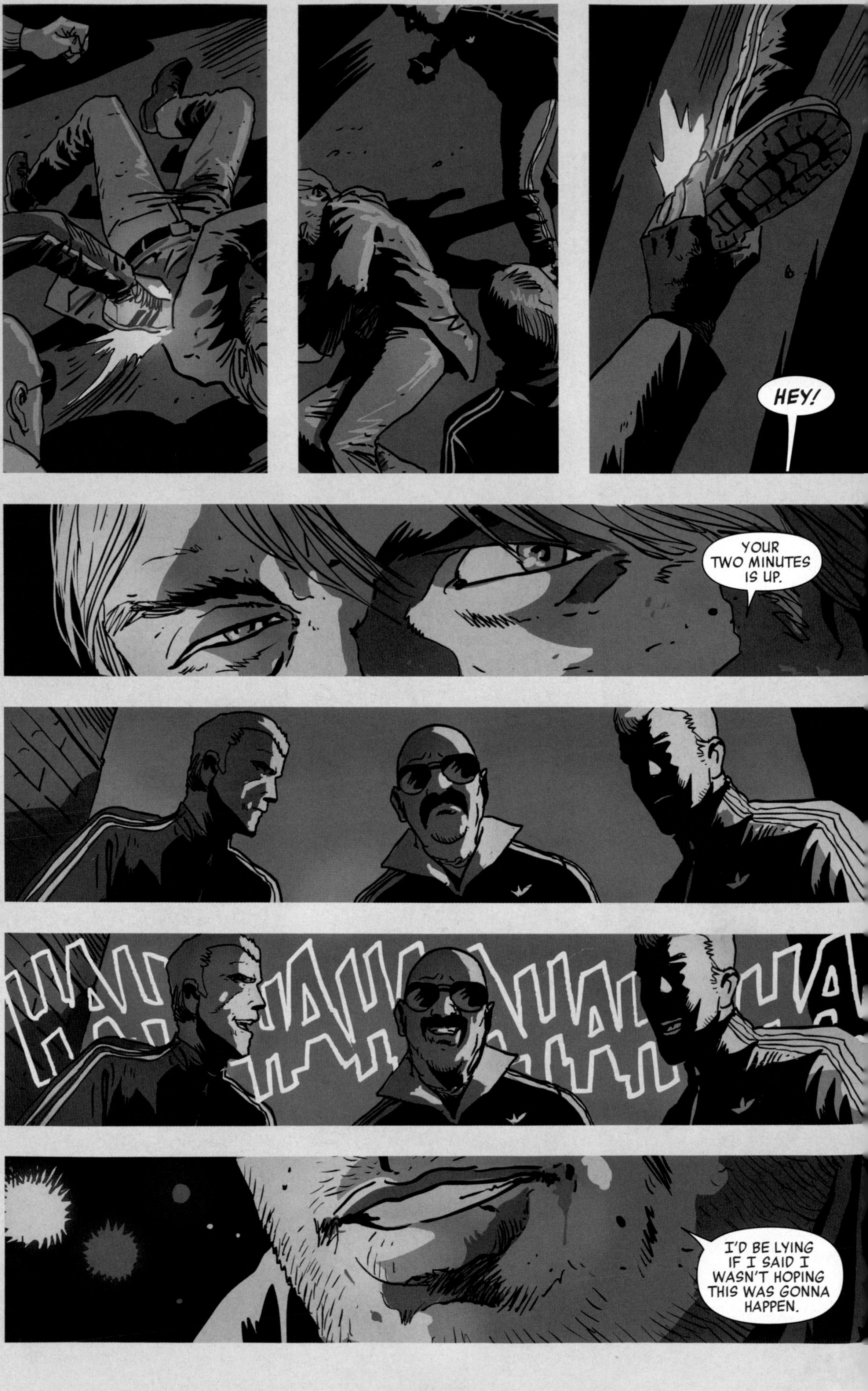
HEY!
YOUR TWO MINUTES IS UP.
HAHAHAHAHAHA
I'D BE LYING IF I SAID I WASN'T HOPING THIS WAS GONNA HAPPEN.

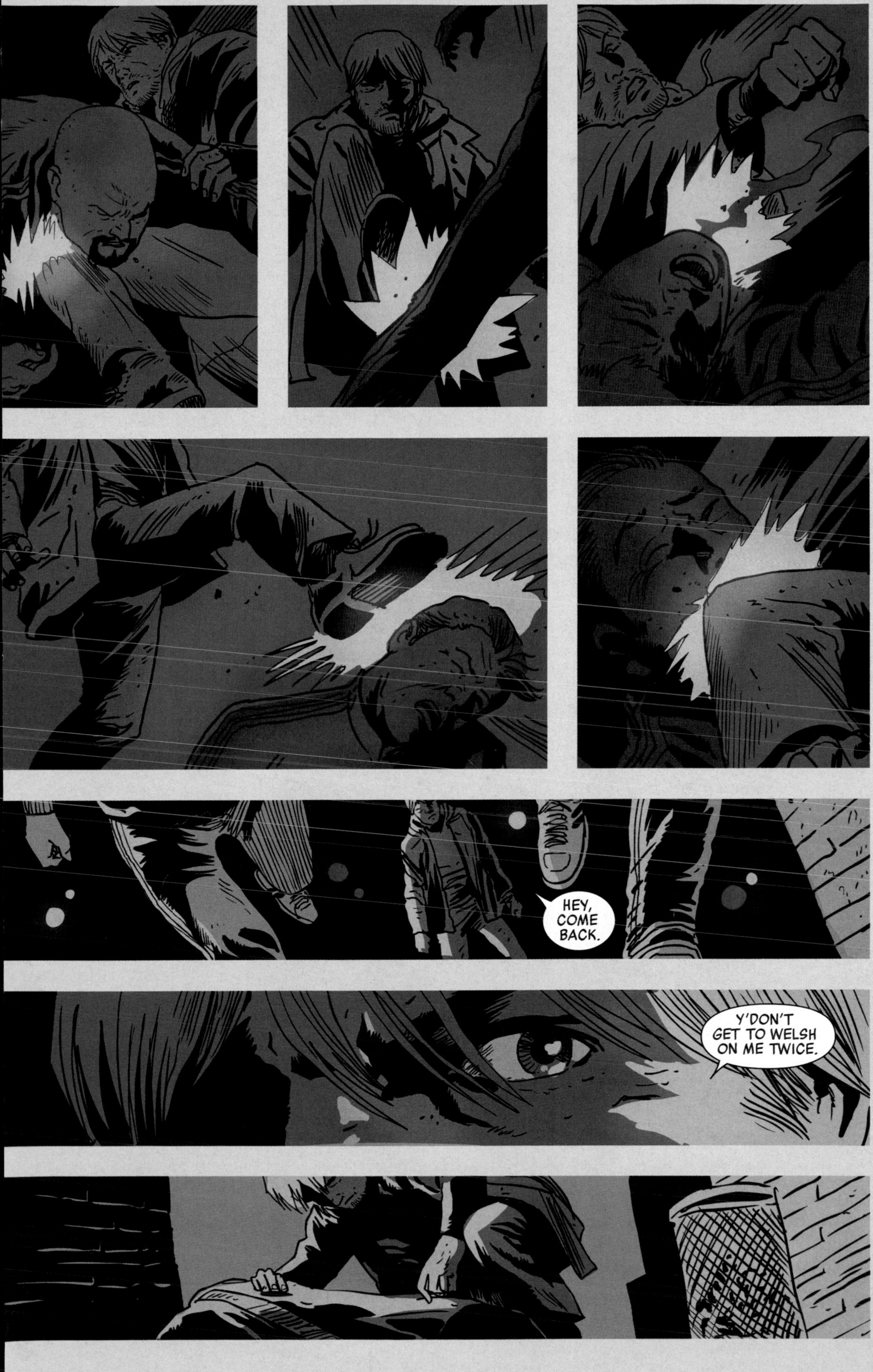
HEY, COME BACK.
Y'DON'T GET TO WELSH ON ME TWICE.

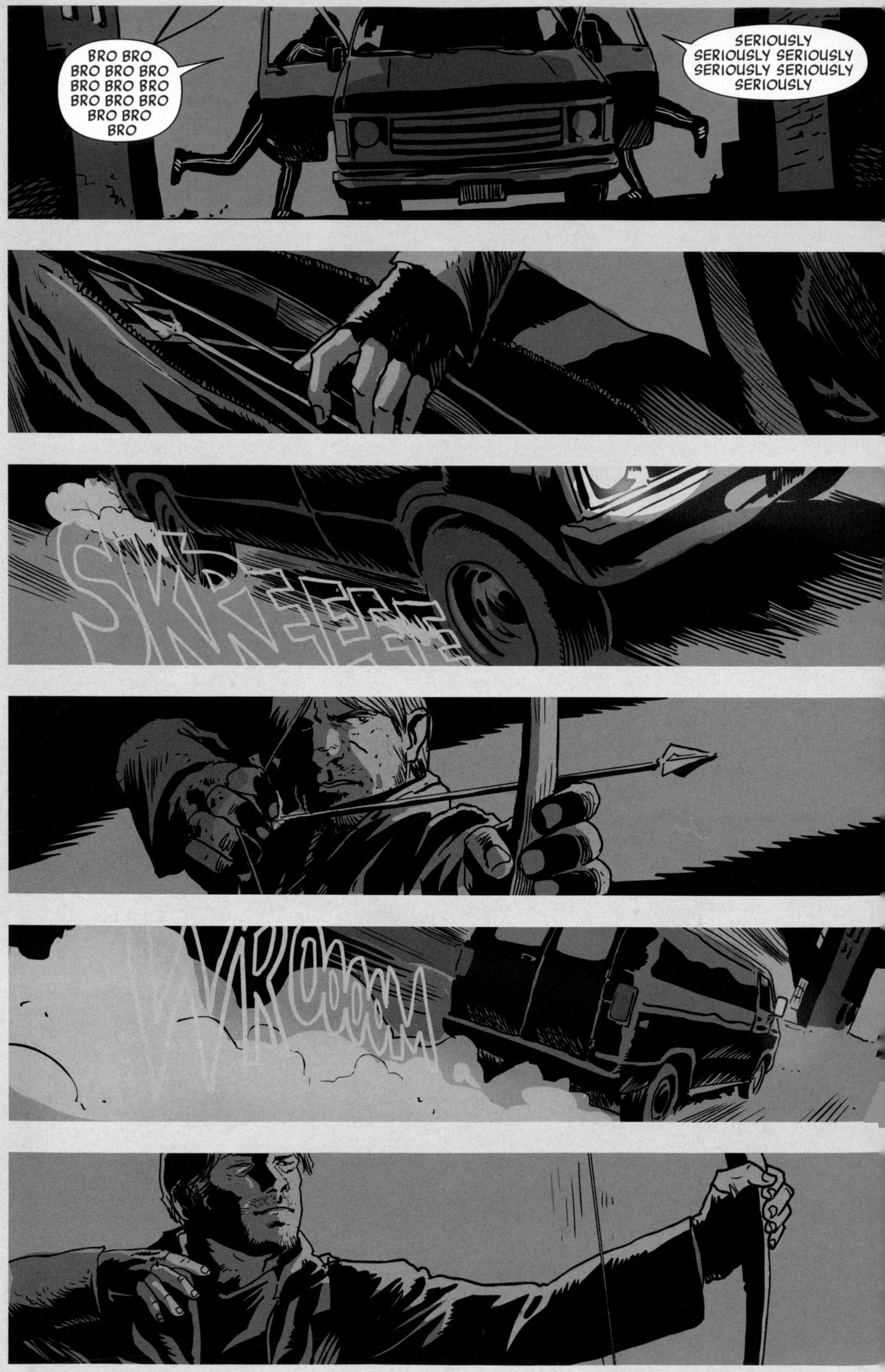
BRO BRO BRO BRO BRO BRO BRO BRO BRO BRO BRO BRO BRO BRO
SERIOUSLY SERIOUSLY SERIOUSLY SERIOUSLY SERIOUSLY SERIOUSLY
SKREEEE
VROOOOM

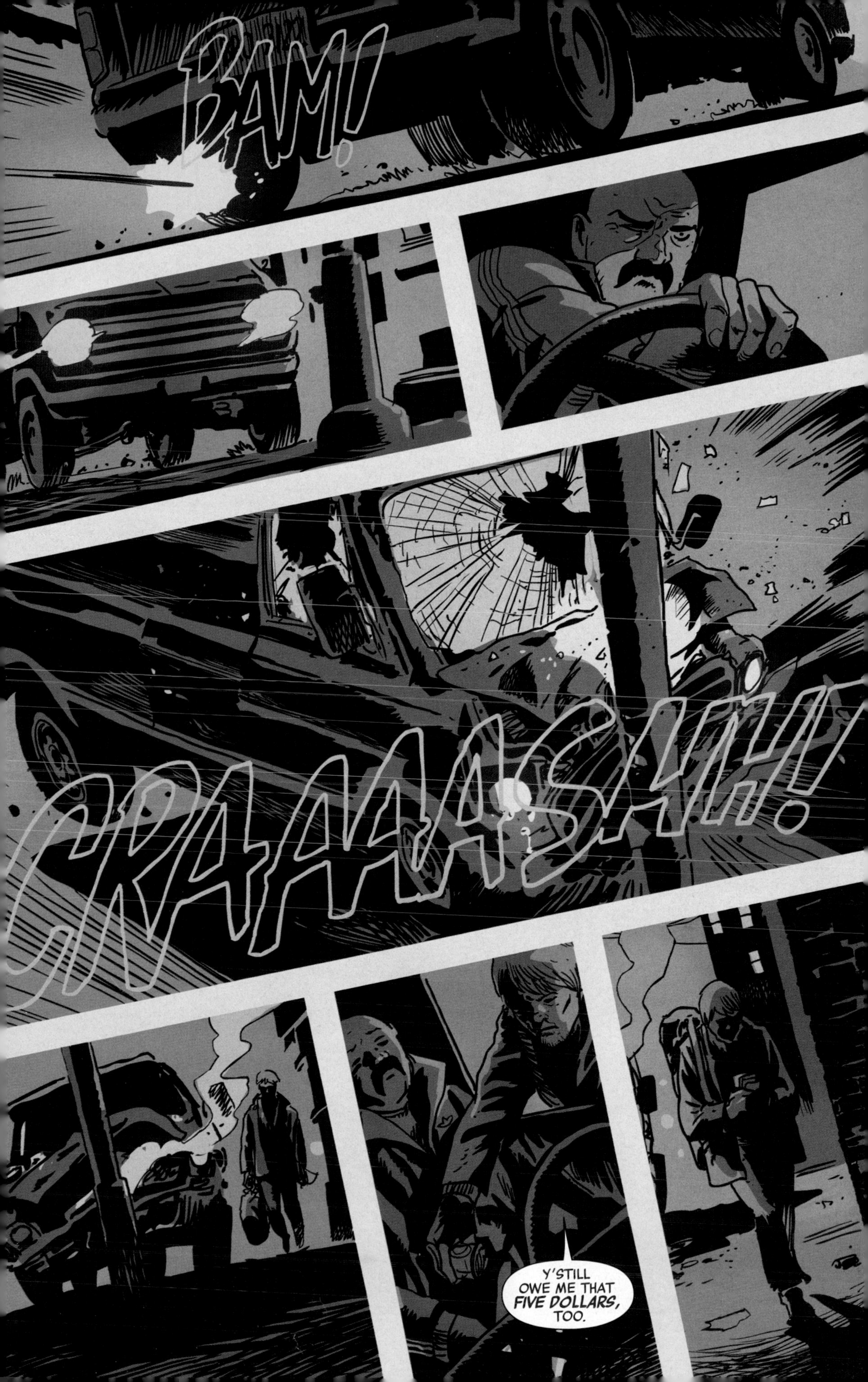
BAM!
CRAAAASHH!
Y'STILL OWE ME THAT FIVE DOLLARS, TOO.

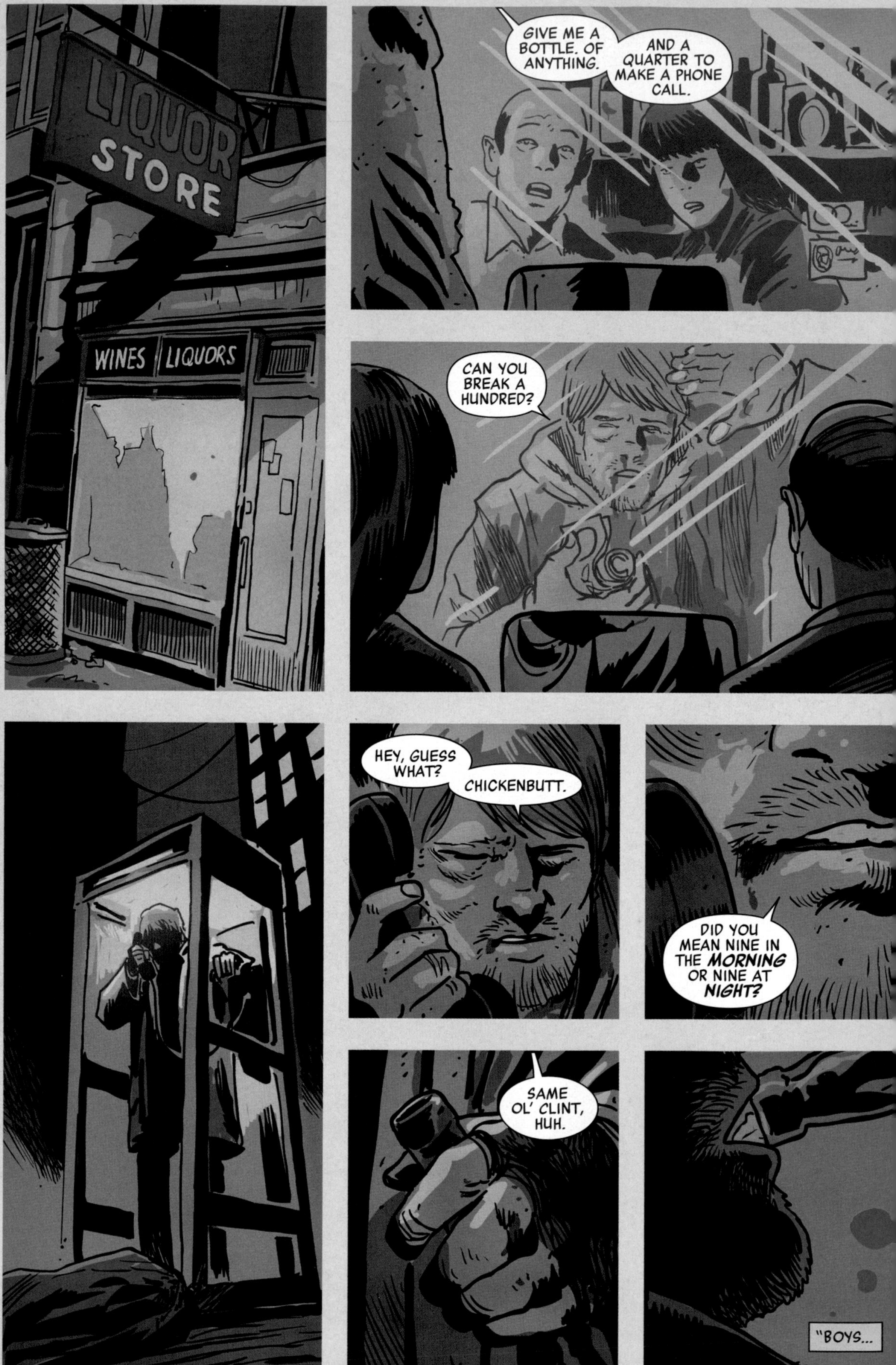
LIQUOR STORE
WINES LIQUORS
GIVE ME A BOTTLE. OF ANYTHING.
AND A QUARTER TO MAKE A PHONE CALL.
CAN YOU BREAK A HUNDRED?
HEY, GUESS WHAT?
CHICKENBUTT.
DID YOU MEAN NINE IN THE MORNING OR NINE AT NIGHT?
SAME OL' CLINT, HUH.
"BOYS...

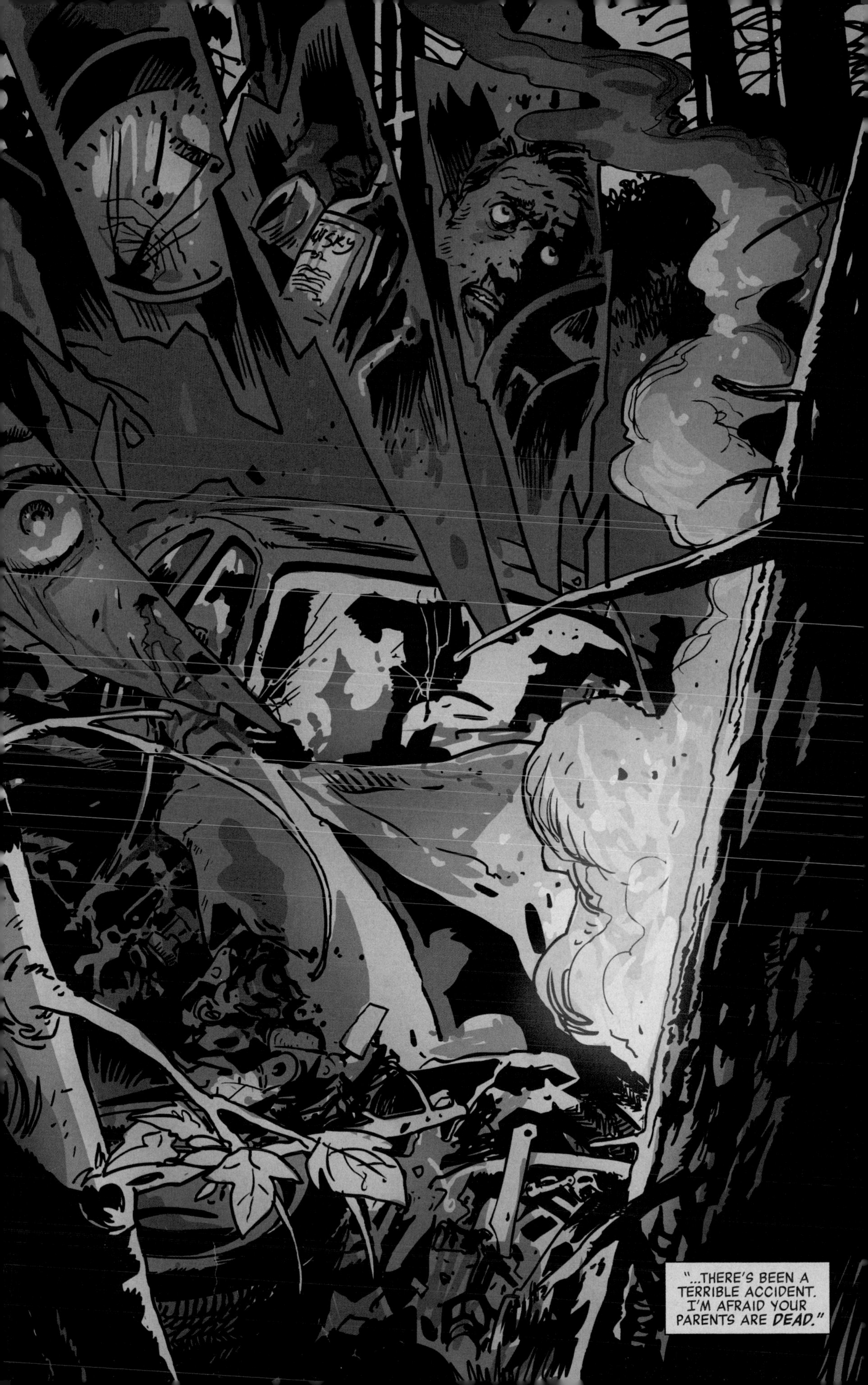
"...THERE'S BEEN A TERRIBLE ACCIDENT. I'M AFRAID YOUR PARENTS ARE *DEAD.*"

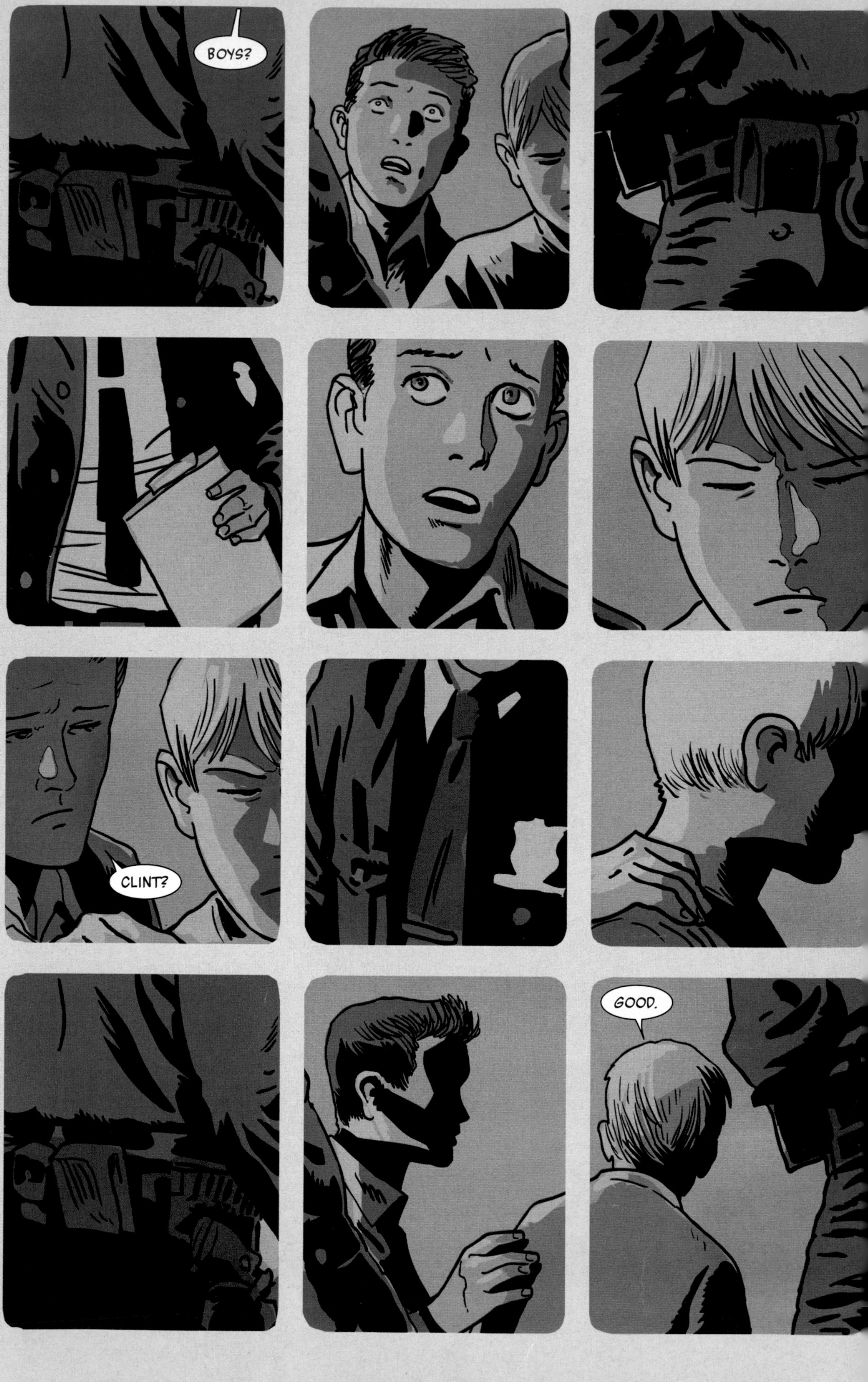
BOYS?
CLINT?
GOOD.

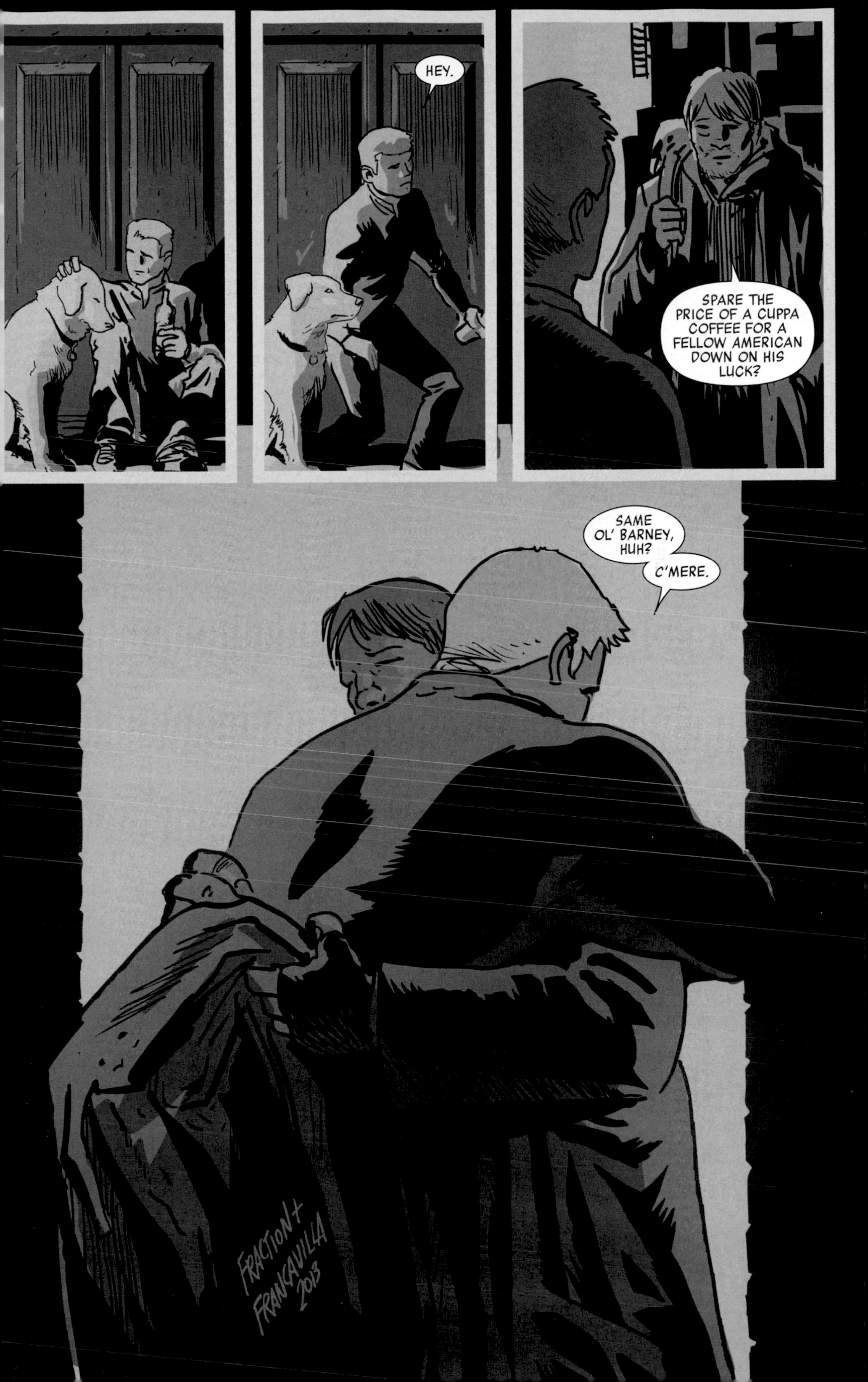
HEY.
SPARE THE PRICE OF A CUPPA COFFEE FOR A FELLOW AMERICAN DOWN ON HIS LUCK?
SAME OL' BARNEY, HUH?
C'MERE.
FRACTION + FRANCAVILLA 2013

13

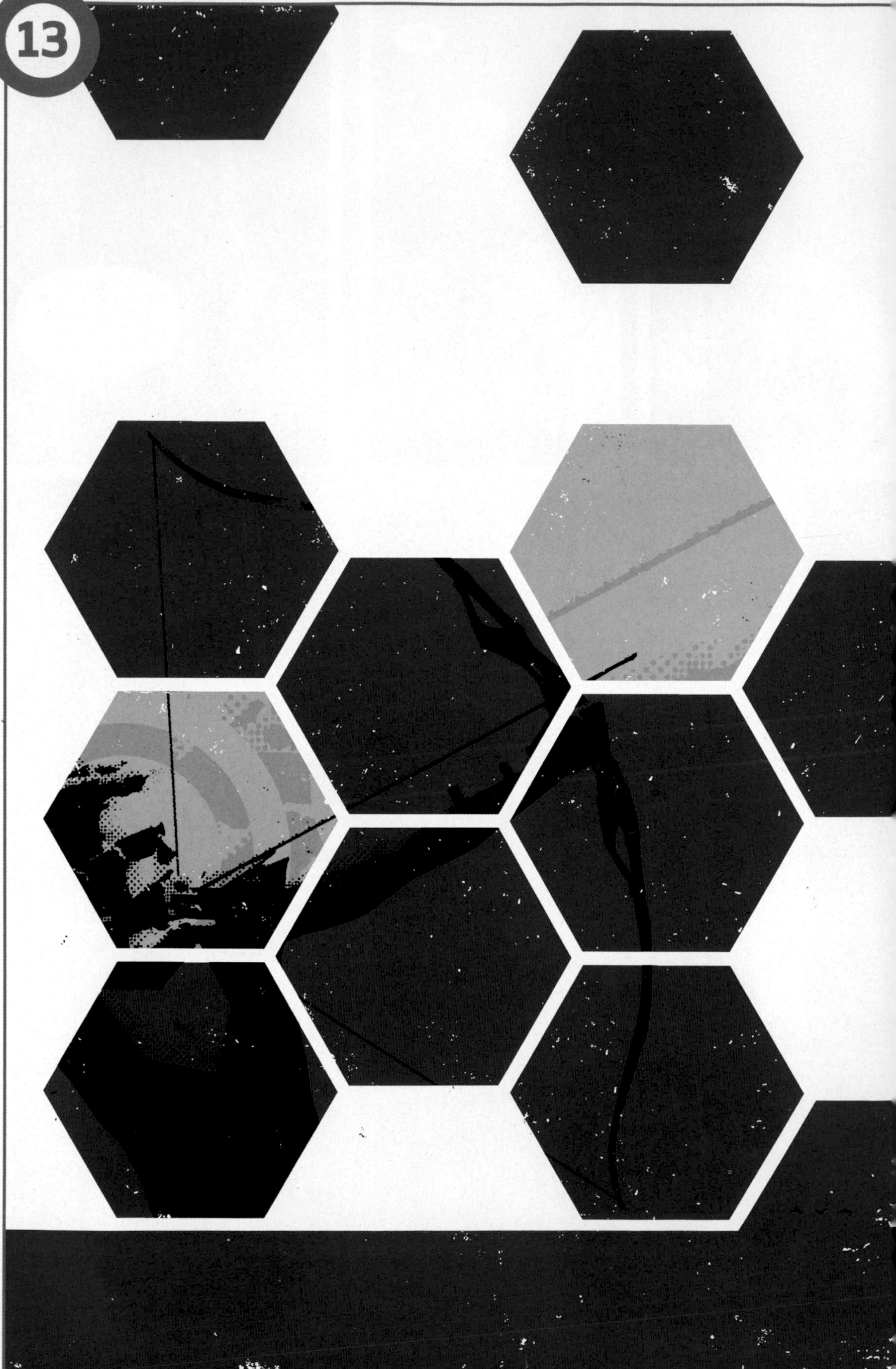

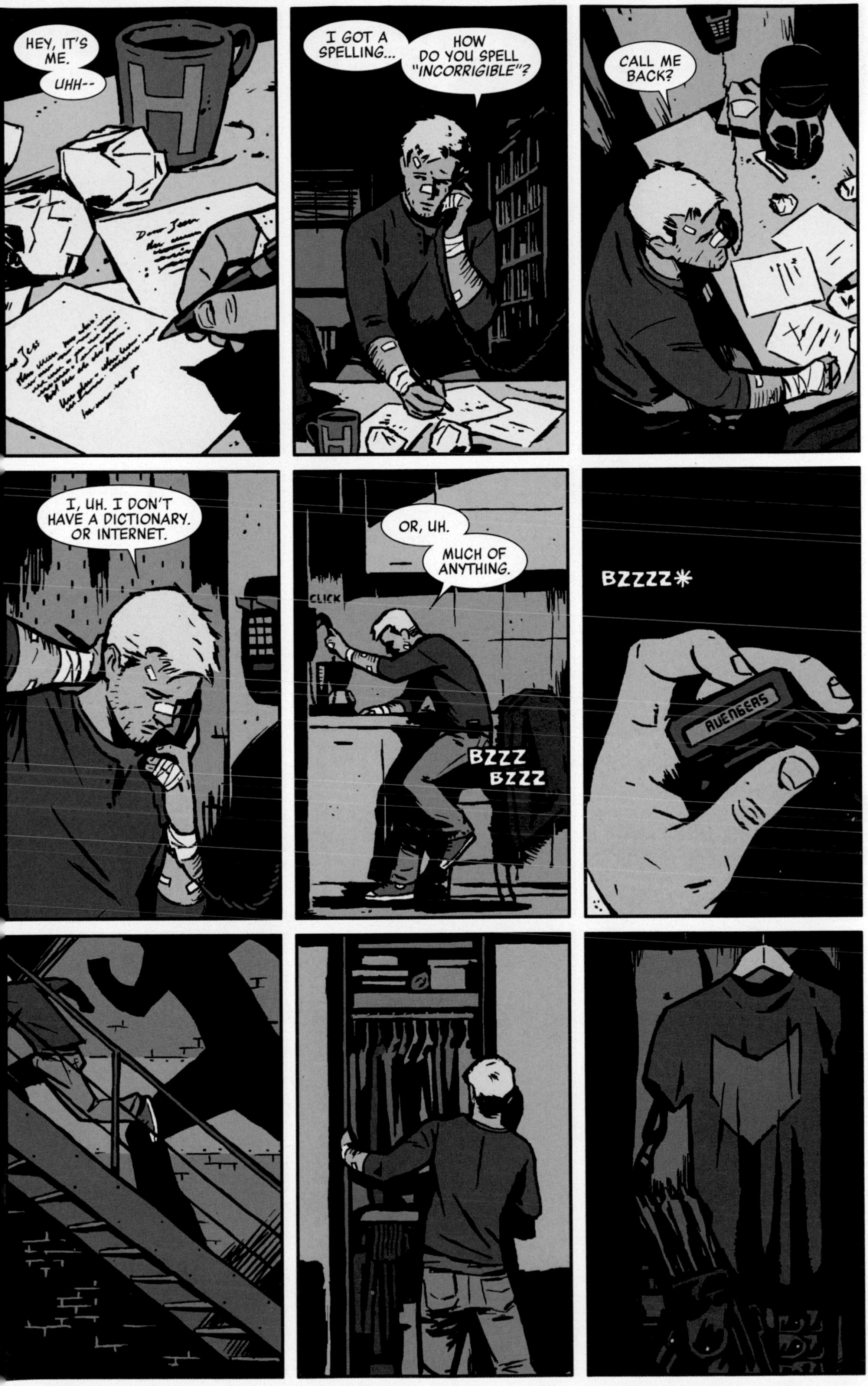
HEY, IT'S ME.
UHH--
I GOT A SPELLING...
HOW DO YOU SPELL "INCORRIGIBLE"?
CALL ME BACK?
I, UH. I DON'T HAVE A DICTIONARY. OR INTERNET.
OR, UH.
MUCH OF ANYTHING.
CLICK
BZZZ BZZZ
BZZZZ*
AVENGERS

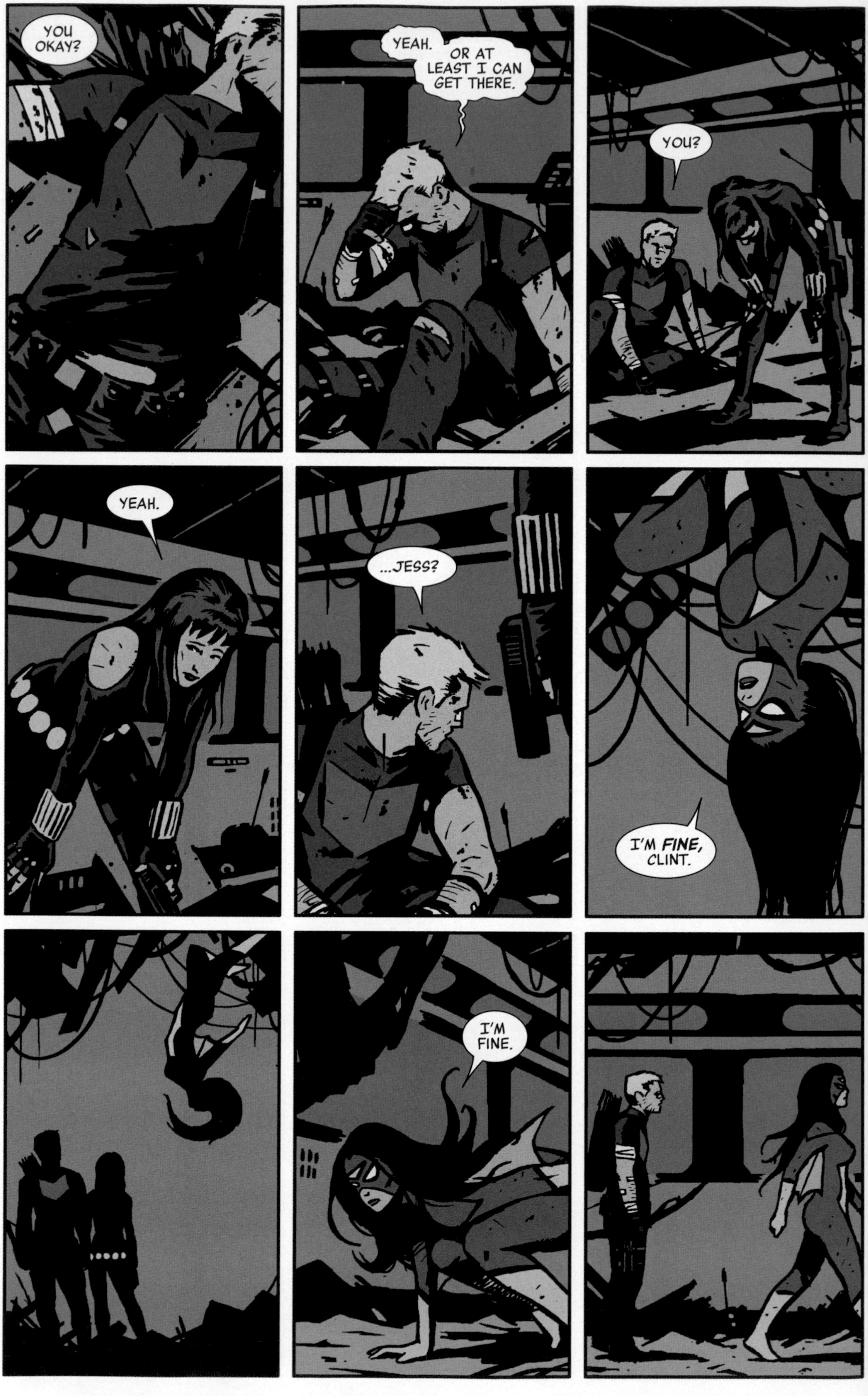
YOU OKAY?
YEAH.
OR AT LEAST I CAN GET THERE.
YOU?
YEAH.
...JESS?
I'M *FINE*, CLINT.
I'M FINE.

...
JE--
--BARTON!
IT'S YOUR SIDEKICK.
I DON'T HAVE A SIDE--
BISHOP, DUMMY. WHAT ARE YOU, CONCUSSED?
...ACTUALLY--
--PHONE.
HEY.
...
SOMETHING HAPPENED.

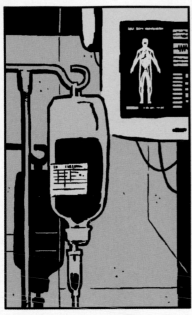

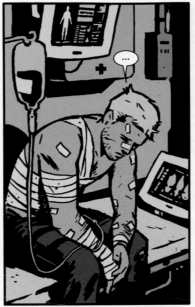

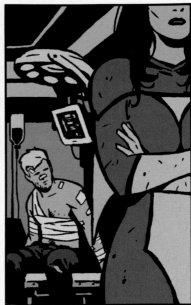

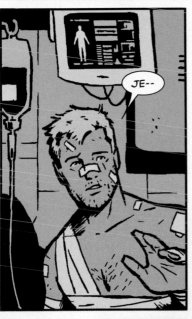

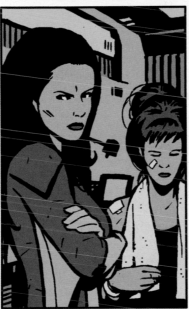

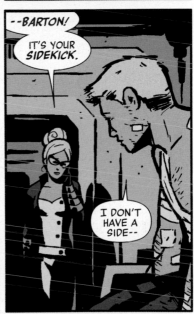

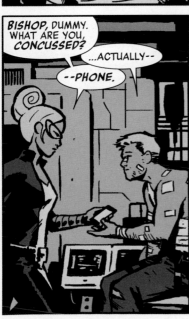

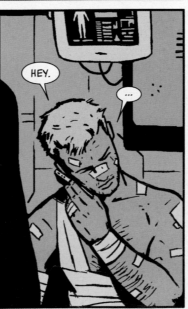

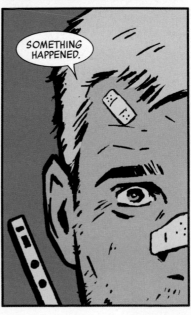

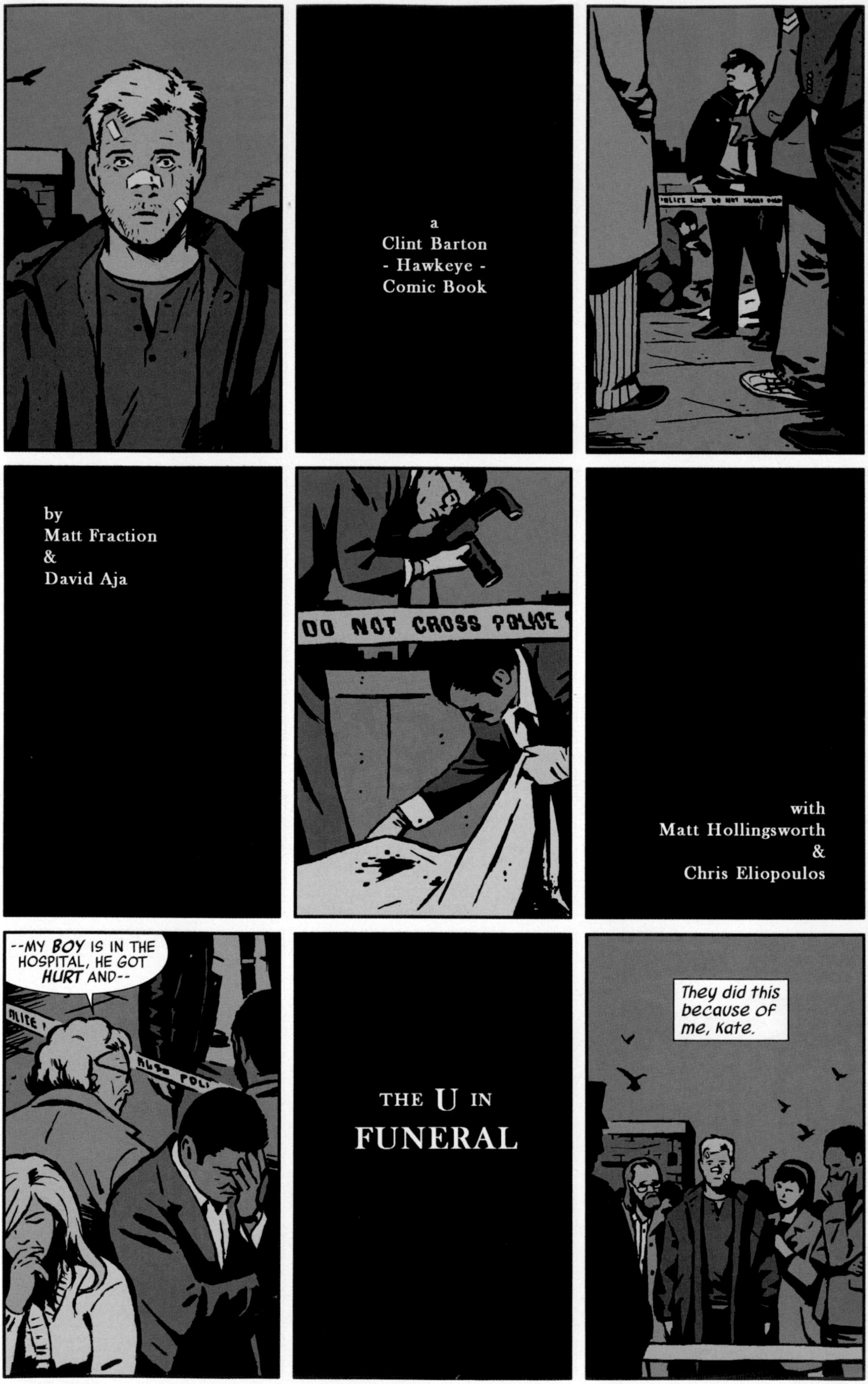
a
Clint Barton
- Hawkeye -
Comic Book
by
Matt Fraction
&
David Aja
DO NOT CROSS POLICE
with
Matt Hollingsworth
&
Chris Eliopoulos
--MY BOY IS IN THE HOSPITAL, HE GOT HURT AND--
THE U IN FUNERAL
They did this because of me, Kate.

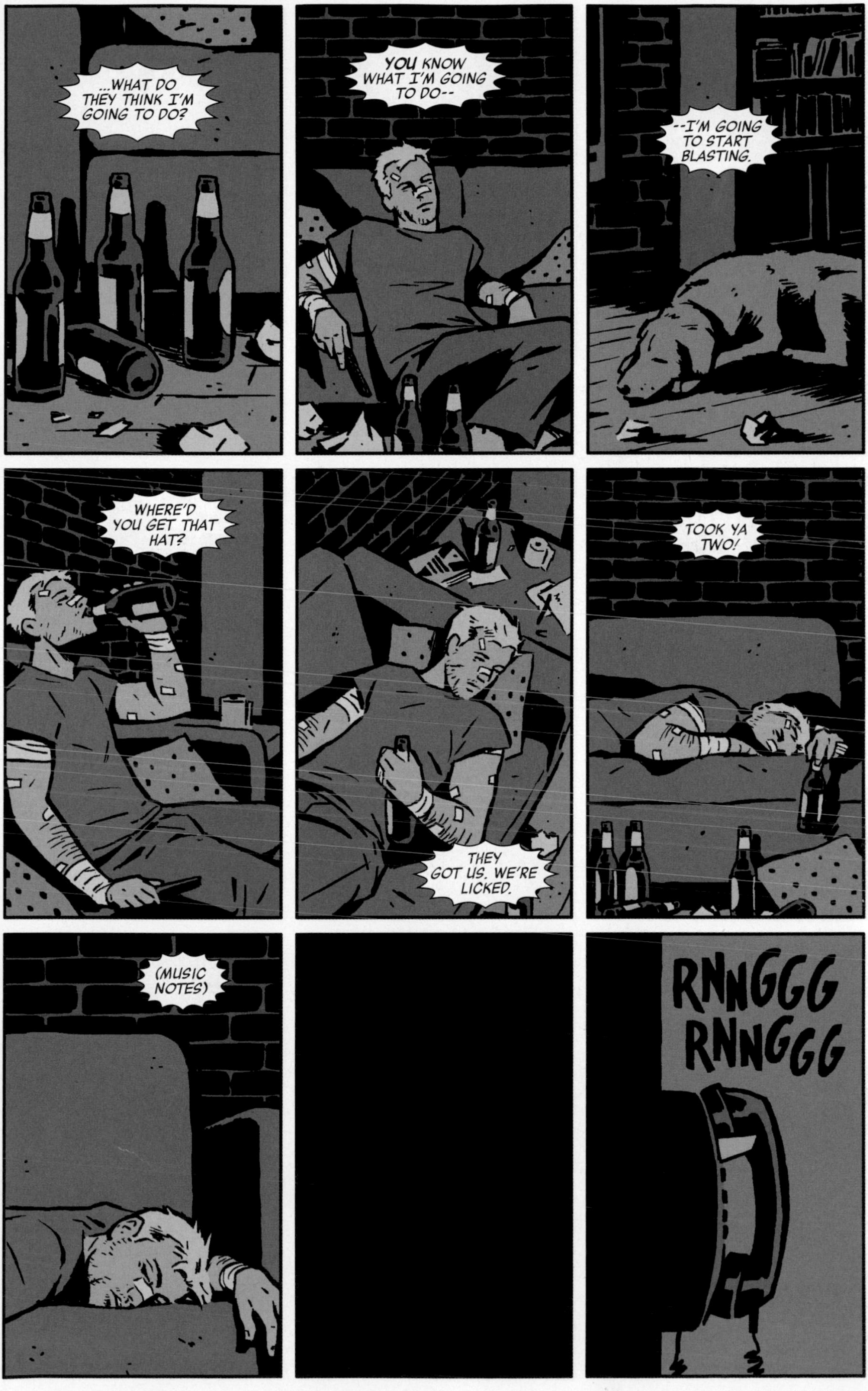
...WHAT DO THEY THINK I'M GOING TO DO?
YOU KNOW WHAT I'M GOING TO DO--
--I'M GOING TO START BLASTING.
WHERE'D YOU GET THAT HAT?
THEY GOT US. WE'RE LICKED.
TOOK YA TWO!
(MUSIC NOTES)
RNNGGG RNNGGG

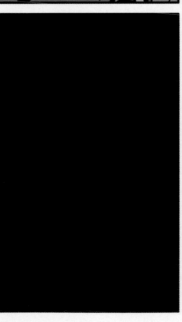

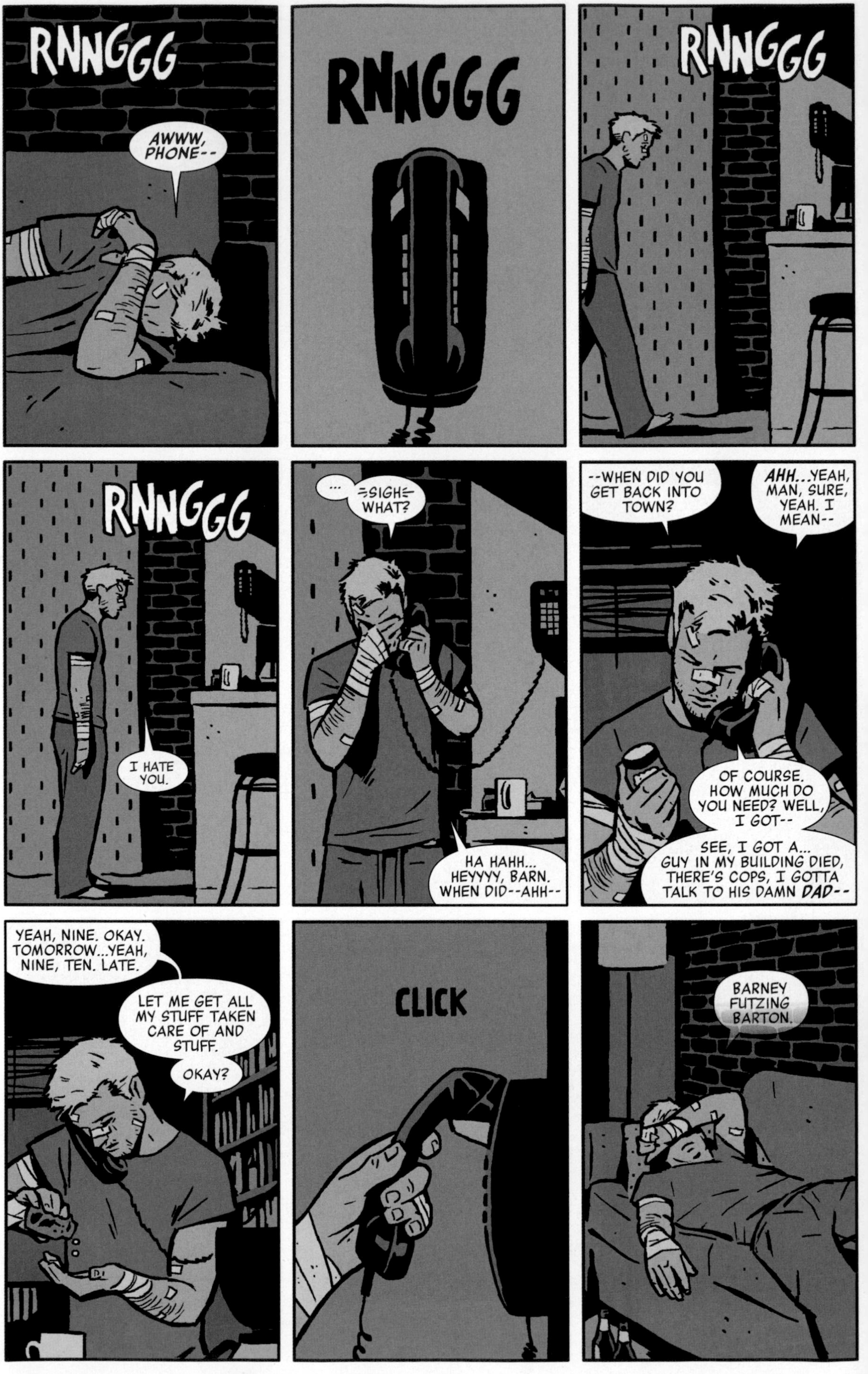
RNNGGG
AWWW, PHONE--
RNNGGG
RNNGGG
RNNGGG
I HATE YOU.
...
=SIGH= WHAT?
HA HAHH... HEYYYY, BARN. WHEN DID--AHH--
--WHEN DID YOU GET BACK INTO TOWN?
AHH...YEAH, MAN, SURE, YEAH. I MEAN--
OF COURSE. HOW MUCH DO YOU NEED? WELL, I GOT--
SEE, I GOT A... GUY IN MY BUILDING DIED, THERE'S COPS, I GOTTA TALK TO HIS DAMN DAD--
YEAH, NINE. OKAY. TOMORROW...YEAH, NINE, TEN. LATE.
LET ME GET ALL MY STUFF TAKEN CARE OF AND STUFF.
OKAY?
CLICK
BARNEY FUTZING BARTON.

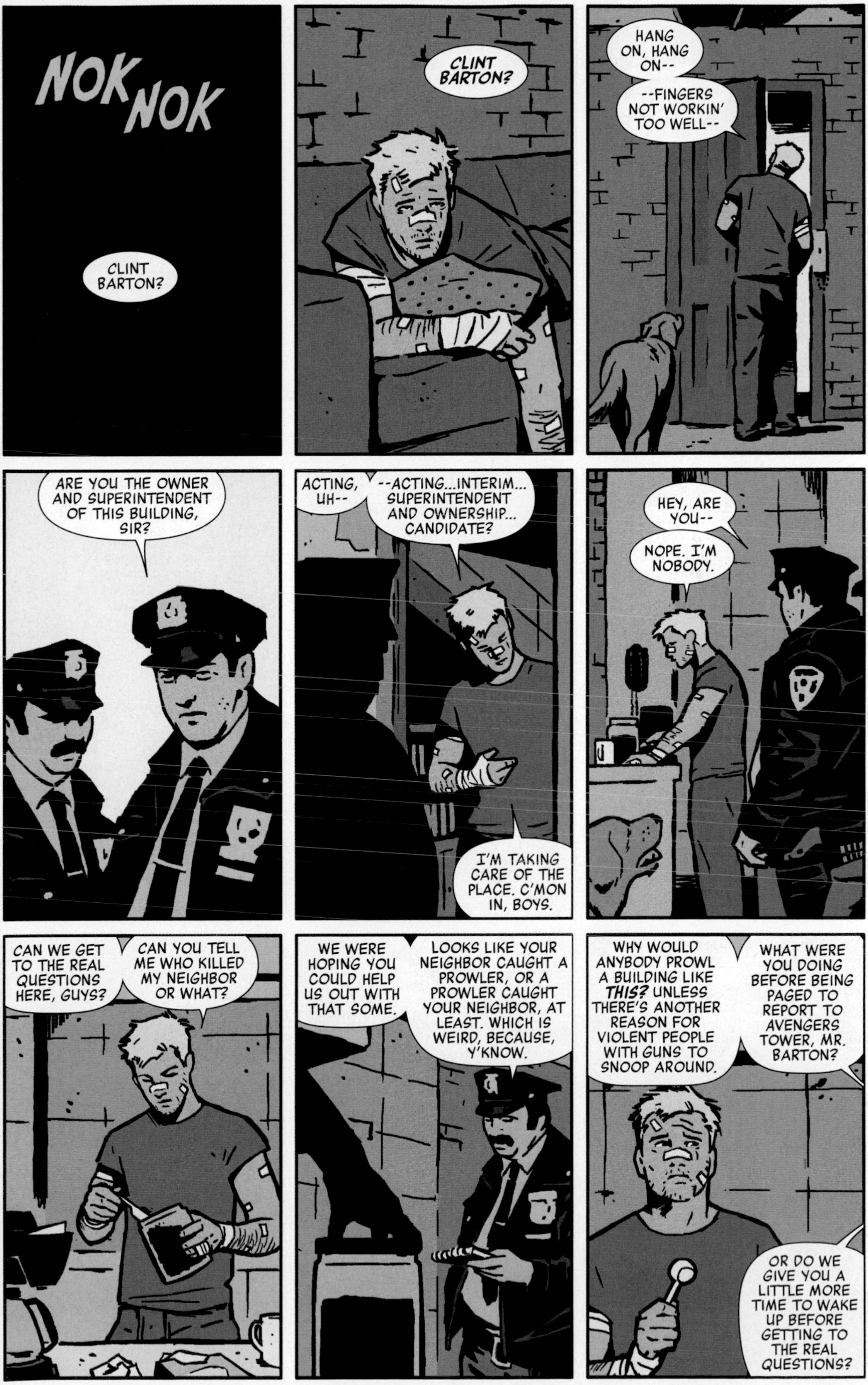
NOK NOK
CLINT BARTON?
CLINT BARTON?
HANG ON, HANG ON--
--FINGERS NOT WORKIN' TOO WELL--
ARE YOU THE OWNER AND SUPERINTENDENT OF THIS BUILDING, SIR?
ACTING, UH--
--ACTING...INTERIM... SUPERINTENDENT AND OWNERSHIP... CANDIDATE?
I'M TAKING CARE OF THE PLACE. C'MON IN, BOYS.
HEY, ARE YOU--
NOPE. I'M NOBODY.
CAN WE GET TO THE REAL QUESTIONS HERE, GUYS?
CAN YOU TELL ME WHO KILLED MY NEIGHBOR OR WHAT?
WE WERE HOPING YOU COULD HELP US OUT WITH THAT SOME.
LOOKS LIKE YOUR NEIGHBOR CAUGHT A PROWLER, OR A PROWLER CAUGHT YOUR NEIGHBOR, AT LEAST. WHICH IS WEIRD, BECAUSE, Y'KNOW.
WHY WOULD ANYBODY PROWL A BUILDING LIKE THIS? UNLESS THERE'S ANOTHER REASON FOR VIOLENT PEOPLE WITH GUNS TO SNOOP AROUND.
WHAT WERE YOU DOING BEFORE BEING PAGED TO REPORT TO AVENGERS TOWER, MR. BARTON?
OR DO WE GIVE YOU A LITTLE MORE TIME TO WAKE UP BEFORE GETTING TO THE REAL QUESTIONS?

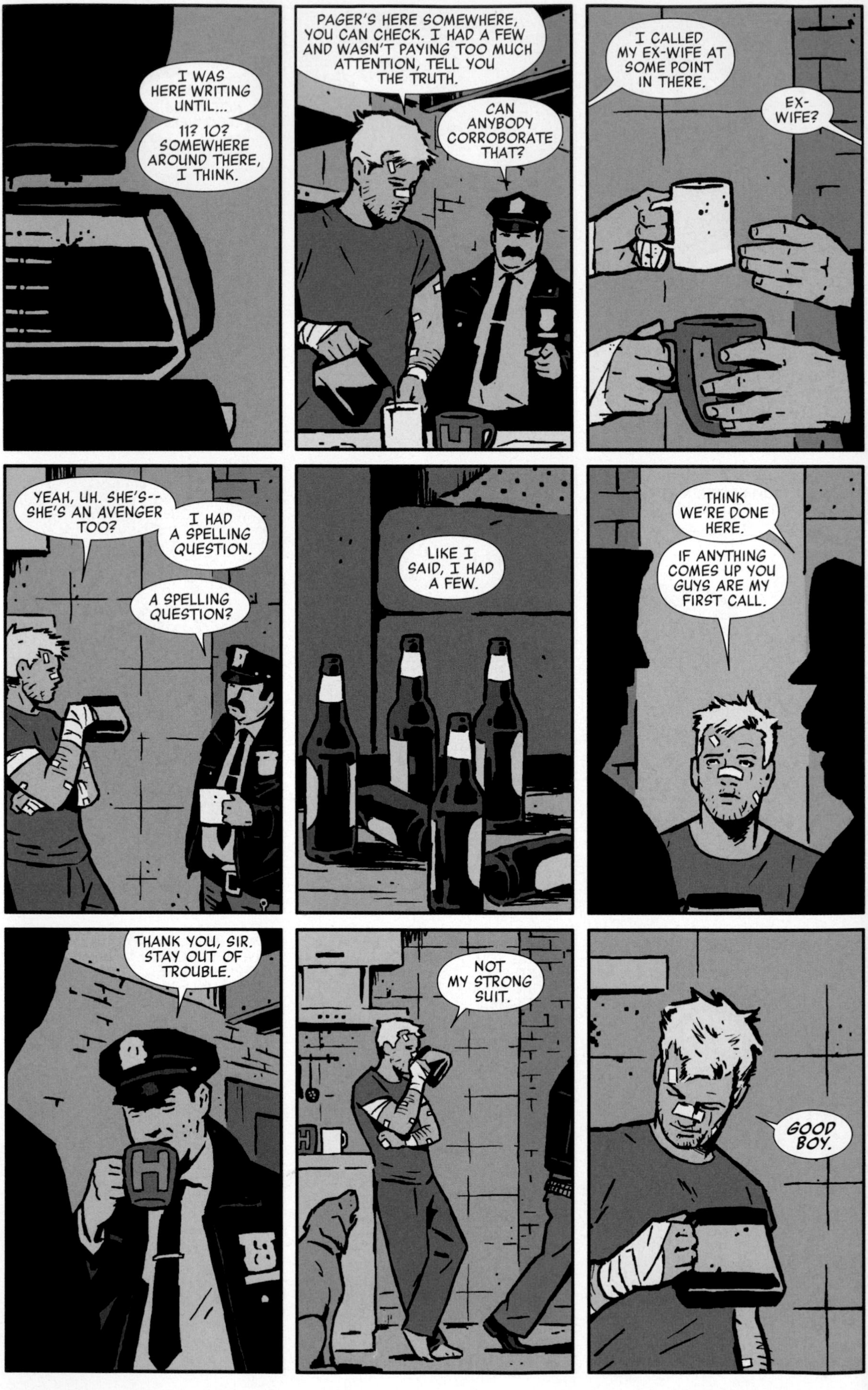
I WAS HERE WRITING UNTIL...
11? 10? SOMEWHERE AROUND THERE, I THINK.
PAGER'S HERE SOMEWHERE, YOU CAN CHECK. I HAD A FEW AND WASN'T PAYING TOO MUCH ATTENTION, TELL YOU THE TRUTH.
CAN ANYBODY CORROBORATE THAT?
I CALLED MY EX-WIFE AT SOME POINT IN THERE.
EX-WIFE?
YEAH, UH. SHE'S-- SHE'S AN AVENGER TOO?
I HAD A SPELLING QUESTION.
A SPELLING QUESTION?
LIKE I SAID, I HAD A FEW.
THINK WE'RE DONE HERE.
IF ANYTHING COMES UP YOU GUYS ARE MY FIRST CALL.
THANK YOU, SIR. STAY OUT OF TROUBLE.
NOT MY STRONG SUIT.
GOOD BOY.

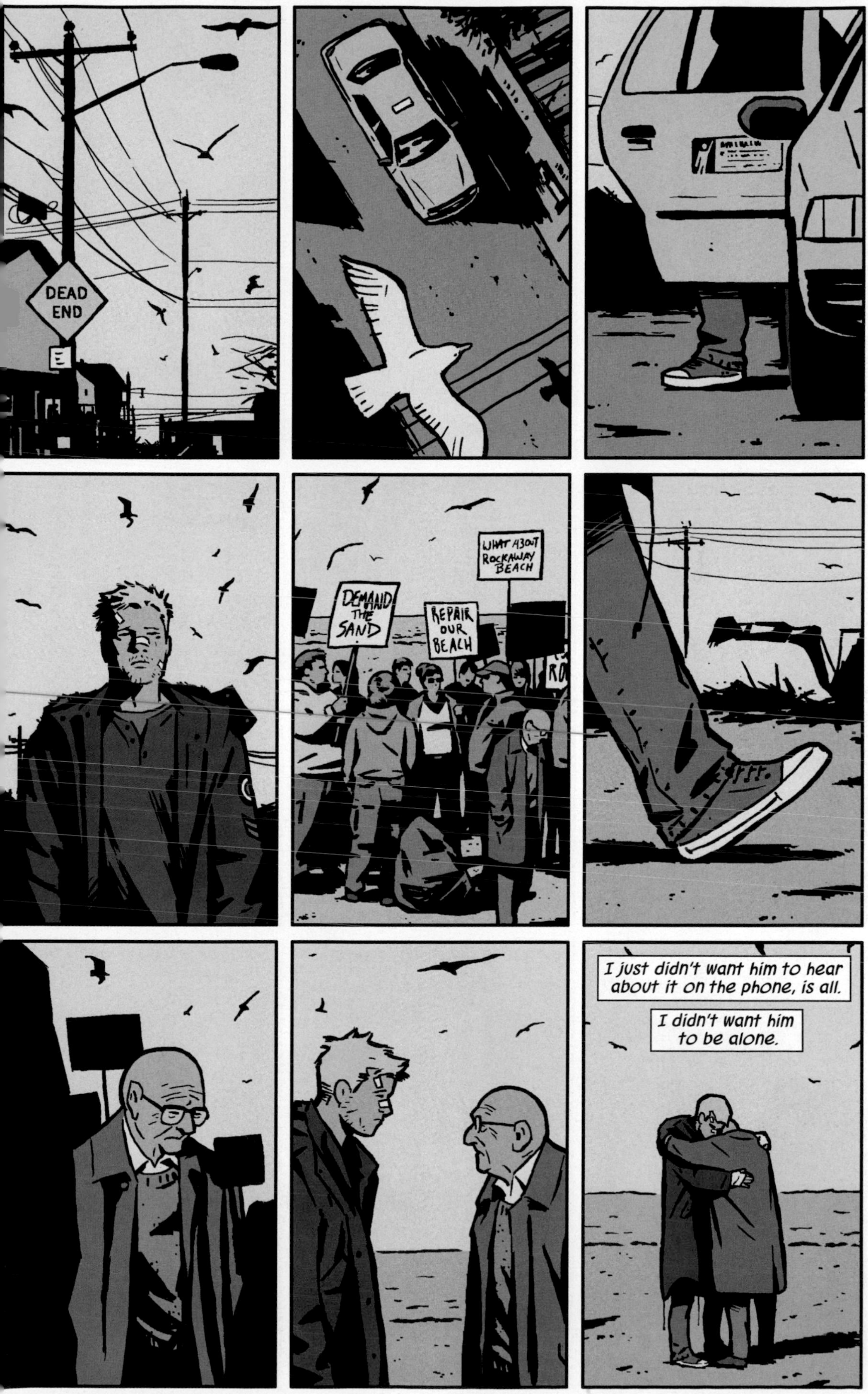
DEAD END
WHAT ABOUT ROCKAWAY BEACH
DEMAND THE SAND
REPAIR OUR BEACH
I just didn't want him to hear about it on the phone, is all.
I didn't want him to be alone.

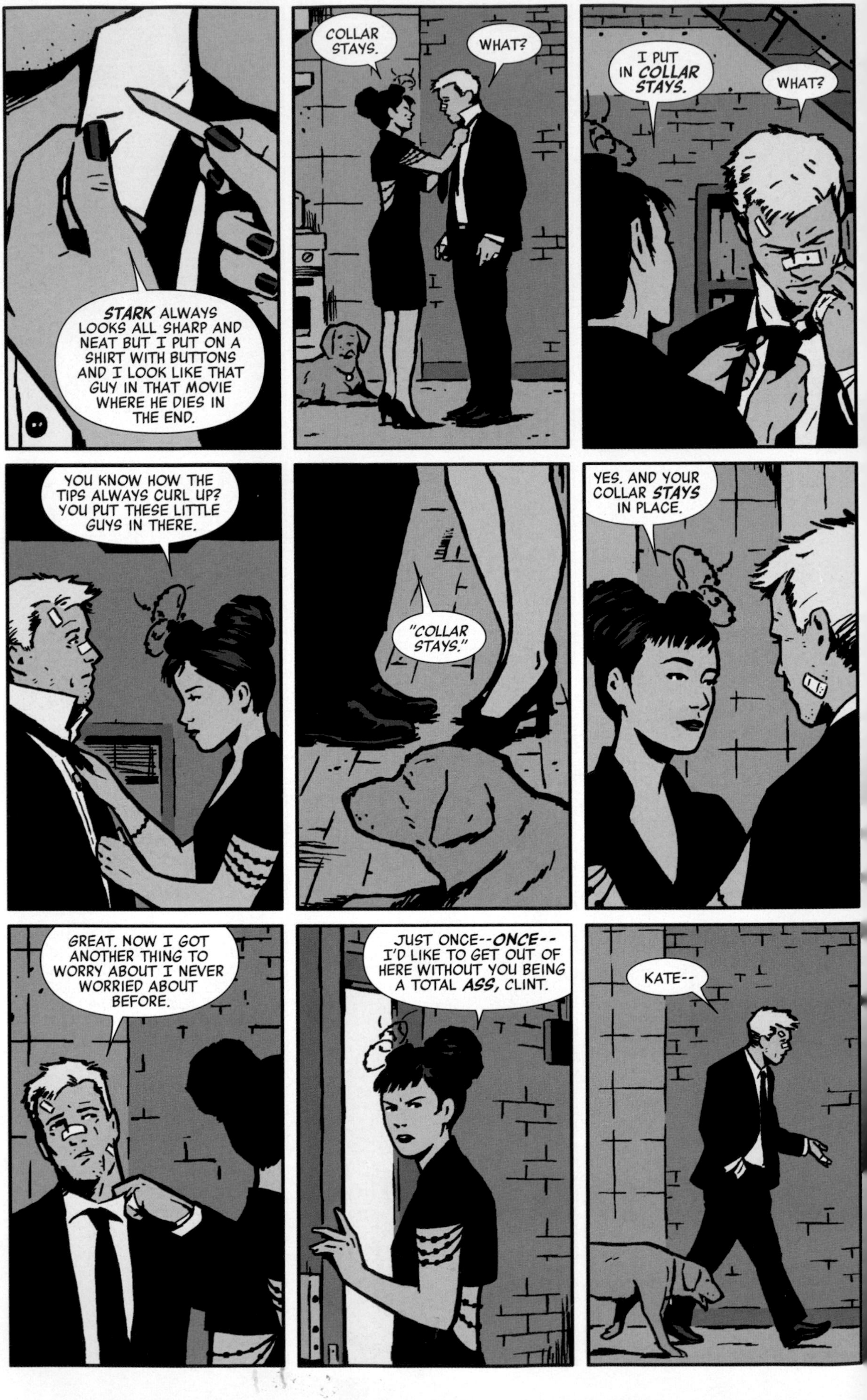
STARK ALWAYS LOOKS ALL SHARP AND NEAT BUT I PUT ON A SHIRT WITH BUTTONS AND I LOOK LIKE THAT GUY IN THAT MOVIE WHERE HE DIES IN THE END.
COLLAR STAYS.
WHAT?
I PUT IN COLLAR STAYS.
WHAT?
YOU KNOW HOW THE TIPS ALWAYS CURL UP? YOU PUT THESE LITTLE GUYS IN THERE.
"COLLAR STAYS."
YES. AND YOUR COLLAR STAYS IN PLACE.
GREAT. NOW I GOT ANOTHER THING TO WORRY ABOUT I NEVER WORRIED ABOUT BEFORE.
JUST ONCE--ONCE--I'D LIKE TO GET OUT OF HERE WITHOUT YOU BEING A TOTAL ASS, CLINT.
KATE--

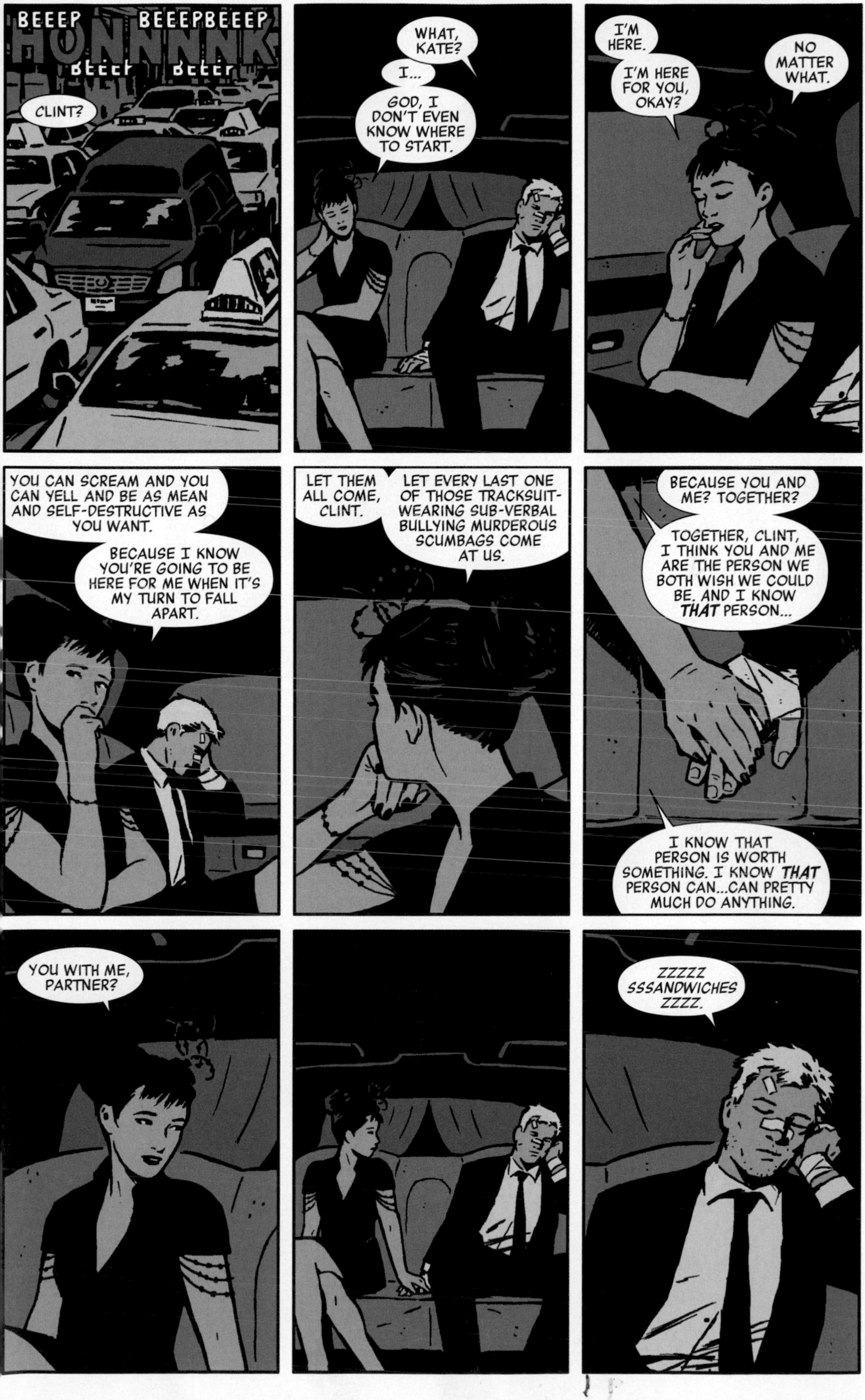
BEEEP BEEEPBEEEP
HONNNNK
CLINT?
WHAT, KATE?
I...
GOD, I DON'T EVEN KNOW WHERE TO START.
I'M HERE.
I'M HERE FOR YOU, OKAY?
NO MATTER WHAT.
YOU CAN SCREAM AND YOU CAN YELL AND BE AS MEAN AND SELF-DESTRUCTIVE AS YOU WANT.
BECAUSE I KNOW YOU'RE GOING TO BE HERE FOR ME WHEN IT'S MY TURN TO FALL APART.
LET THEM ALL COME, CLINT.
LET EVERY LAST ONE OF THOSE TRACKSUIT-WEARING SUB-VERBAL BULLYING MURDEROUS SCUMBAGS COME AT US.
BECAUSE YOU AND ME? TOGETHER?
TOGETHER, CLINT, I THINK YOU AND ME ARE THE PERSON WE BOTH WISH WE COULD BE. AND I KNOW THAT PERSON...
I KNOW THAT PERSON IS WORTH SOMETHING. I KNOW THAT PERSON CAN...CAN PRETTY MUCH DO ANYTHING.
YOU WITH ME, PARTNER?
ZZZZZ SSSANDWICHES ZZZZ.

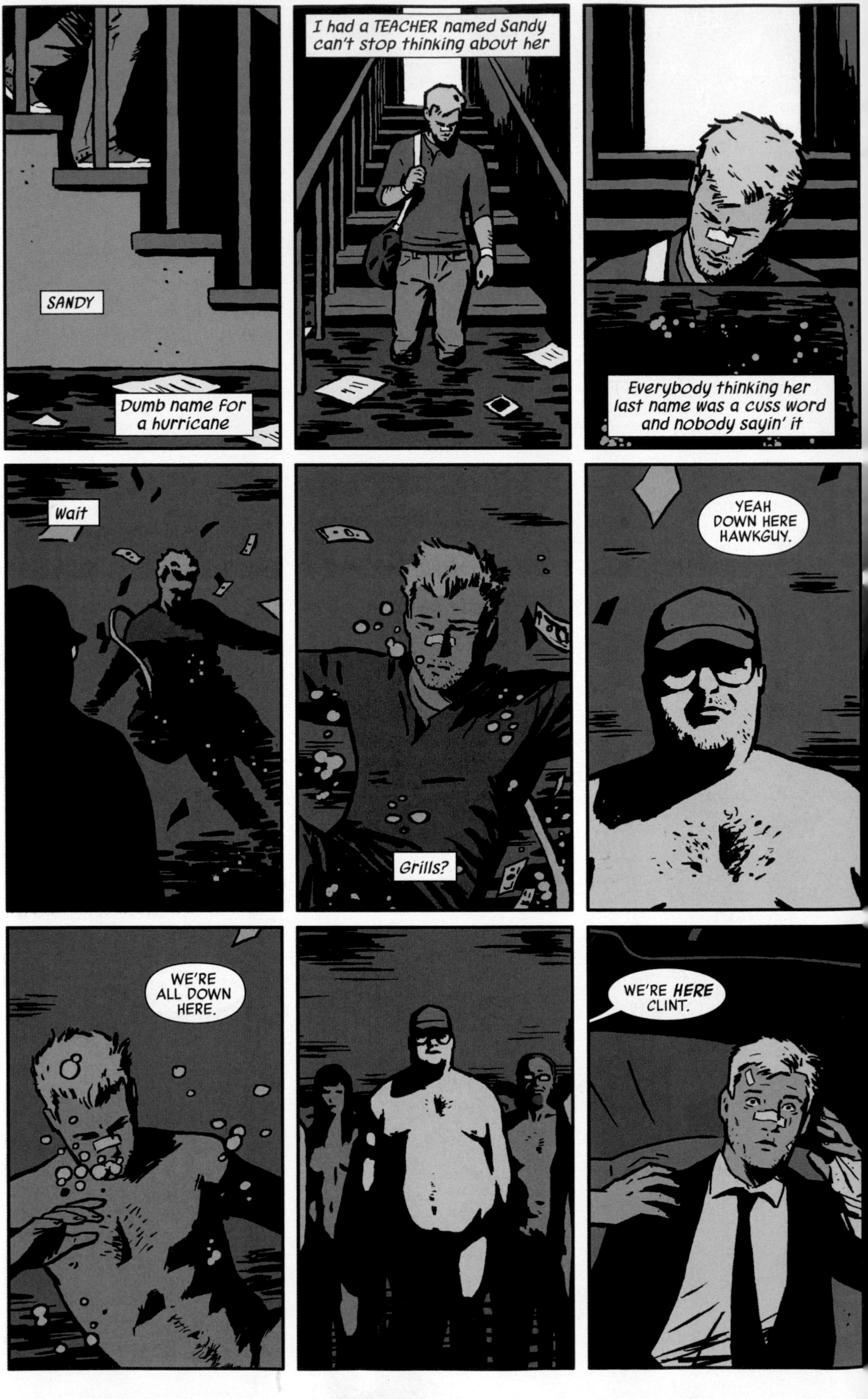
SANDY
Dumb name for a hurricane
I had a TEACHER named Sandy can't stop thinking about her
Everybody thinking her last name was a cuss word and nobody sayin' it
Wait
Grills?
YEAH DOWN HERE HAWKGUY.
WE'RE ALL DOWN HERE.
WE'RE HERE CLINT.

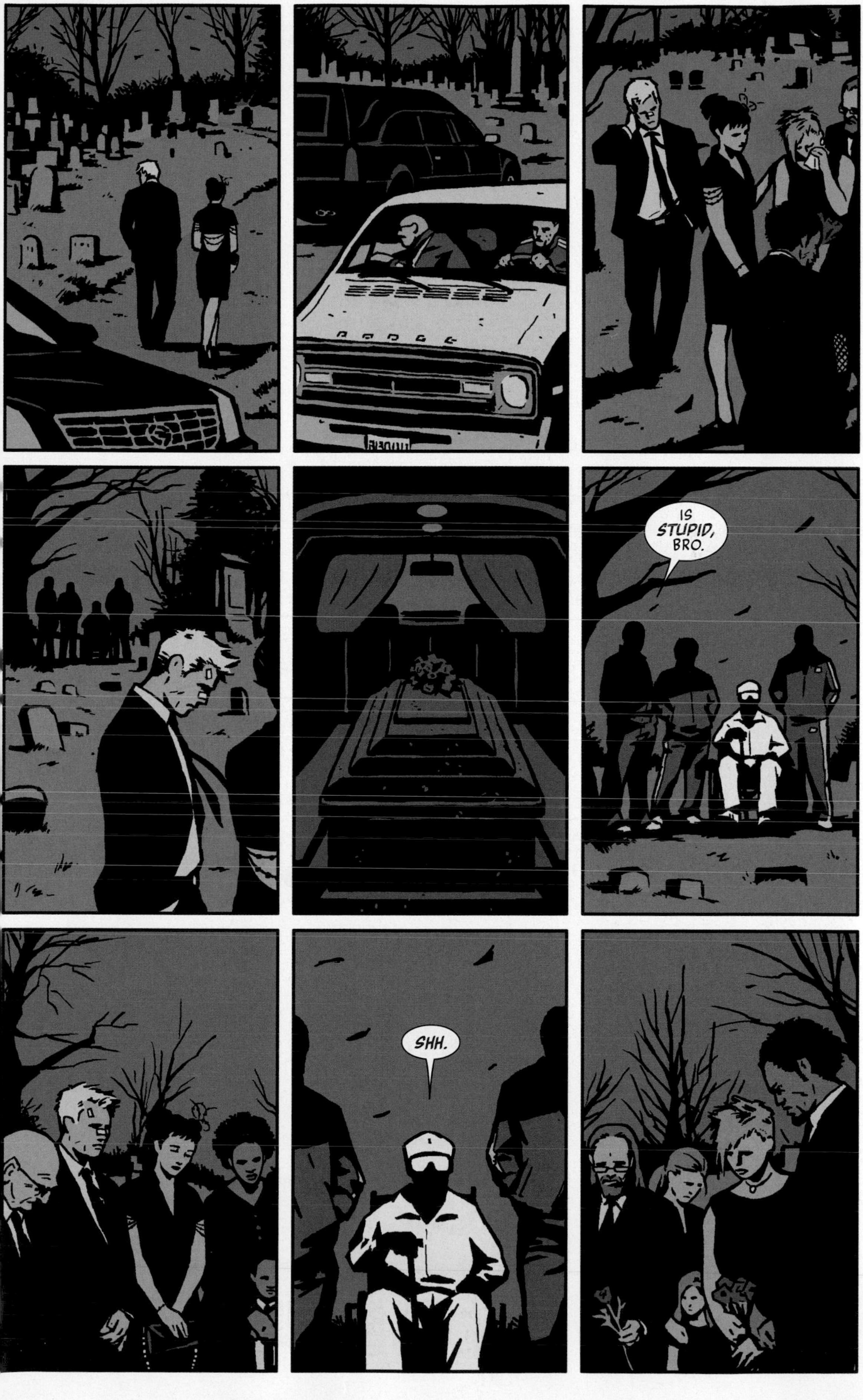
IS STUPID, BRO.
SHH.

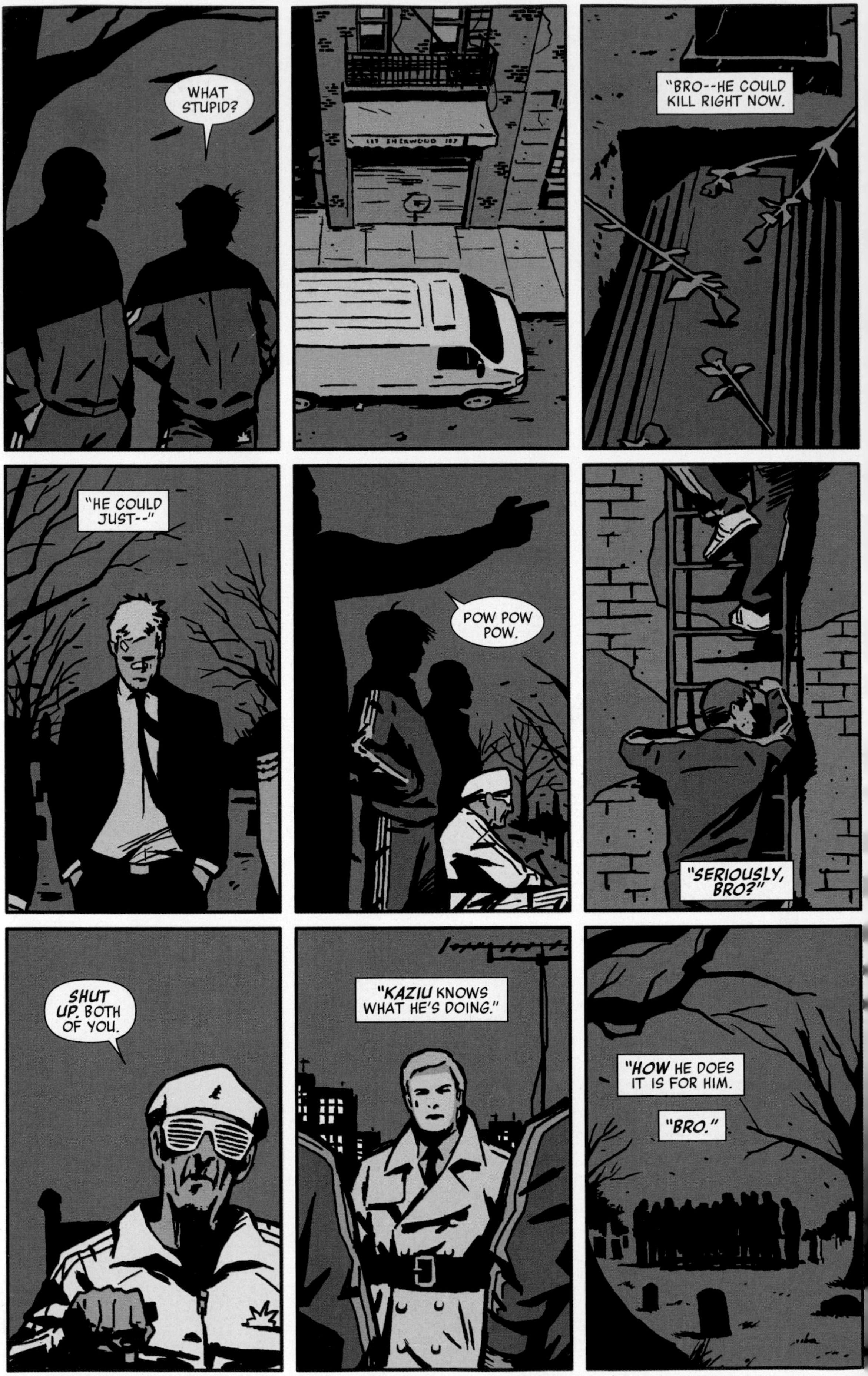
WHAT STUPID?
"BRO--HE COULD KILL RIGHT NOW.
"HE COULD JUST--"
POW POW POW.
"SERIOUSLY, BRO?"
SHUT UP. BOTH OF YOU.
"KAZIU KNOWS WHAT HE'S DOING."
"HOW HE DOES IT IS FOR HIM.
"BRO."

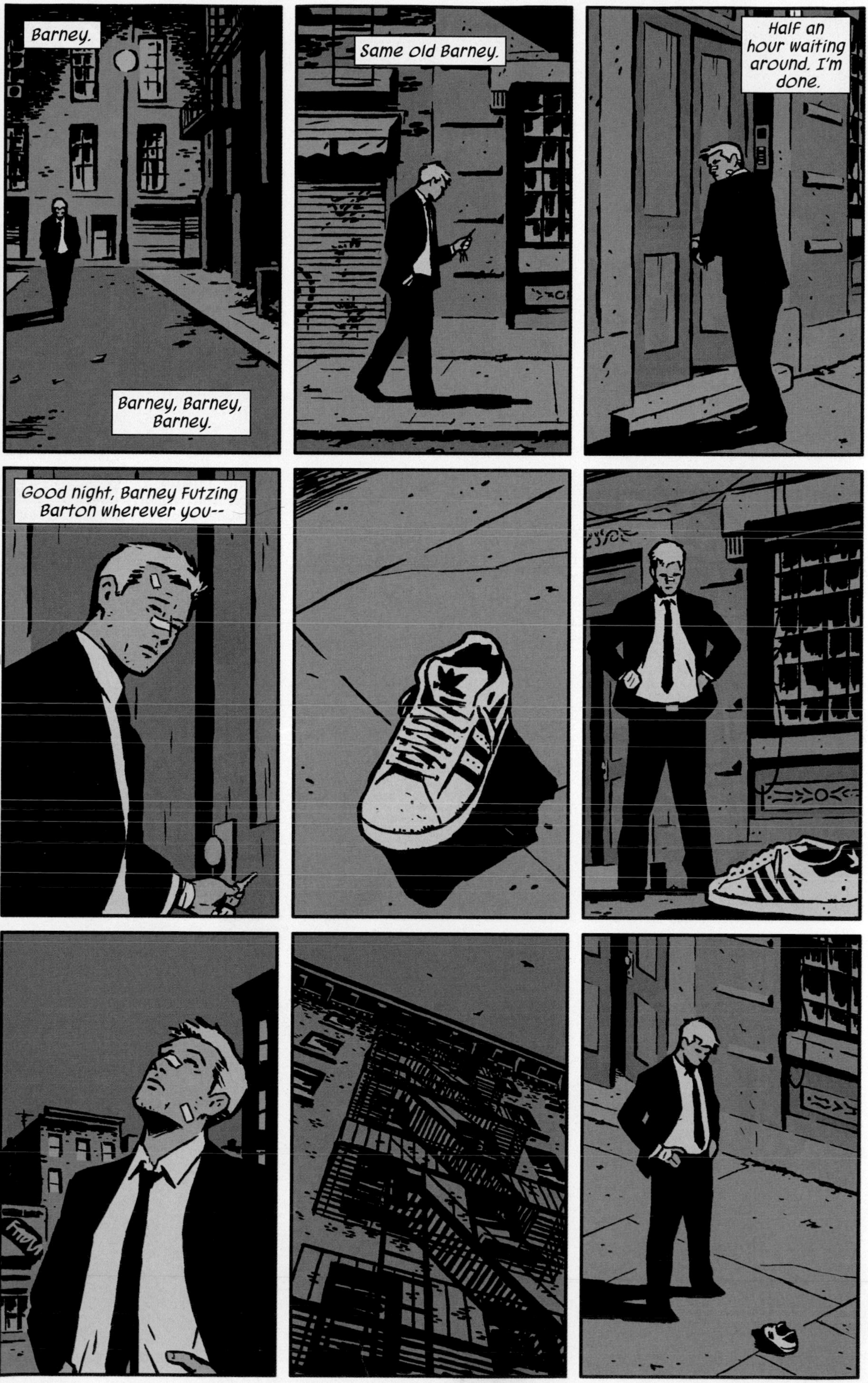
Barney.
Barney, Barney, Barney.
Same old Barney.
Half an hour waiting around. I'm done.
Good night, Barney Futzing Barton wherever you--

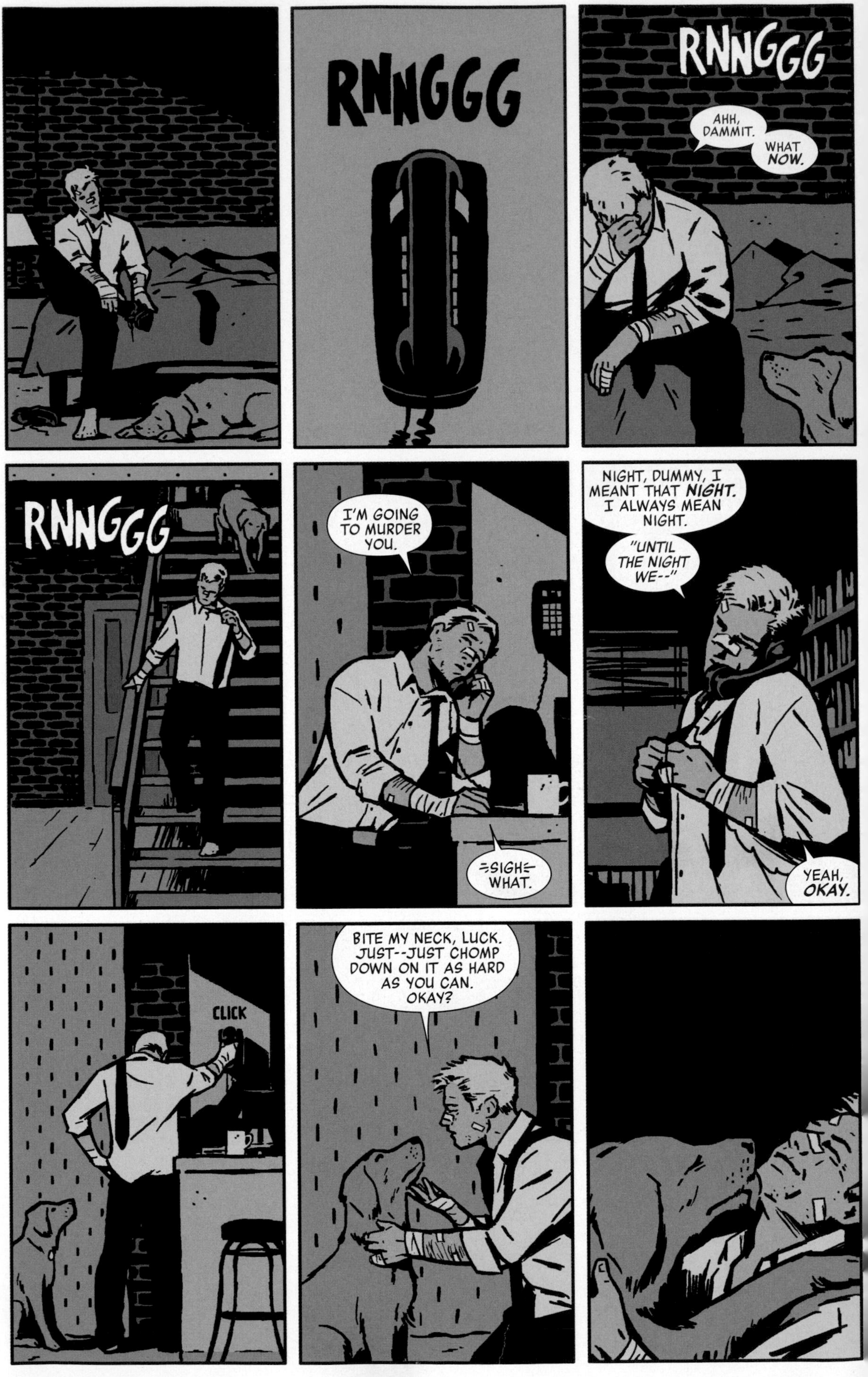
RNNGGG
RNNGGG
AHH, DAMMIT.
WHAT NOW.
RNNGGG
I'M GOING TO MURDER YOU.
=SIGH= WHAT.
NIGHT, DUMMY, I MEANT THAT NIGHT. I ALWAYS MEAN NIGHT.
"UNTIL THE NIGHT WE--"
YEAH, OKAY.
CLICK
BITE MY NECK, LUCK. JUST--JUST CHOMP DOWN ON IT AS HARD AS YOU CAN. OKAY?

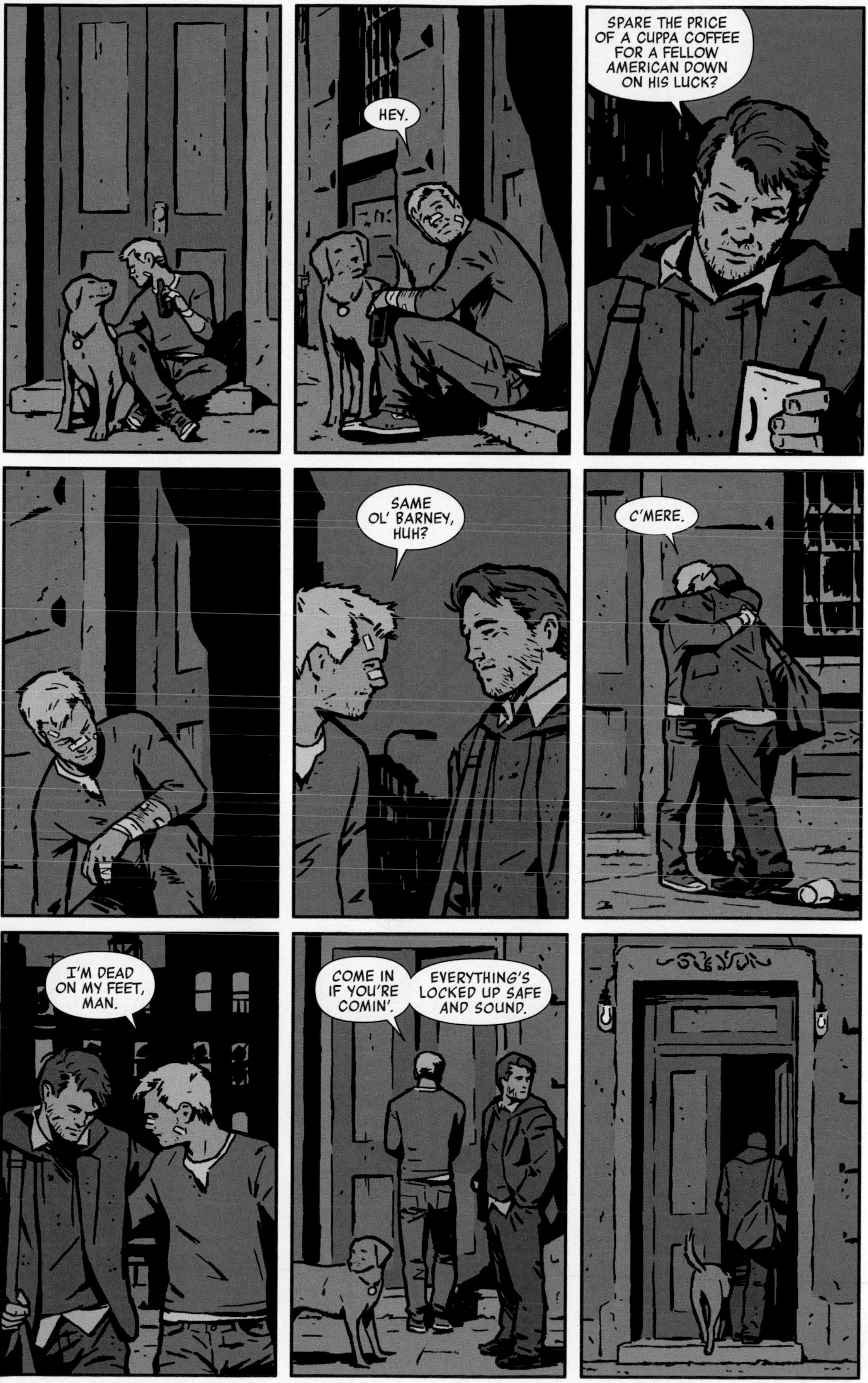
HEY.
SPARE THE PRICE OF A CUPPA COFFEE FOR A FELLOW AMERICAN DOWN ON HIS LUCK?
SAME OL' BARNEY, HUH?
C'MERE.
I'M DEAD ON MY FEET, MAN.
COME IN IF YOU'RE COMIN'.
EVERYTHING'S LOCKED UP SAFE AND SOUND.

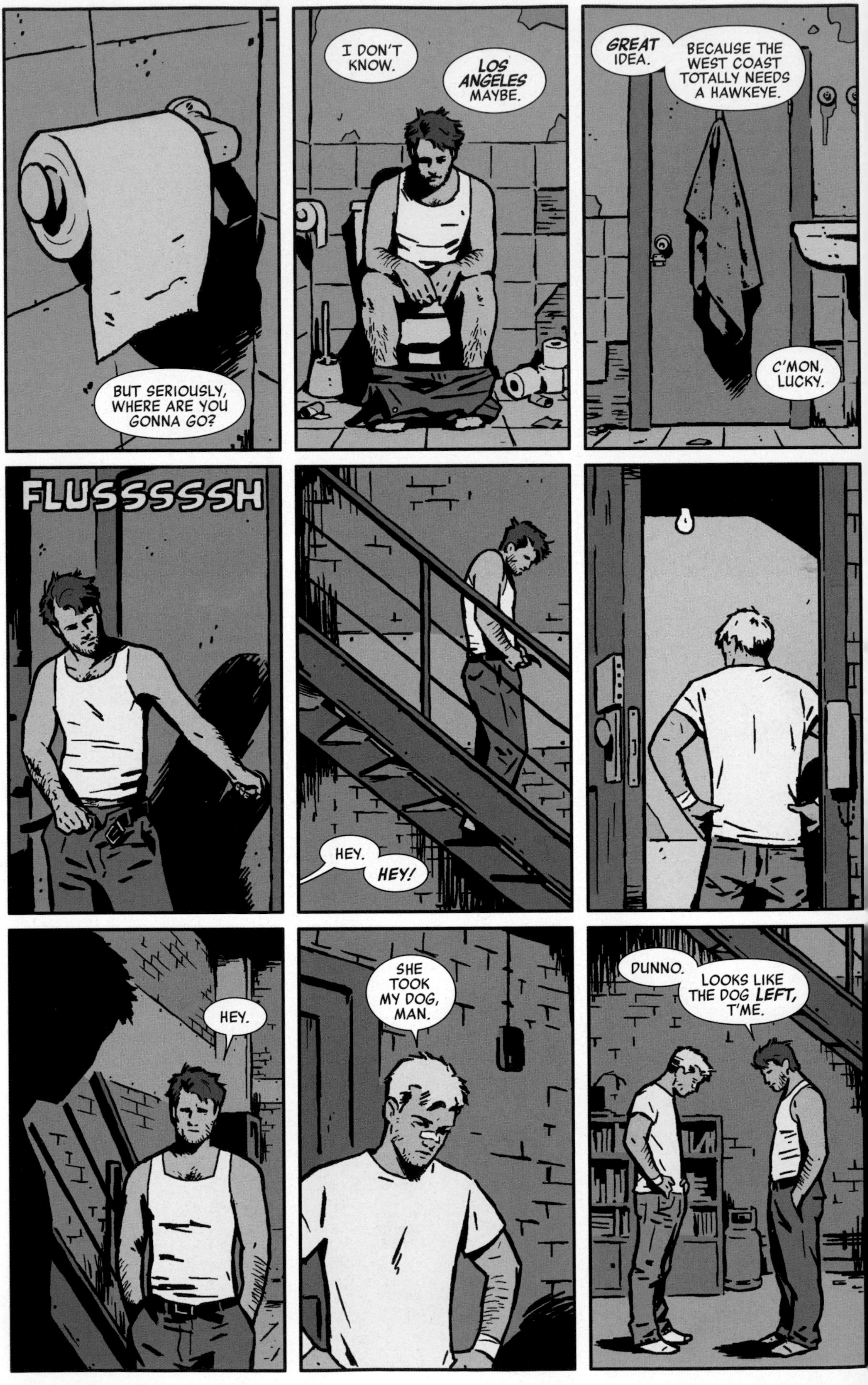
BUT SERIOUSLY, WHERE ARE YOU GONNA GO?
I DON'T KNOW.
LOS ANGELES MAYBE.
GREAT IDEA.
BECAUSE THE WEST COAST TOTALLY NEEDS A HAWKEYE.
C'MON, LUCKY.
FLUSSSSSH
HEY.
HEY!
HEY.
SHE TOOK MY DOG, MAN.
DUNNO.
LOOKS LIKE THE DOG LEFT, T'ME.

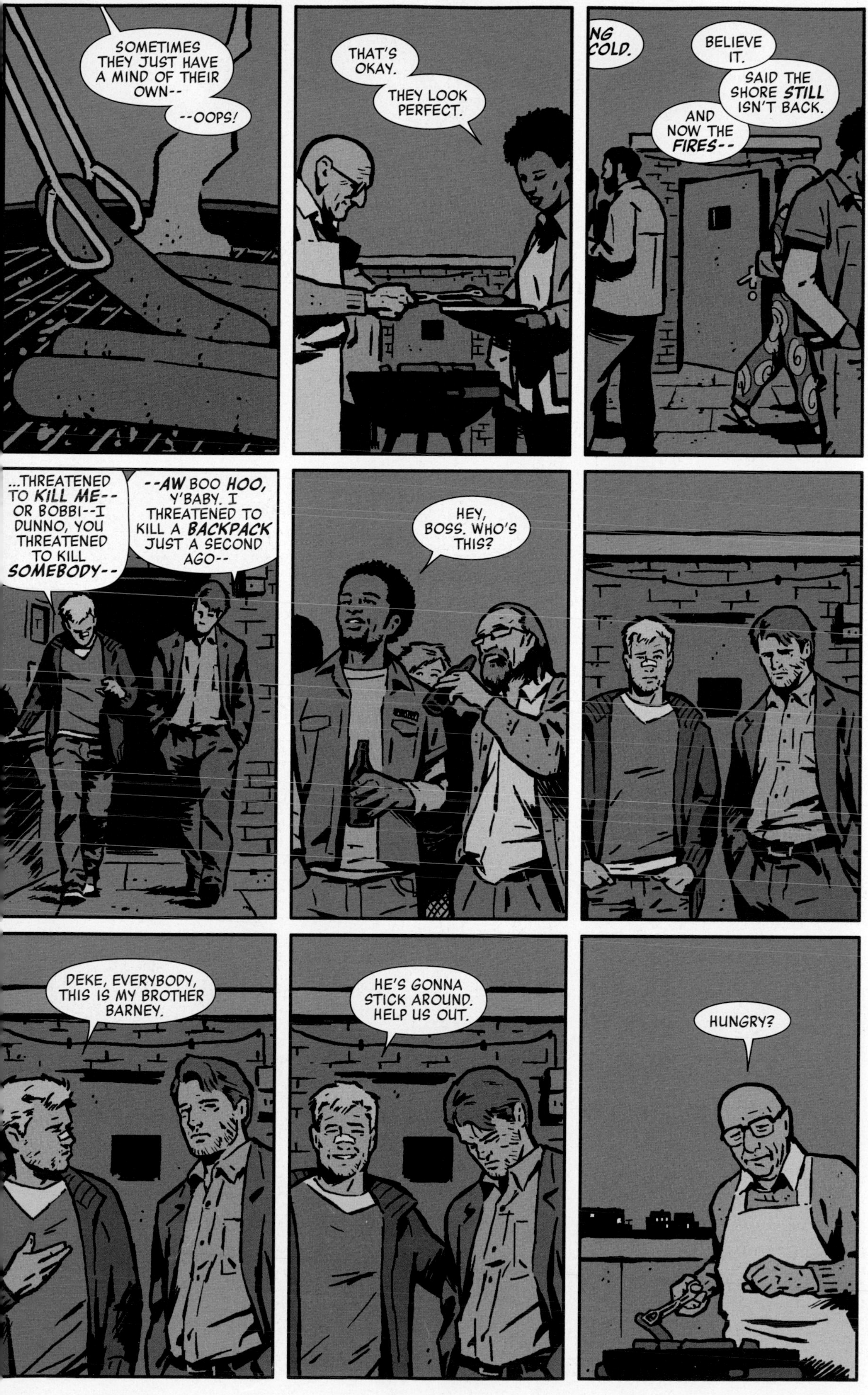

SOMETIMES THEY JUST HAVE A MIND OF THEIR OWN--
--OOPS!
THAT'S OKAY.
THEY LOOK PERFECT.
NG COLD.
BELIEVE IT.
SAID THE SHORE STILL ISN'T BACK.
AND NOW THE FIRES--
...THREATENED TO KILL ME--OR BOBBI--I DUNNO, YOU THREATENED TO KILL SOMEBODY--
--AW BOO HOO, Y'BABY. I THREATENED TO KILL A BACKPACK JUST A SECOND AGO--
HEY, BOSS. WHO'S THIS?
DEKE, EVERYBODY, THIS IS MY BROTHER BARNEY.
HE'S GONNA STICK AROUND. HELP US OUT.
HUNGRY?

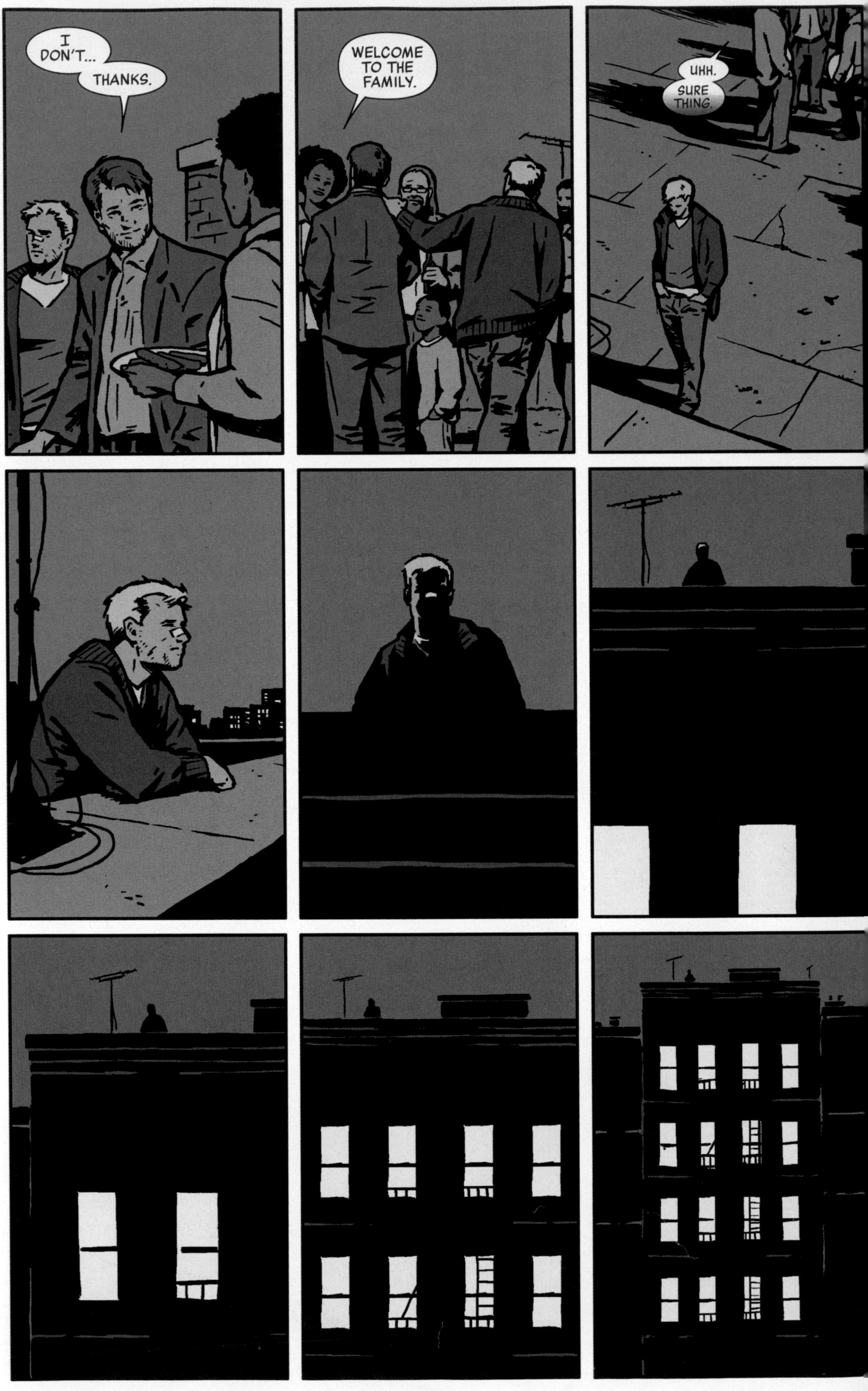
I DON'T...
THANKS.
WELCOME TO THE FAMILY.
UHH.
SURE THING.

fun & games

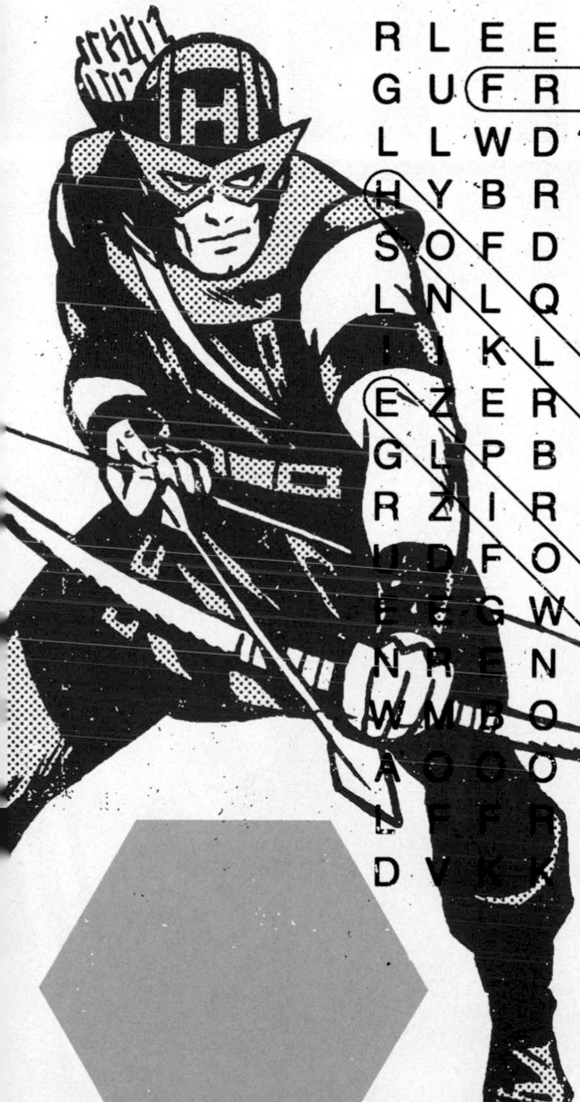

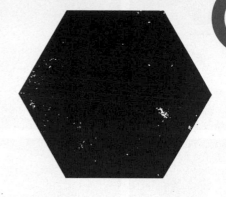

R	L	E	E	A	X	U	M	H	E	C	K	E
G	U	F	R	A	C	T	I	O	N	C	H	G
L	L	W	D	O	A	J	A	C	A	H	N	D
H	Y	B	R	O	L	L	T	R	E	P	M	A
S	O	F	D	E	H	A	W	K	E	Y	E	M
L	N	L	Q	J	R	Z	A	I	D	B	O	A
I	I	K	L	B	D	S	C	A	D	R	L	N
E	Z	E	R	I	A	A	K	V	M	E	O	A
G	L	P	B	C	N	F	E	A	C	N	R	T
R	Z	I	R	E	I	G	R	R	H	N	P	C
U	D	F	O	E	R	O	S	S	T	A	P	A
E	E	G	W	P	A	R	D	W	U	N	M	L
N	R	E	N	C	O	H	C	U	O	U	M	M
W	M	B	O	S	S	U	N	G	P	R	E	S
A	O	O	O	D	P	U	L	I	D	O	T	Q
L	F	F	R	F	R	A	R	O	I	N	G	H
D	V	K	K	B	C	Z	I	I	S	O	I	N

Okay...

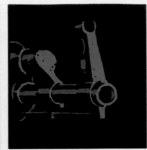

This looks...

completely ridiculous.

Whatever happens to me tonight? However bad it gets?

I had it comin'.

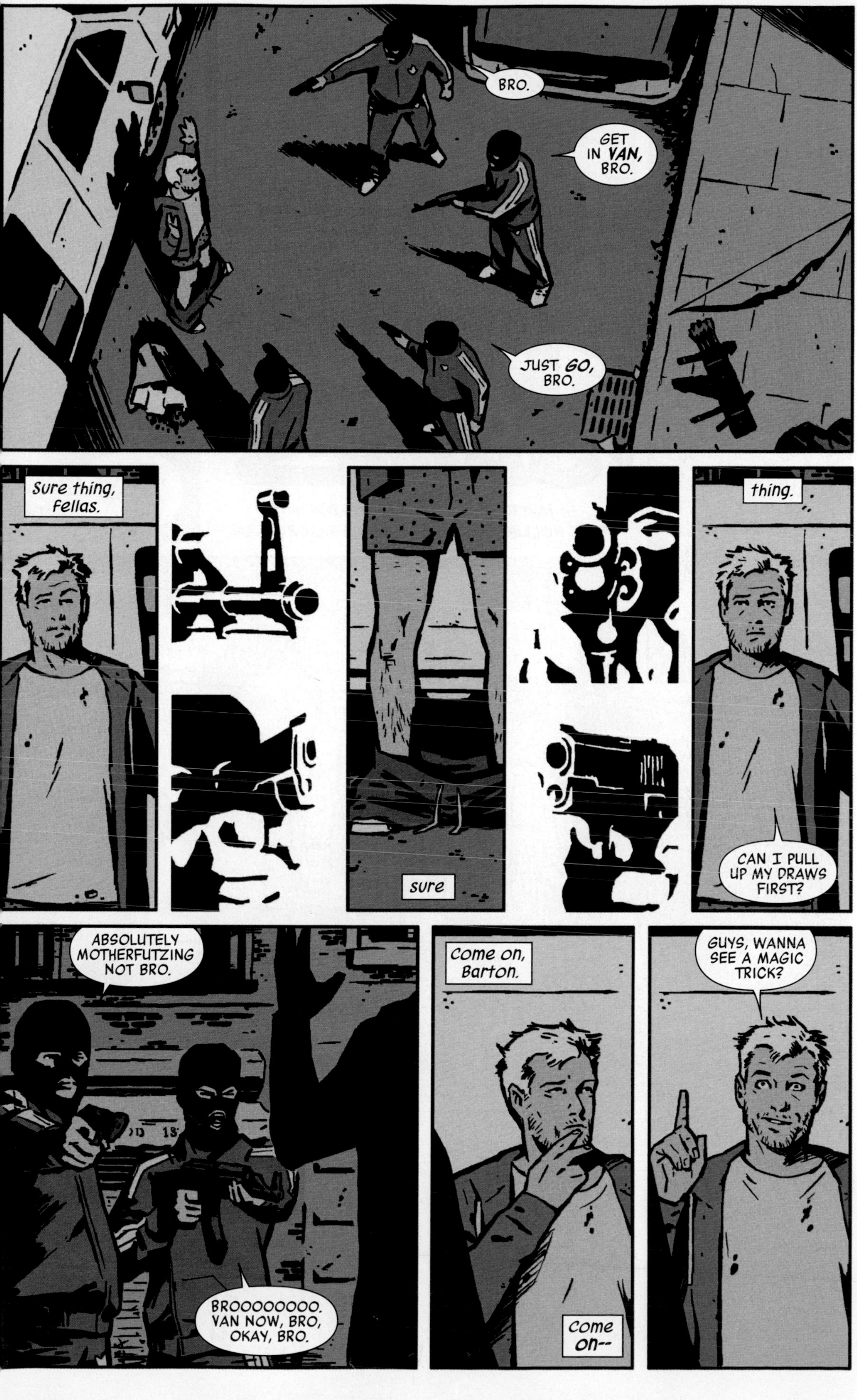
BRO.
GET IN VAN, BRO.
JUST GO, BRO.
Sure thing, fellas.
sure
thing.
CAN I PULL UP MY DRAWS FIRST?
ABSOLUTELY MOTHERFUTZING NOT BRO.
BROOOOOOOO. VAN NOW, BRO, OKAY, BRO.
Come on, Barton.
Come on--
GUYS, WANNA SEE A MAGIC TRICK?

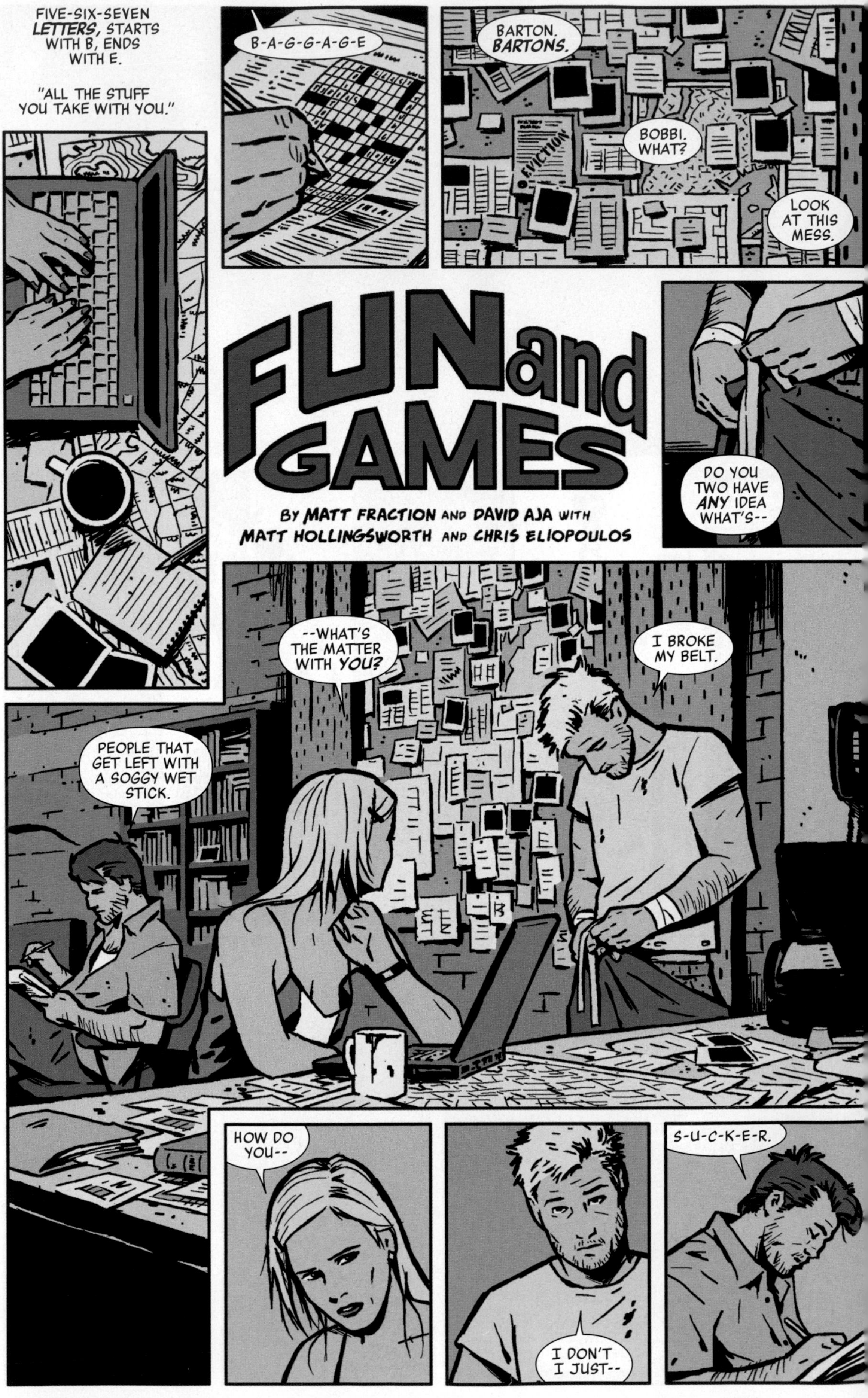
FIVE-SIX-SEVEN LETTERS, STARTS WITH B, ENDS WITH E.
"ALL THE STUFF YOU TAKE WITH YOU."
B-A-G-G-A-G-E
BARTON. BARTONS.
BOBBI. WHAT?
LOOK AT THIS MESS.
FUN and GAMES
BY MATT FRACTION AND DAVID AJA WITH MATT HOLLINGSWORTH AND CHRIS ELIOPOULOS
DO YOU TWO HAVE ANY IDEA WHAT'S--
--WHAT'S THE MATTER WITH YOU?
I BROKE MY BELT.
PEOPLE THAT GET LEFT WITH A SOGGY WET STICK.
HOW DO YOU--
I DON'T I JUST--
S-U-C-K-E-R.

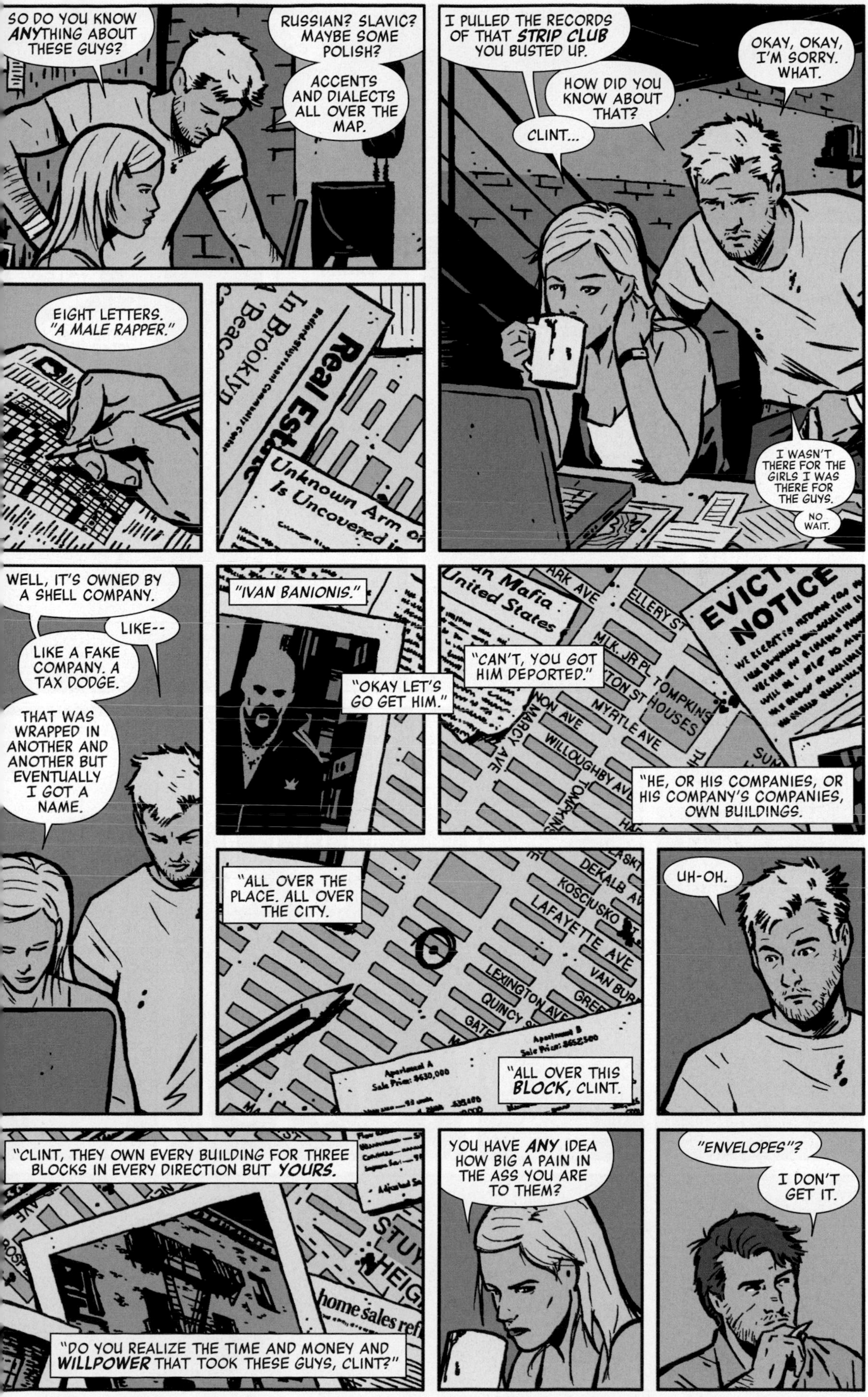
SO DO YOU KNOW ANYTHING ABOUT THESE GUYS?
RUSSIAN? SLAVIC? MAYBE SOME POLISH?
ACCENTS AND DIALECTS ALL OVER THE MAP.
I PULLED THE RECORDS OF THAT STRIP CLUB YOU BUSTED UP.
HOW DID YOU KNOW ABOUT THAT?
CLINT...
OKAY, OKAY, I'M SORRY. WHAT.
EIGHT LETTERS. "A MALE RAPPER."
Real Estate
In Brooklyn
Unknown Arm of
Is Uncovered i
I WASN'T THERE FOR THE GIRLS I WAS THERE FOR THE GUYS.
NO WAIT.
WELL, IT'S OWNED BY A SHELL COMPANY.
LIKE--
LIKE A FAKE COMPANY. A TAX DODGE.
THAT WAS WRAPPED IN ANOTHER AND ANOTHER BUT EVENTUALLY I GOT A NAME.
"IVAN BANIONIS."
"OKAY LET'S GO GET HIM."
"CAN'T, YOU GOT HIM DEPORTED."
United States
EVICTI NOTICE
"HE, OR HIS COMPANIES, OR HIS COMPANY'S COMPANIES, OWN BUILDINGS.
"ALL OVER THE PLACE. ALL OVER THE CITY.
DEKALB AV
KOSCIUSKO
LAFAYETTE AVE
LEXINGTON AVE
QUINCY
"ALL OVER THIS BLOCK, CLINT.
UH-OH.
"CLINT, THEY OWN EVERY BUILDING FOR THREE BLOCKS IN EVERY DIRECTION BUT YOURS.
home sales ref
"DO YOU REALIZE THE TIME AND MONEY AND WILLPOWER THAT TOOK THESE GUYS, CLINT?"
YOU HAVE ANY IDEA HOW BIG A PAIN IN THE ASS YOU ARE TO THEM?
"ENVELOPES"?
I DON'T GET IT.

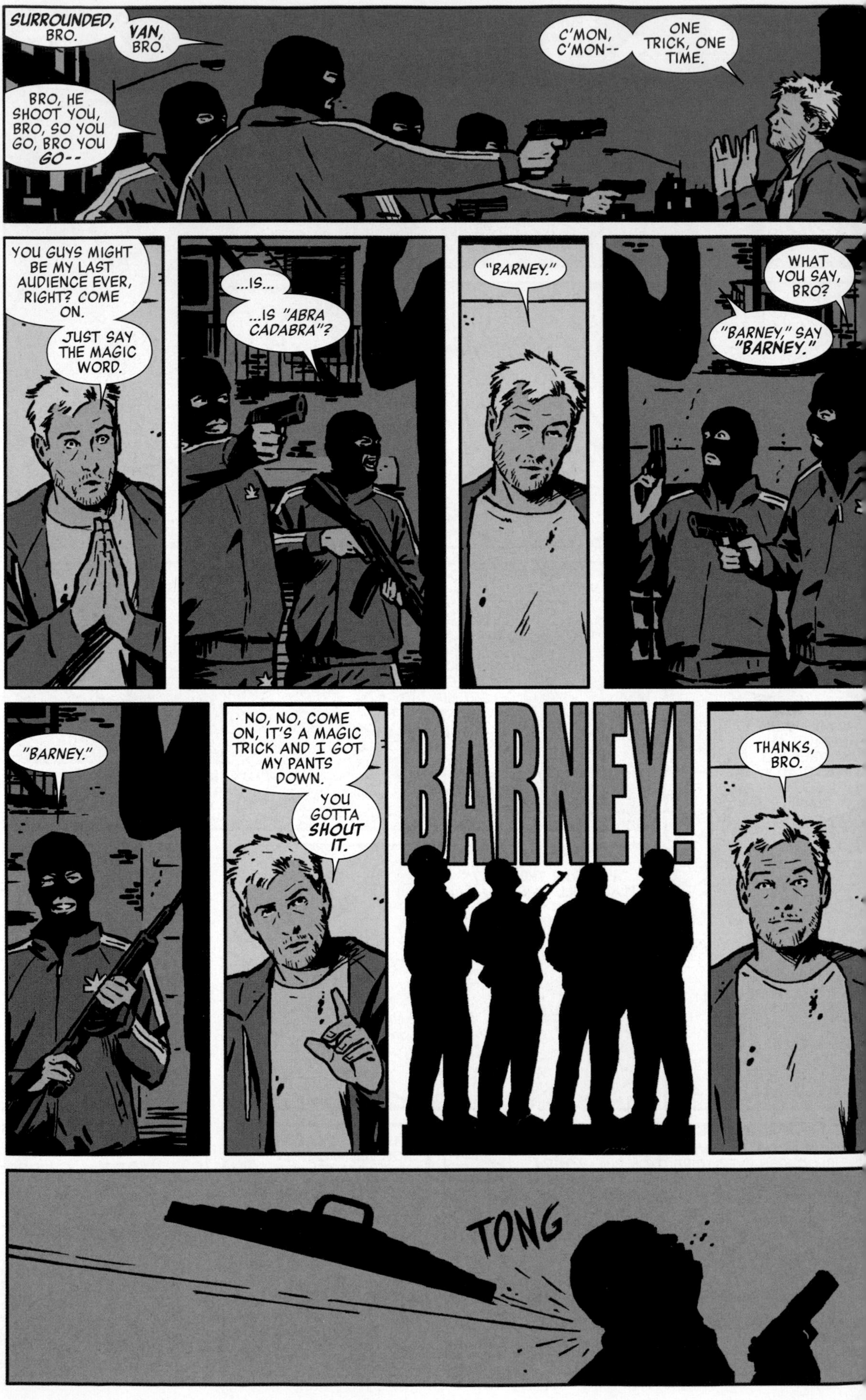
SURROUNDED, BRO.
VAN, BRO.
BRO, HE SHOOT YOU, BRO, SO YOU GO, BRO YOU GO--
C'MON, C'MON--
ONE TRICK, ONE TIME.
YOU GUYS MIGHT BE MY LAST AUDIENCE EVER, RIGHT? COME ON.
JUST SAY THE MAGIC WORD.
...IS...
...IS "ABRA CADABRA"?
"BARNEY."
WHAT YOU SAY, BRO?
"BARNEY," SAY "BARNEY."
"BARNEY."
NO, NO, COME ON, IT'S A MAGIC TRICK AND I GOT MY PANTS DOWN.
YOU GOTTA SHOUT IT.
BARNEY!
THANKS, BRO.
TONG

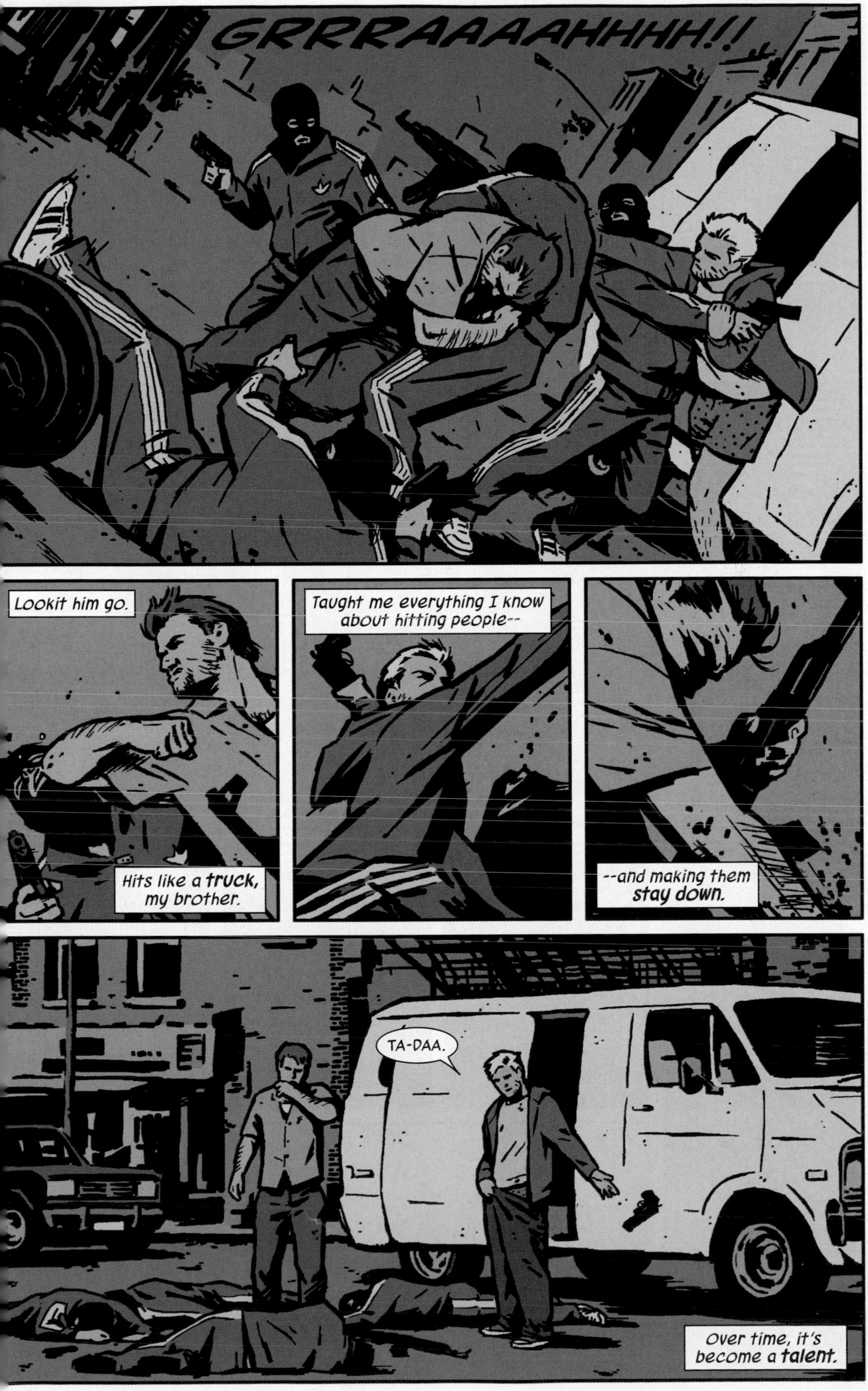
GRRRAAAAHHHH!!
Lookit him go.
Hits like a **truck**, my brother.
Taught me everything I know about hitting people--
--and making them **stay down.**
TA-DAA.
Over time, it's become a **talent.**

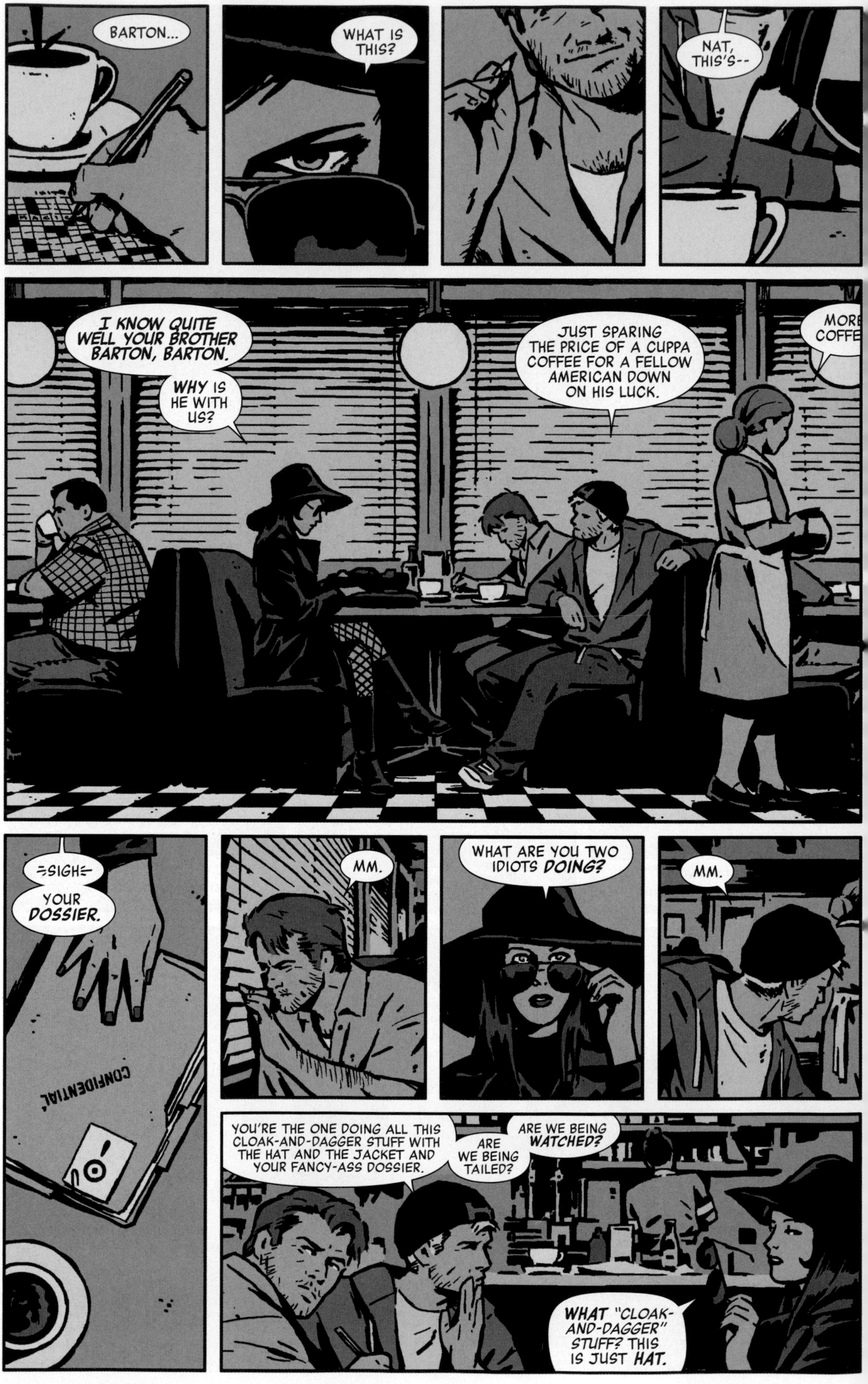
BARTON...
WHAT IS THIS?
NAT, THIS'S--
I KNOW QUITE WELL YOUR BROTHER BARTON, BARTON.
WHY IS HE WITH US?
JUST SPARING THE PRICE OF A CUPPA COFFEE FOR A FELLOW AMERICAN DOWN ON HIS LUCK.
MORE COFFE
=SIGH=
YOUR DOSSIER.
CONFIDENTIAL
MM.
WHAT ARE YOU TWO IDIOTS DOING?
MM.
YOU'RE THE ONE DOING ALL THIS CLOAK-AND-DAGGER STUFF WITH THE HAT AND THE JACKET AND YOUR FANCY-ASS DOSSIER.
ARE WE BEING TAILED?
ARE WE BEING WATCHED?
WHAT "CLOAK-AND-DAGGER" STUFF? THIS IS JUST HAT.

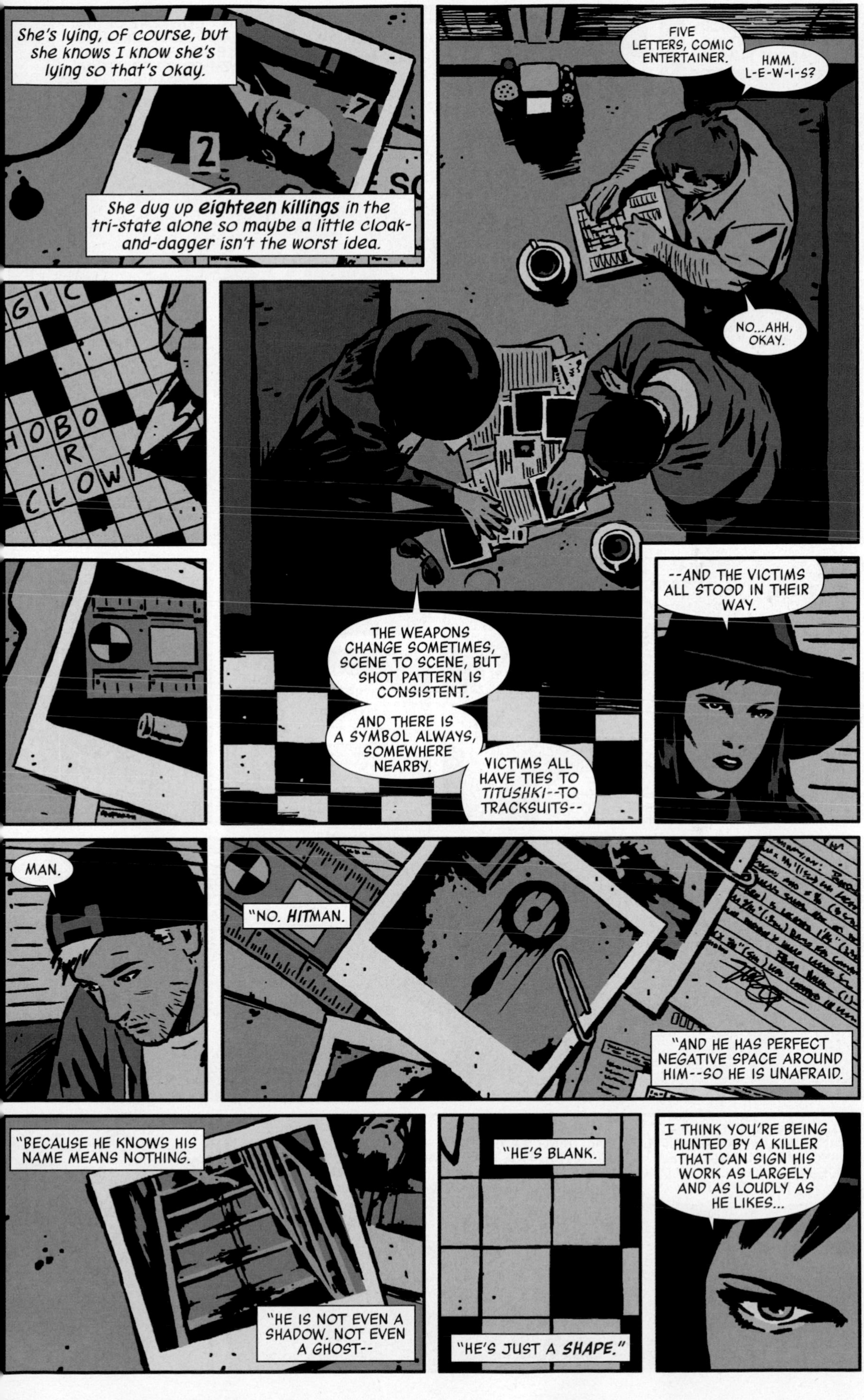
She's lying, of course, but she knows I know she's lying so that's okay.
She dug up **eighteen killings** in the tri-state alone so maybe a little cloak-and-dagger isn't the worst idea.
FIVE LETTERS, COMIC ENTERTAINER.
HMM. L-E-W-I-S?
NO...AHH, OKAY.
THE WEAPONS CHANGE SOMETIMES, SCENE TO SCENE, BUT SHOT PATTERN IS CONSISTENT.
AND THERE IS A SYMBOL ALWAYS, SOMEWHERE NEARBY.
VICTIMS ALL HAVE TIES TO *TITUSHKI*--TO TRACKSUITS--
--AND THE VICTIMS ALL STOOD IN THEIR WAY.
MAN.
"NO. ***HIT***MAN.
"AND HE HAS PERFECT NEGATIVE SPACE AROUND HIM--SO HE IS UNAFRAID.
"BECAUSE HE KNOWS HIS NAME MEANS NOTHING.
"HE IS NOT EVEN A SHADOW. NOT EVEN A GHOST--
"HE'S BLANK.
"HE'S JUST A ***SHAPE.***"
I THINK YOU'RE BEING HUNTED BY A KILLER THAT CAN SIGN HIS WORK AS LARGELY AND AS LOUDLY AS HE LIKES...

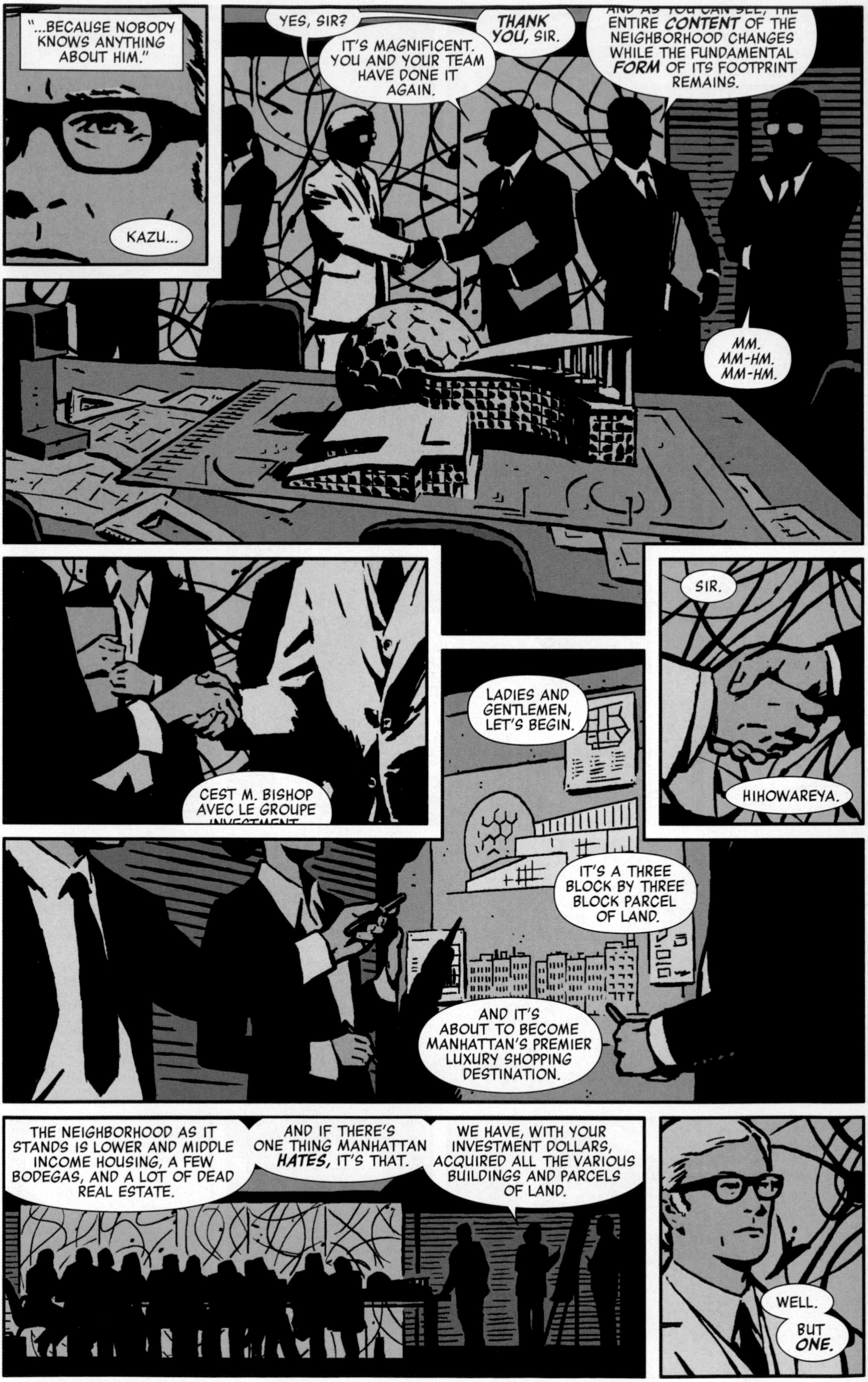
"...BECAUSE NOBODY KNOWS ANYTHING ABOUT HIM."
KAZU...
YES, SIR?
IT'S MAGNIFICENT. YOU AND YOUR TEAM HAVE DONE IT AGAIN.
THANK YOU, SIR.
ENTIRE CONTENT OF THE NEIGHBORHOOD CHANGES WHILE THE FUNDAMENTAL FORM OF ITS FOOTPRINT REMAINS.
MM. MM-HM. MM-HM.
CEST M. BISHOP AVEC LE GROUPE
SIR.
HIHOWAREYA.
LADIES AND GENTLEMEN, LET'S BEGIN.
IT'S A THREE BLOCK BY THREE BLOCK PARCEL OF LAND.
AND IT'S ABOUT TO BECOME MANHATTAN'S PREMIER LUXURY SHOPPING DESTINATION.
THE NEIGHBORHOOD AS IT STANDS IS LOWER AND MIDDLE INCOME HOUSING, A FEW BODEGAS, AND A LOT OF DEAD REAL ESTATE.
AND IF THERE'S ONE THING MANHATTAN HATES, IT'S THAT.
WE HAVE, WITH YOUR INVESTMENT DOLLARS, ACQUIRED ALL THE VARIOUS BUILDINGS AND PARCELS OF LAND.
WELL.
BUT ONE.

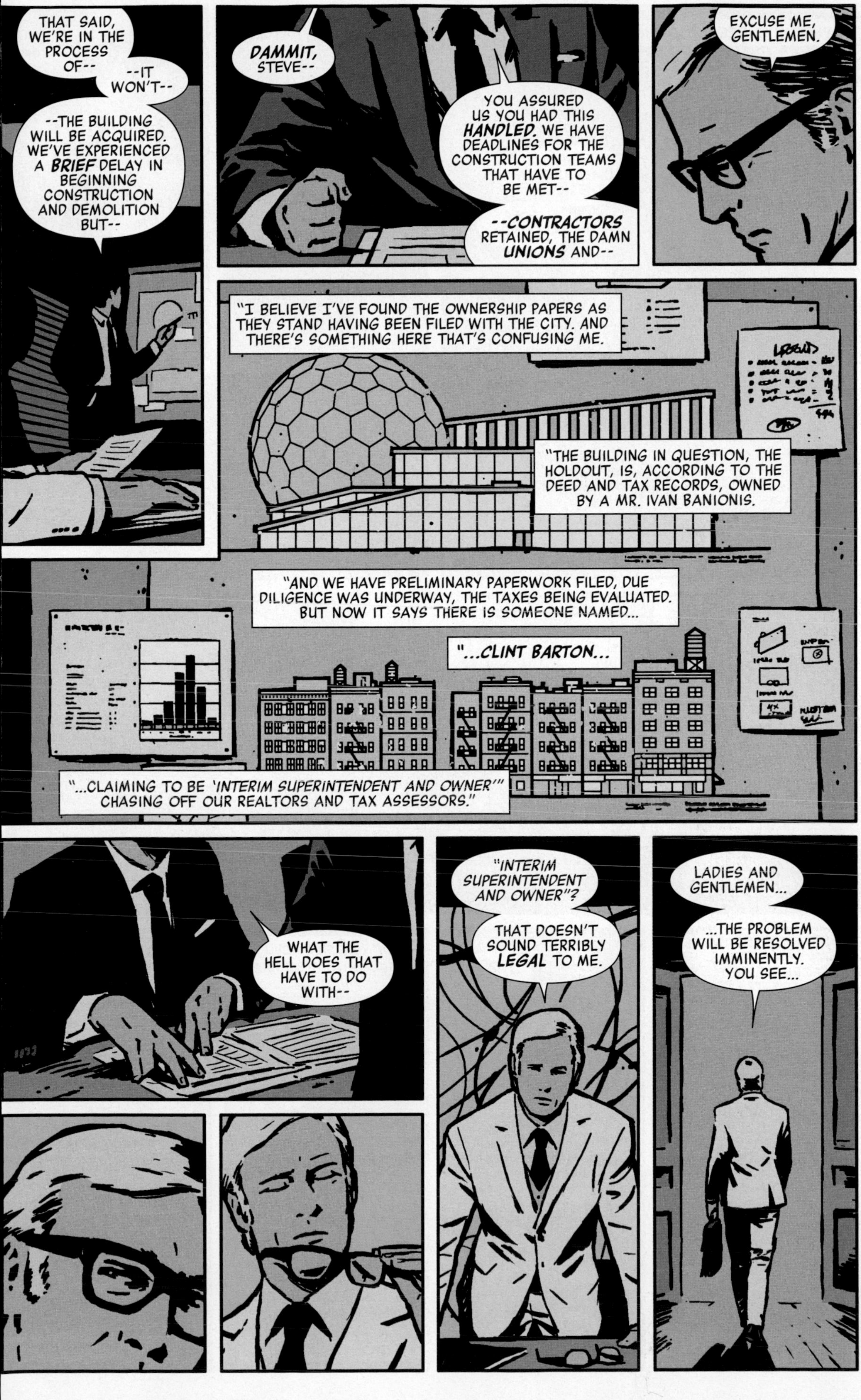
THAT SAID, WE'RE IN THE PROCESS OF--
--IT WON'T--
--THE BUILDING WILL BE ACQUIRED. WE'VE EXPERIENCED A BRIEF DELAY IN BEGINNING CONSTRUCTION AND DEMOLITION BUT--
DAMMIT, STEVE--
YOU ASSURED US YOU HAD THIS HANDLED. WE HAVE DEADLINES FOR THE CONSTRUCTION TEAMS THAT HAVE TO BE MET--
--CONTRACTORS RETAINED, THE DAMN UNIONS AND--
EXCUSE ME, GENTLEMEN.
"I BELIEVE I'VE FOUND THE OWNERSHIP PAPERS AS THEY STAND HAVING BEEN FILED WITH THE CITY. AND THERE'S SOMETHING HERE THAT'S CONFUSING ME.
"THE BUILDING IN QUESTION, THE HOLDOUT, IS, ACCORDING TO THE DEED AND TAX RECORDS, OWNED BY A MR. IVAN BANIONIS.
"AND WE HAVE PRELIMINARY PAPERWORK FILED, DUE DILIGENCE WAS UNDERWAY, THE TAXES BEING EVALUATED. BUT NOW IT SAYS THERE IS SOMEONE NAMED...
"...CLINT BARTON...
"...CLAIMING TO BE 'INTERIM SUPERINTENDENT AND OWNER'" CHASING OFF OUR REALTORS AND TAX ASSESSORS."
WHAT THE HELL DOES THAT HAVE TO DO WITH--
"INTERIM SUPERINTENDENT AND OWNER"?
THAT DOESN'T SOUND TERRIBLY LEGAL TO ME.
LADIES AND GENTLEMEN...
...THE PROBLEM WILL BE RESOLVED IMMINENTLY. YOU SEE...

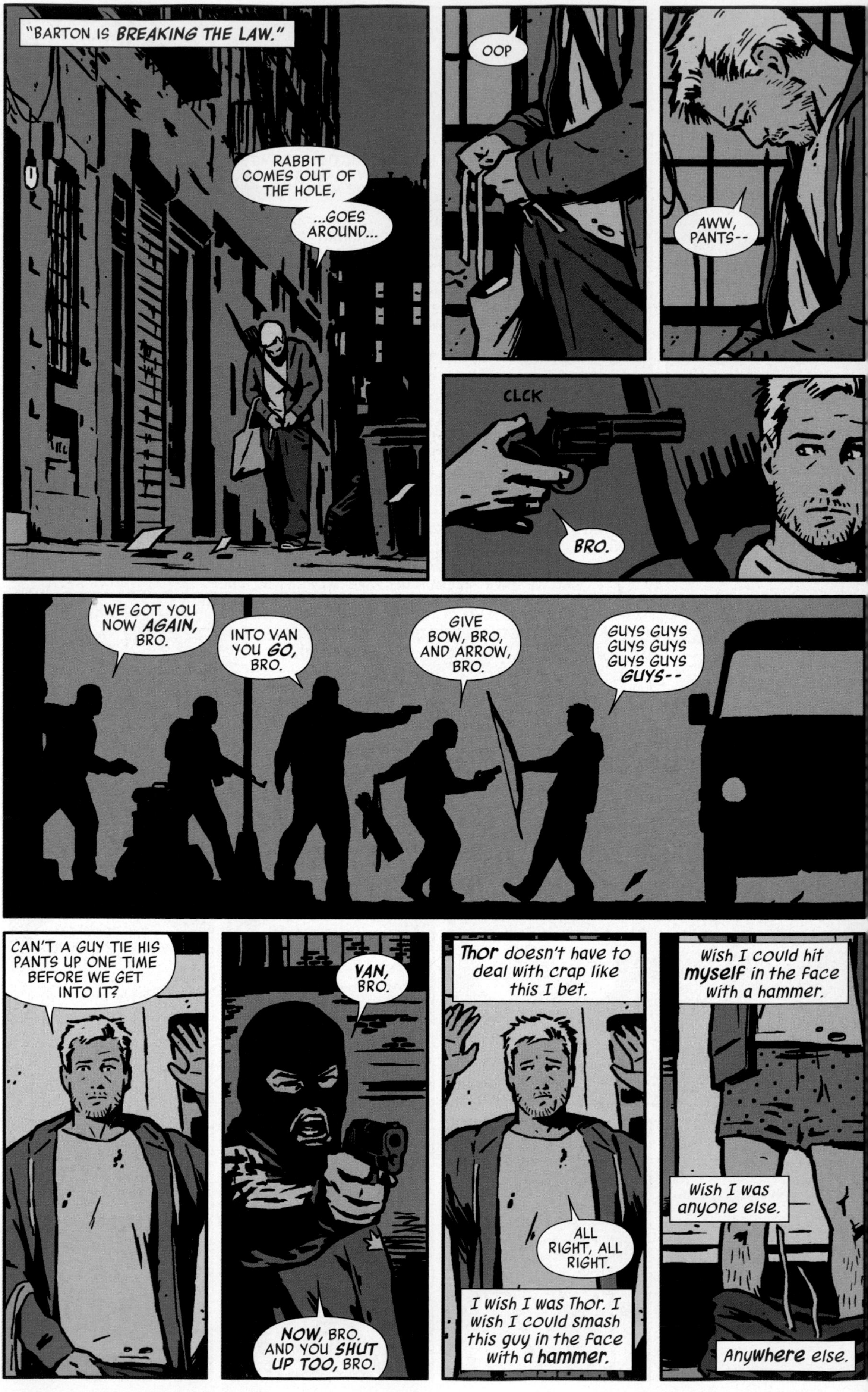
"BARTON IS BREAKING THE LAW."
RABBIT COMES OUT OF THE HOLE,
...GOES AROUND...
OOP
AWW, PANTS--
CLCK
BRO.
WE GOT YOU NOW AGAIN, BRO.
INTO VAN YOU GO, BRO.
GIVE BOW, BRO, AND ARROW, BRO.
GUYS GUYS GUYS GUYS GUYS GUYS GUYS--
CAN'T A GUY TIE HIS PANTS UP ONE TIME BEFORE WE GET INTO IT?
VAN, BRO.
NOW, BRO. AND YOU SHUT UP TOO, BRO.
Thor doesn't have to deal with crap like this I bet.
ALL RIGHT, ALL RIGHT.
I wish I was Thor. I wish I could smash this guy in the face with a hammer.
Wish I could hit myself in the face with a hammer.
Wish I was anyone else.
Anywhere else.

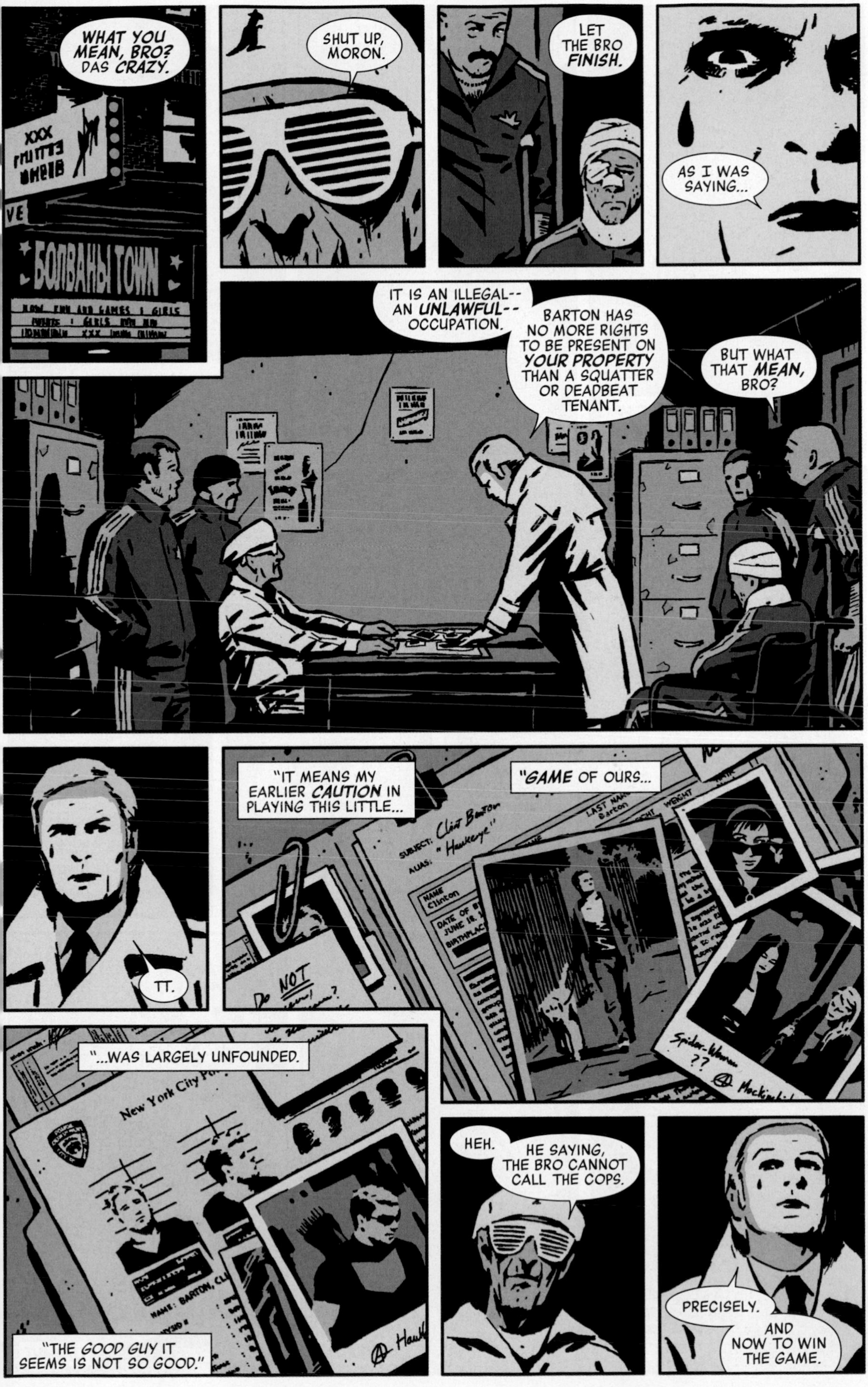
WHAT YOU MEAN, BRO? DAS CRAZY.
XXX
БОЛВАНЫ TOWN
SHUT UP, MORON.
LET THE BRO FINISH.
AS I WAS SAYING...
IT IS AN ILLEGAL-- AN UNLAWFUL-- OCCUPATION.
BARTON HAS NO MORE RIGHTS TO BE PRESENT ON YOUR PROPERTY THAN A SQUATTER OR DEADBEAT TENANT.
BUT WHAT THAT MEAN, BRO?
TT.
"IT MEANS MY EARLIER CAUTION IN PLAYING THIS LITTLE...
"GAME OF OURS...
"...WAS LARGELY UNFOUNDED.
"THE GOOD GUY IT SEEMS IS NOT SO GOOD."
HEH.
HE SAYING, THE BRO CANNOT CALL THE COPS.
PRECISELY.
AND NOW TO WIN THE GAME.

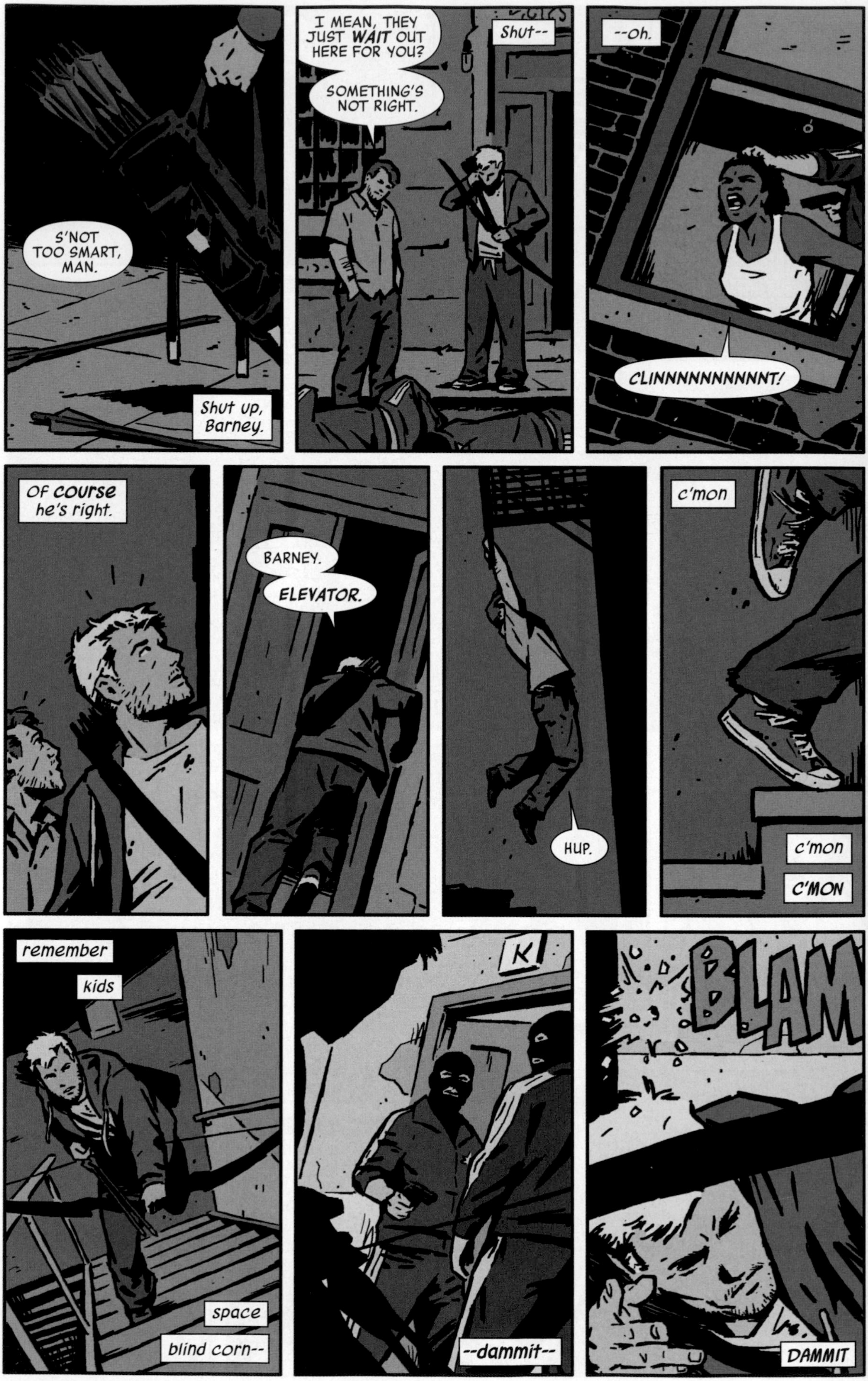
S'NOT TOO SMART, MAN.
Shut up, Barney.
I MEAN, THEY JUST WAIT OUT HERE FOR YOU?
SOMETHING'S NOT RIGHT.
Shut--
--oh.
CLINNNNNNNNNNT!
Of course he's right.
BARNEY.
ELEVATOR.
HUP.
c'mon
c'mon
C'MON
remember
kids
space
blind corn--
K
--dammit--
BLAM
DAMMIT

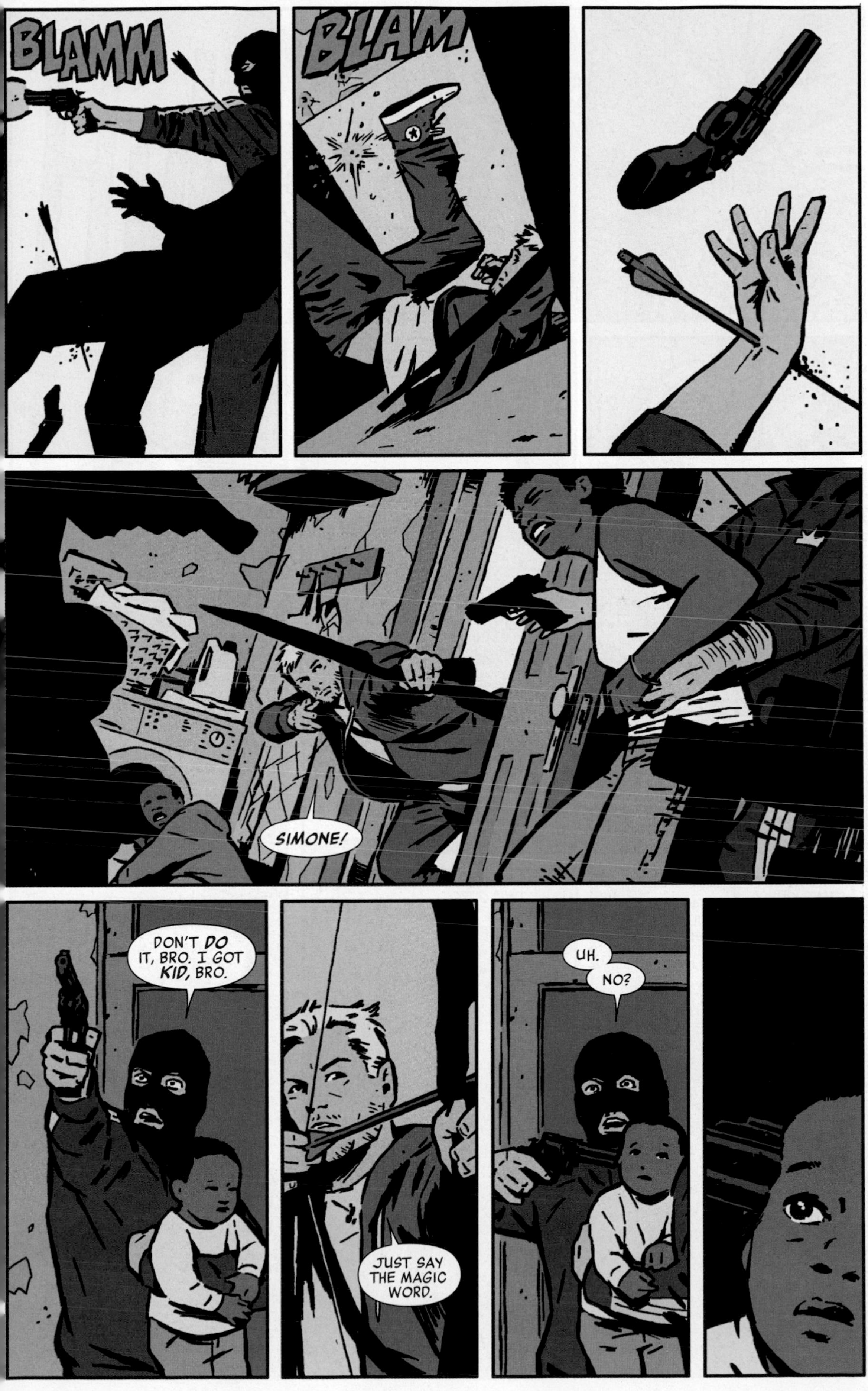

BLAMM
BLAM
SIMONE!
DON'T DO IT, BRO. I GOT KID, BRO.
JUST SAY THE MAGIC WORD.
UH.
NO?

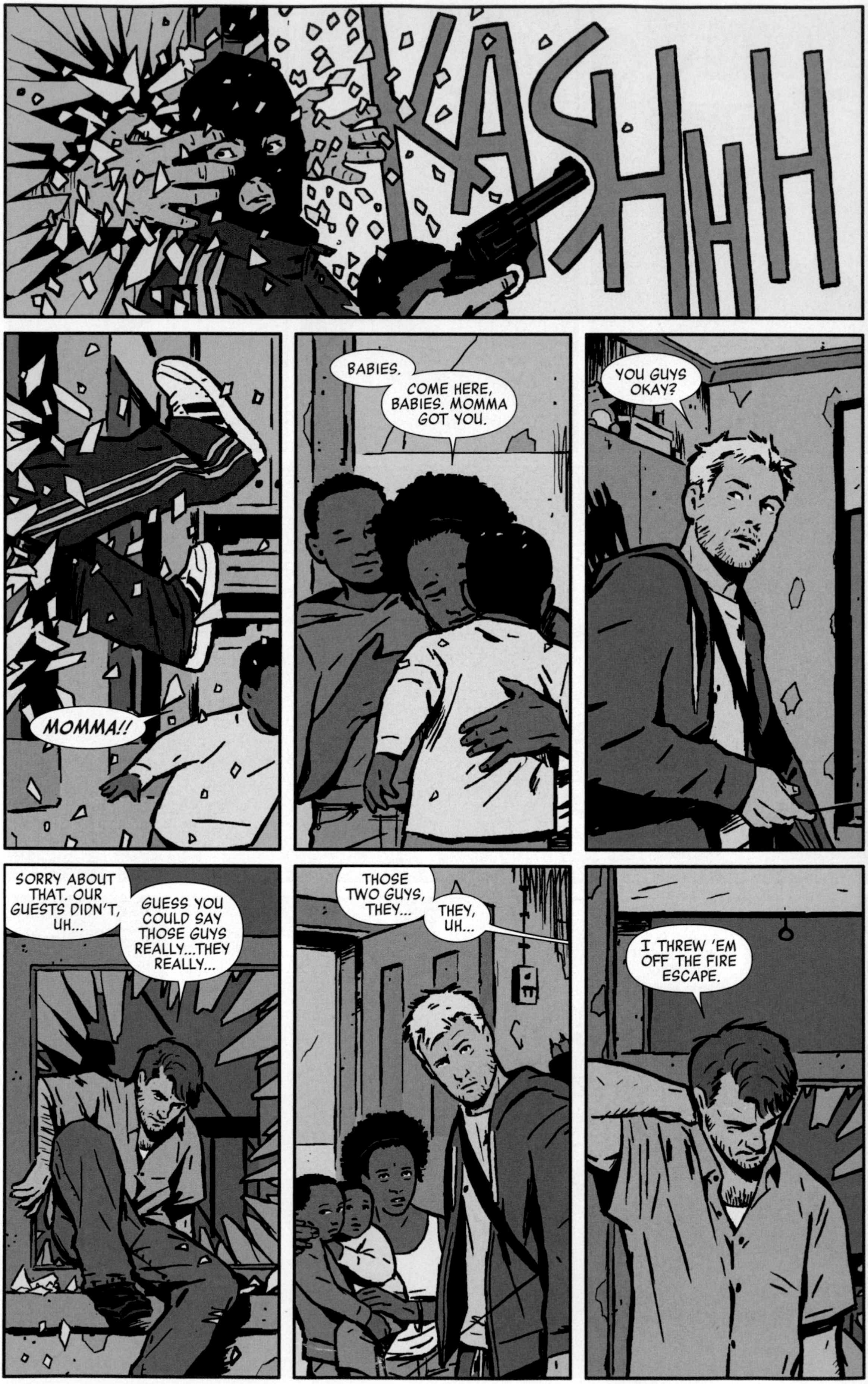
KASHHH
MOMMA!!
BABIES.
COME HERE, BABIES. MOMMA GOT YOU.
YOU GUYS OKAY?
SORRY ABOUT THAT. OUR GUESTS DIDN'T, UH...
GUESS YOU COULD SAY THOSE GUYS REALLY...THEY REALLY...
THOSE TWO GUYS, THEY...
THEY, UH...
I THREW 'EM OFF THE FIRE ESCAPE.

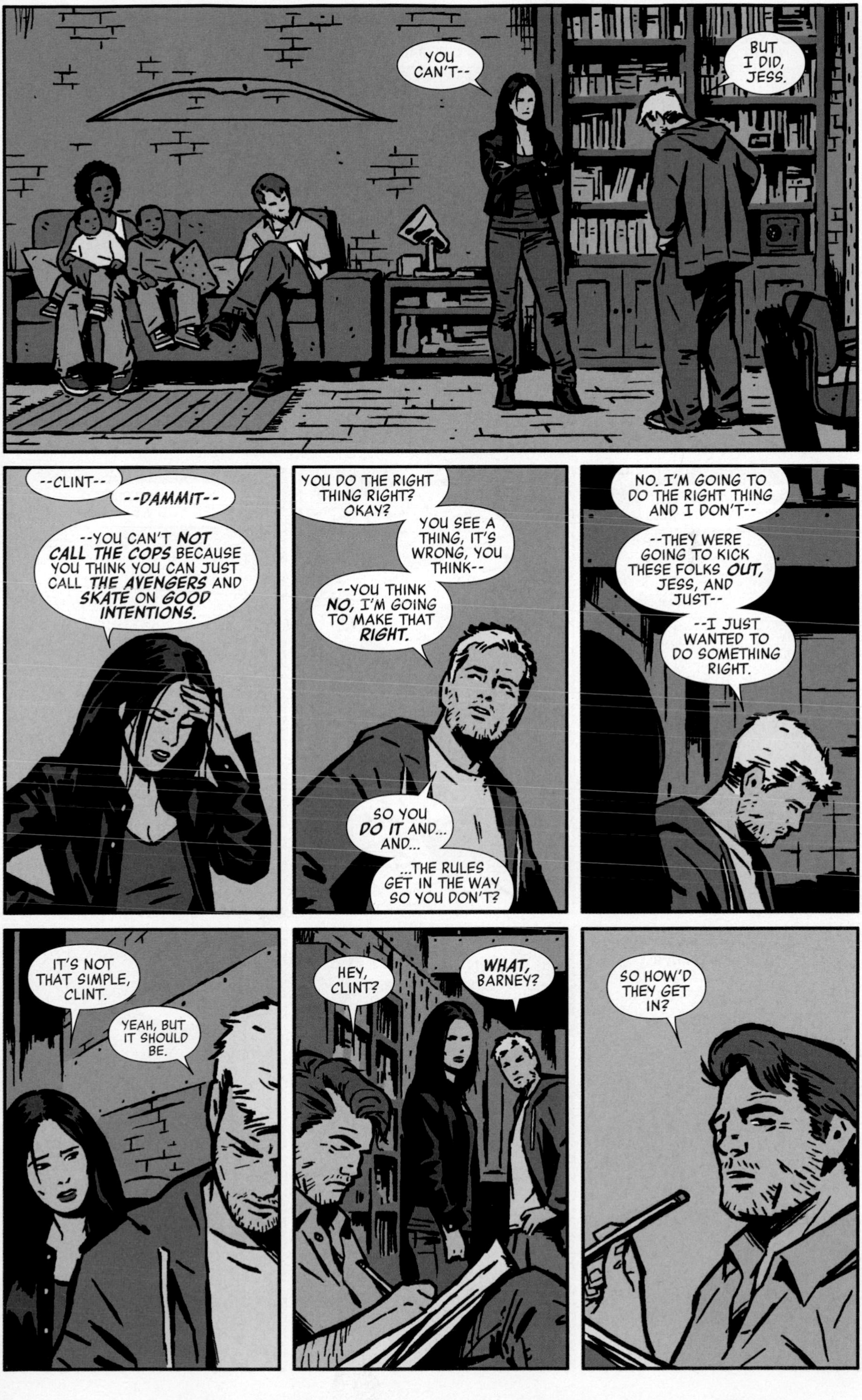

YOU CAN'T--
BUT I DID, JESS.
--CLINT--
--DAMMIT--
--YOU CAN'T NOT CALL THE COPS BECAUSE YOU THINK YOU CAN JUST CALL THE AVENGERS AND SKATE ON GOOD INTENTIONS.
YOU DO THE RIGHT THING RIGHT? OKAY?
YOU SEE A THING, IT'S WRONG, YOU THINK--
--YOU THINK NO, I'M GOING TO MAKE THAT RIGHT.
SO YOU DO IT AND... AND...
...THE RULES GET IN THE WAY SO YOU DON'T?
NO. I'M GOING TO DO THE RIGHT THING AND I DON'T--
--THEY WERE GOING TO KICK THESE FOLKS OUT, JESS, AND JUST--
--I JUST WANTED TO DO SOMETHING RIGHT.
IT'S NOT THAT SIMPLE, CLINT.
YEAH, BUT IT SHOULD BE.
HEY, CLINT?
WHAT, BARNEY?
SO HOW'D THEY GET IN?

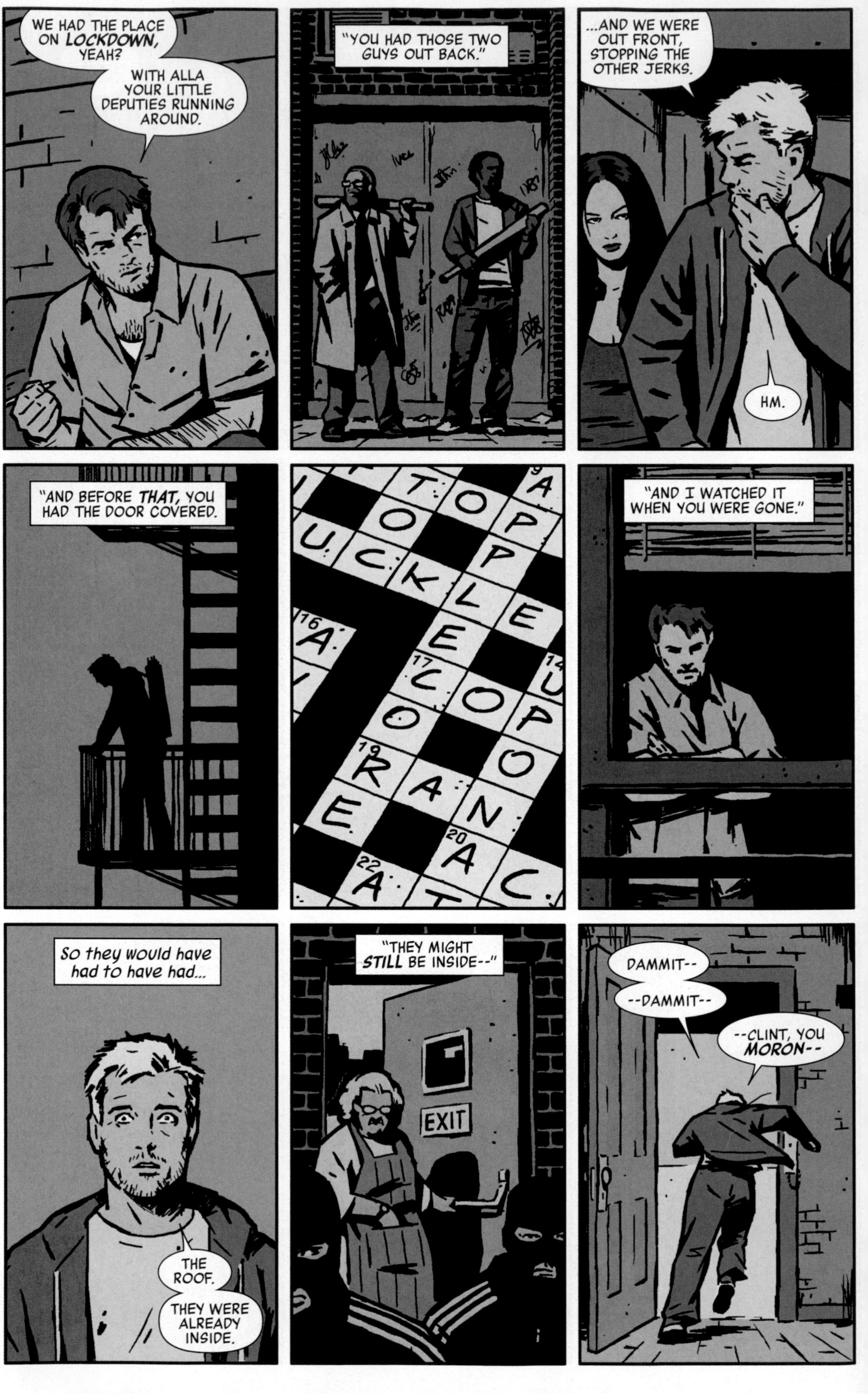
WE HAD THE PLACE ON LOCKDOWN, YEAH?
WITH ALLA YOUR LITTLE DEPUTIES RUNNING AROUND.
"YOU HAD THOSE TWO GUYS OUT BACK."
...AND WE WERE OUT FRONT, STOPPING THE OTHER JERKS.
HM.
"AND BEFORE THAT, YOU HAD THE DOOR COVERED.
"AND I WATCHED IT WHEN YOU WERE GONE."
So they would have had to have had...
THE ROOF.
THEY WERE ALREADY INSIDE.
"THEY MIGHT STILL BE INSIDE--"
EXIT
DAMMIT--
--DAMMIT--
--CLINT, YOU MORON--

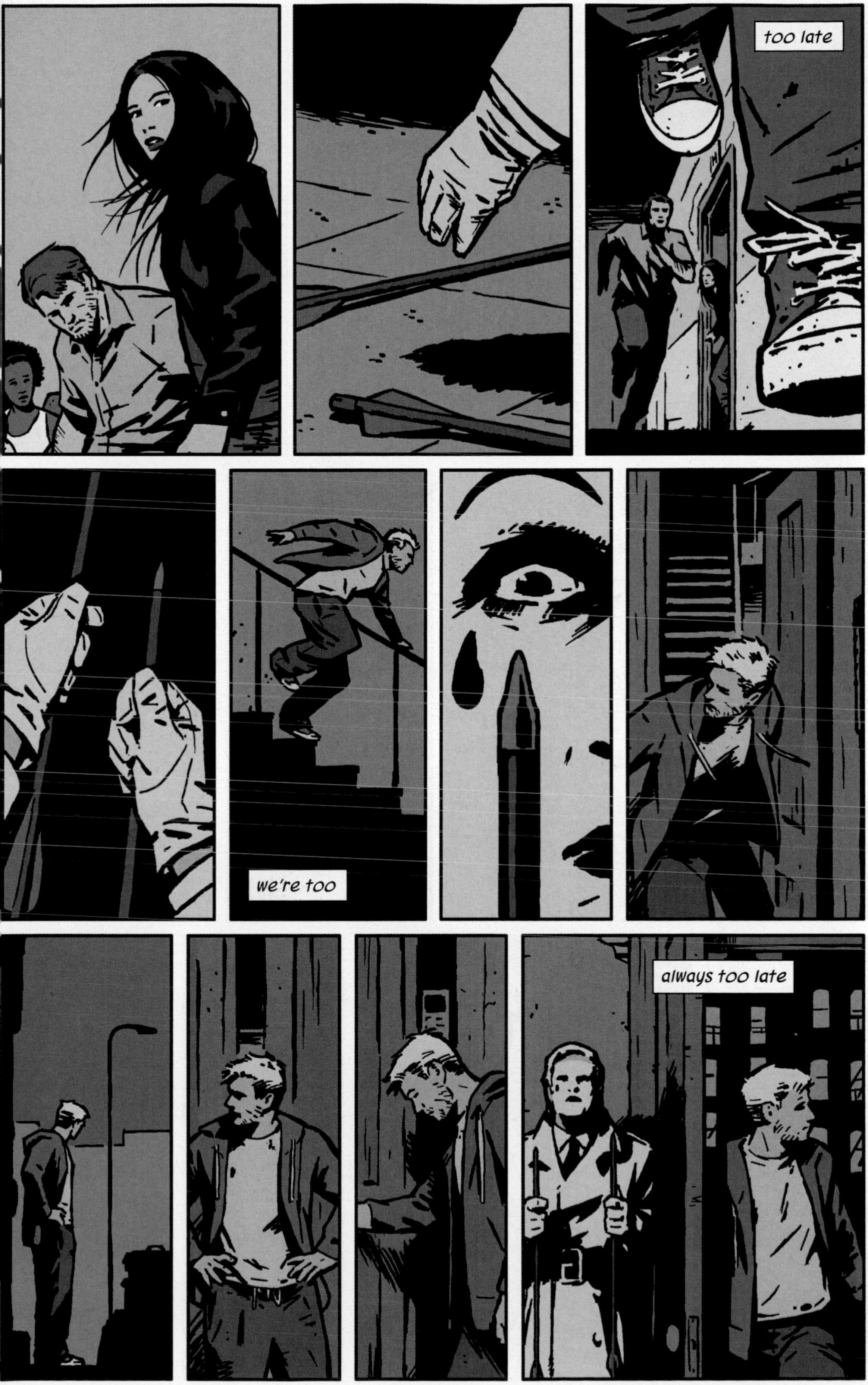
too late
we're too
always too late

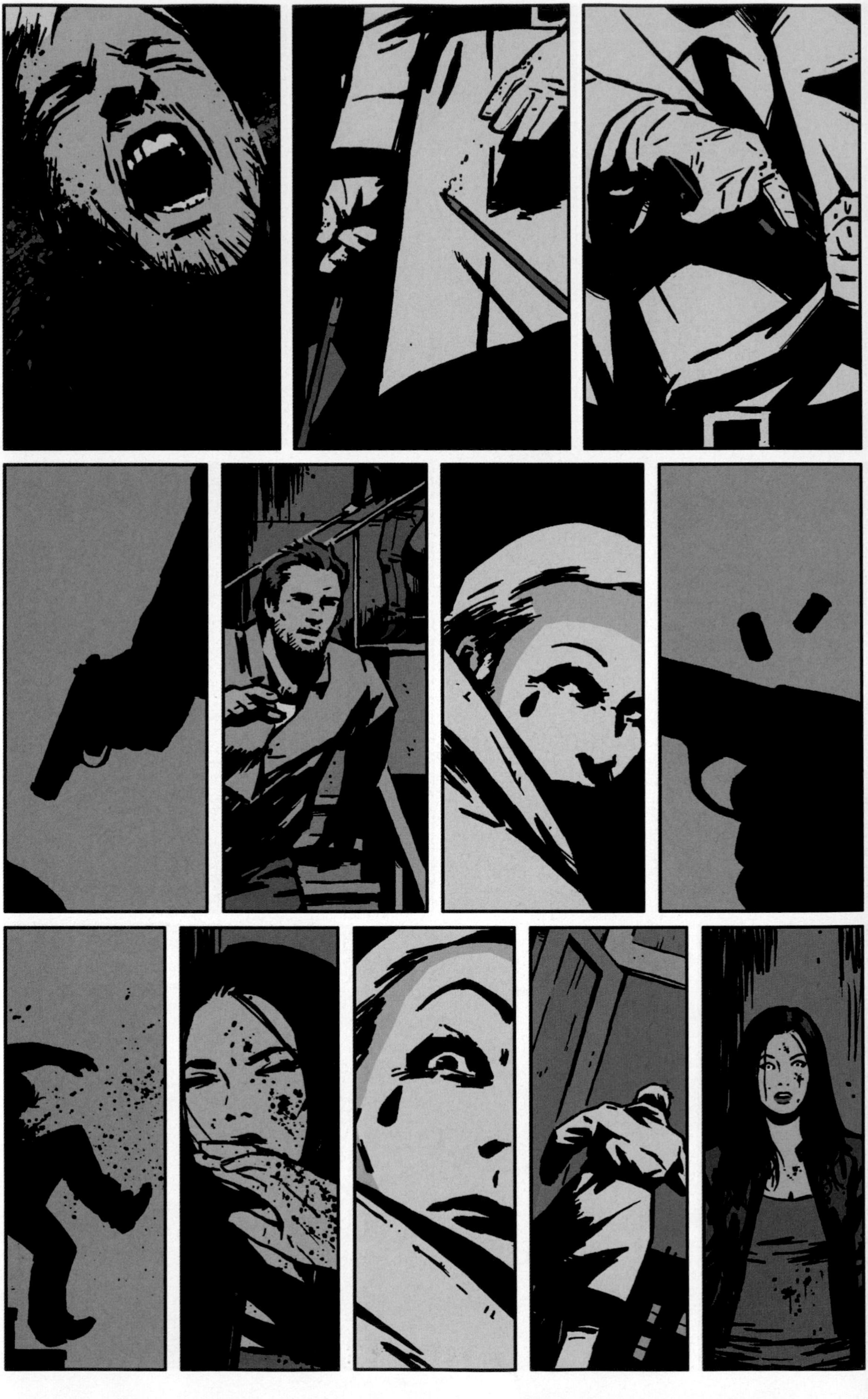

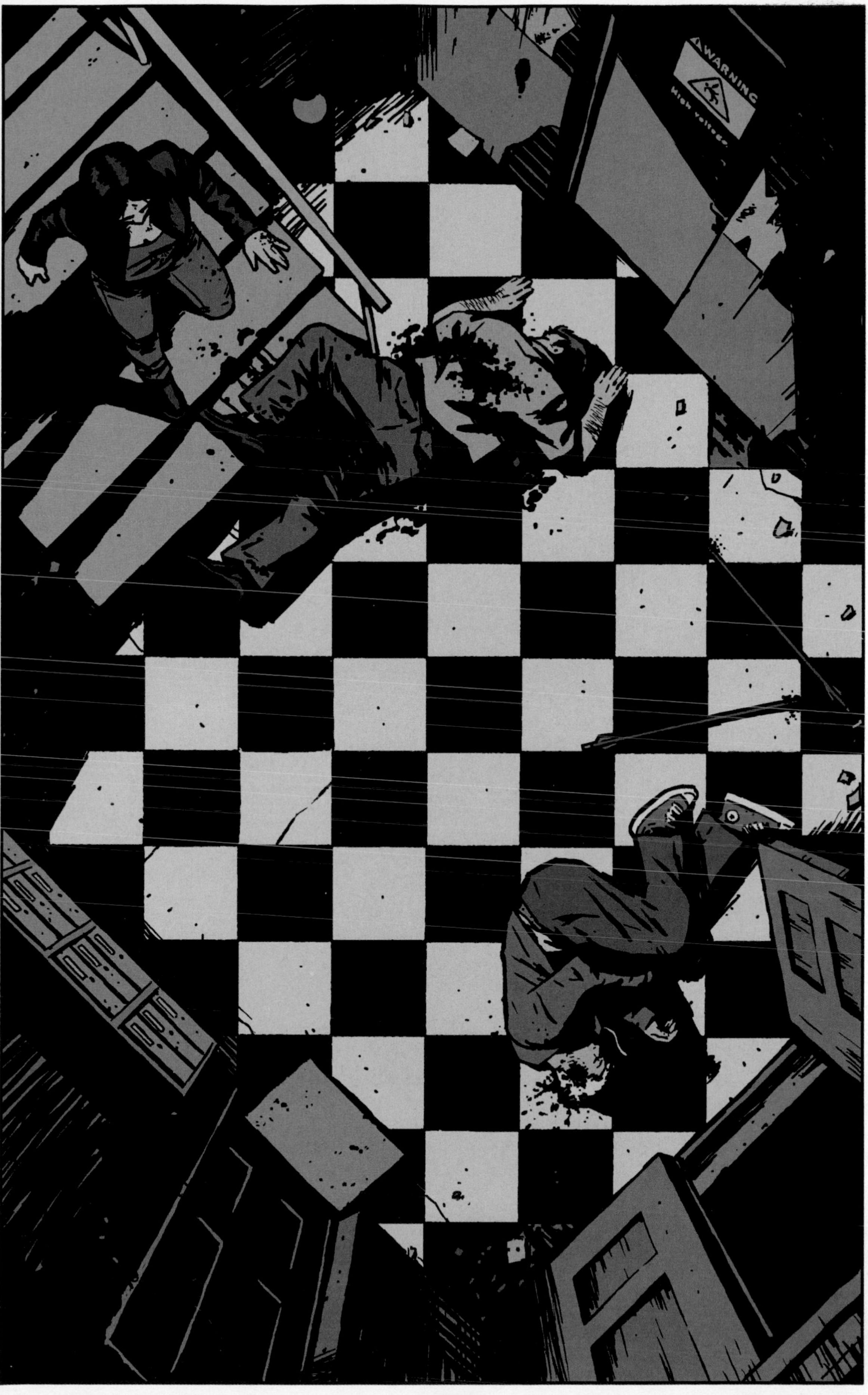
WARNING
High voltage.

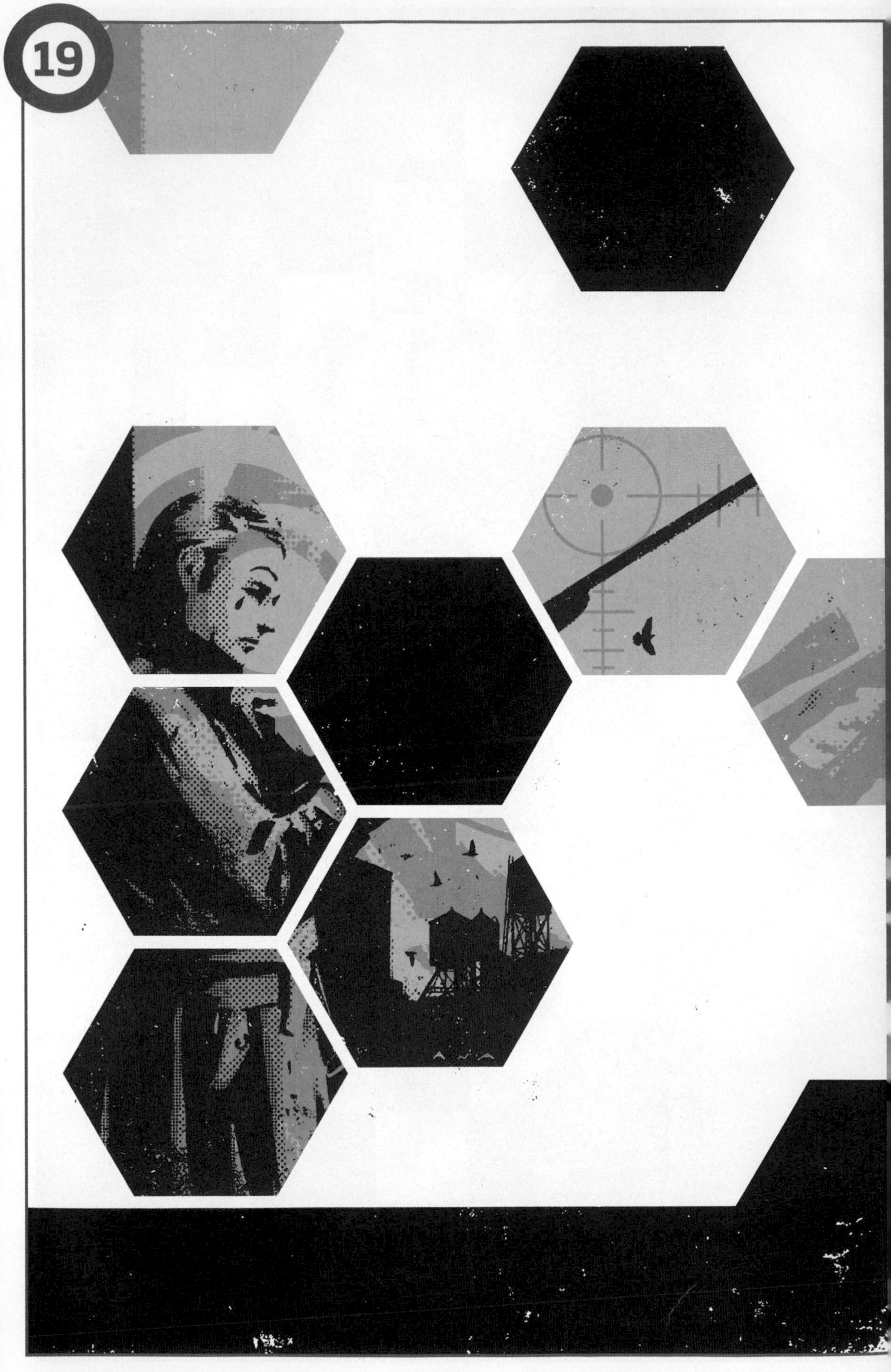
19

in)
deaf
midd
damaged.
the injury
been deafened
lly and I hope
mporarily
r inner and middle
ear were damaged.
Because of the injury
you have been deafene
partially and I hop
temporarily.
With
r inner and middle
ear were damaged.
Because of the injury
you have been deafened
partially and I hope
temporarily.
With care and
E
F P
T O Z

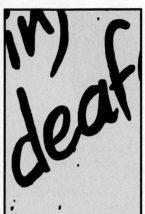

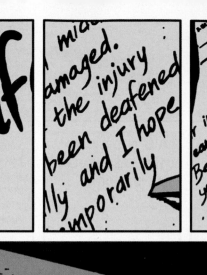

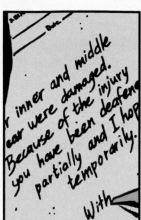

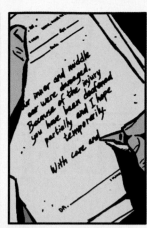

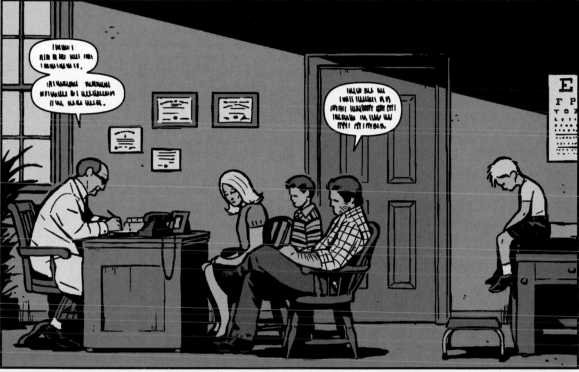

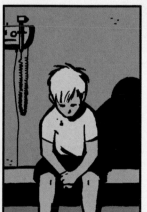

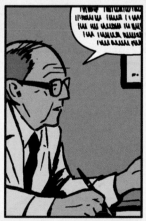

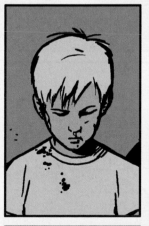

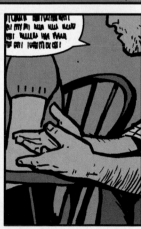

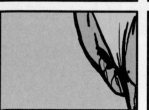

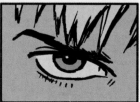

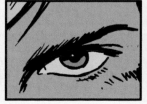

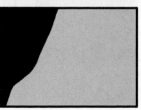

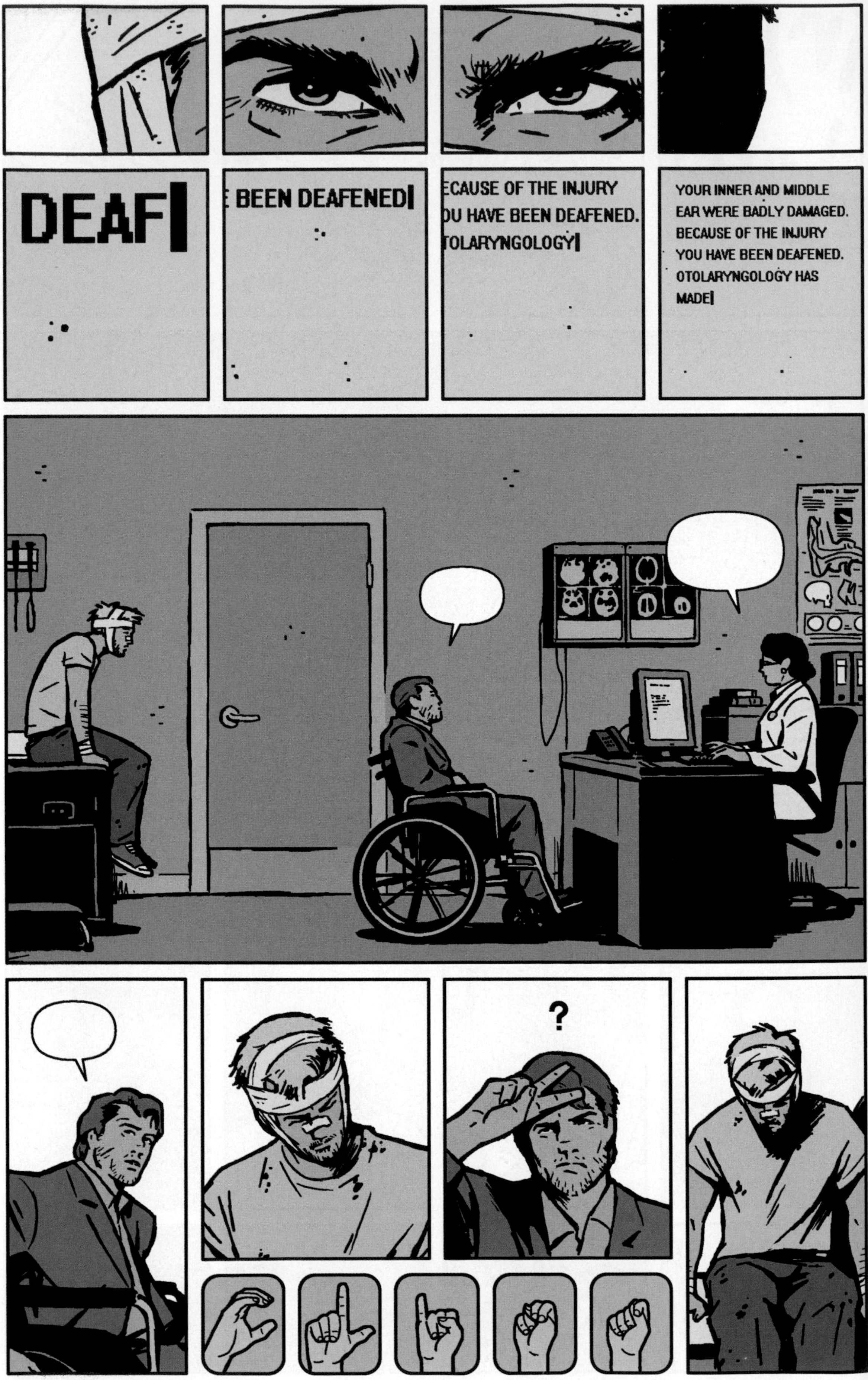
DEAF
E BEEN DEAFENED
ECAUSE OF THE INJURY
OU HAVE BEEN DEAFENED.
OTOLARYNGOLOGY
YOUR INNER AND MIDDLE
EAR WERE BADLY DAMAGED.
BECAUSE OF THE INJURY
YOU HAVE BEEN DEAFENED.
OTOLARYNGOLOGY HAS
MADE
?

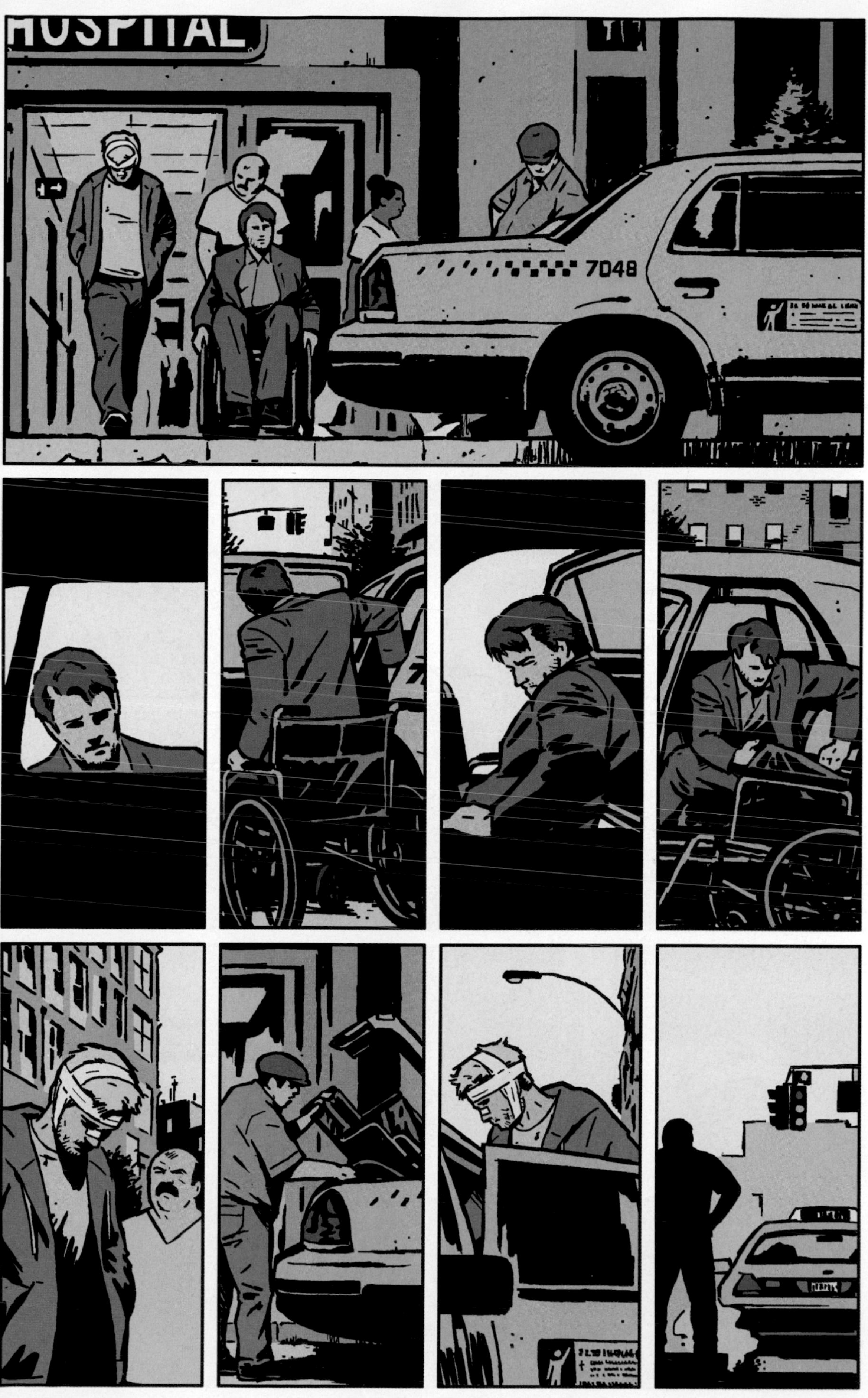
HOSPITAL
7048

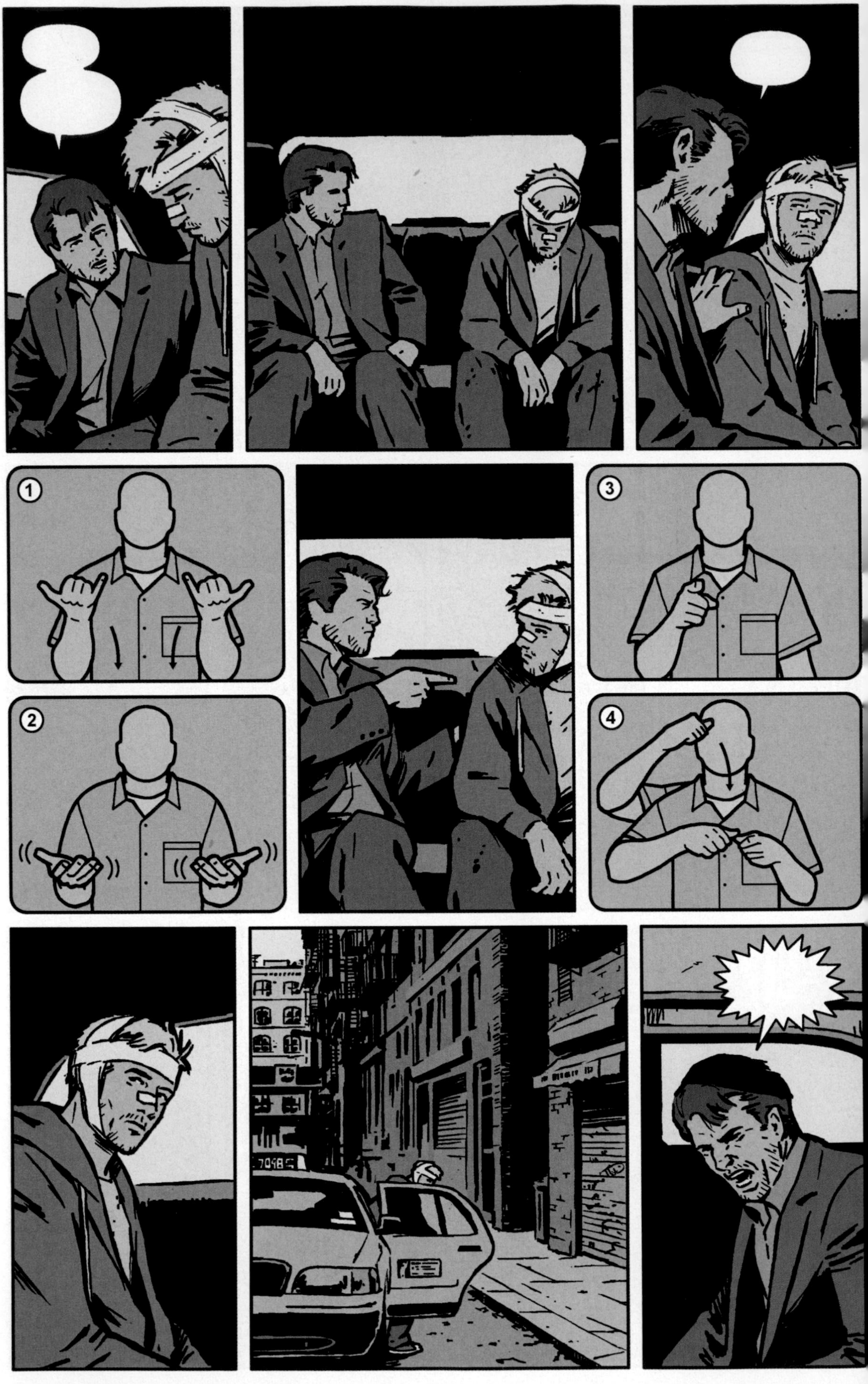
1
2
3
4

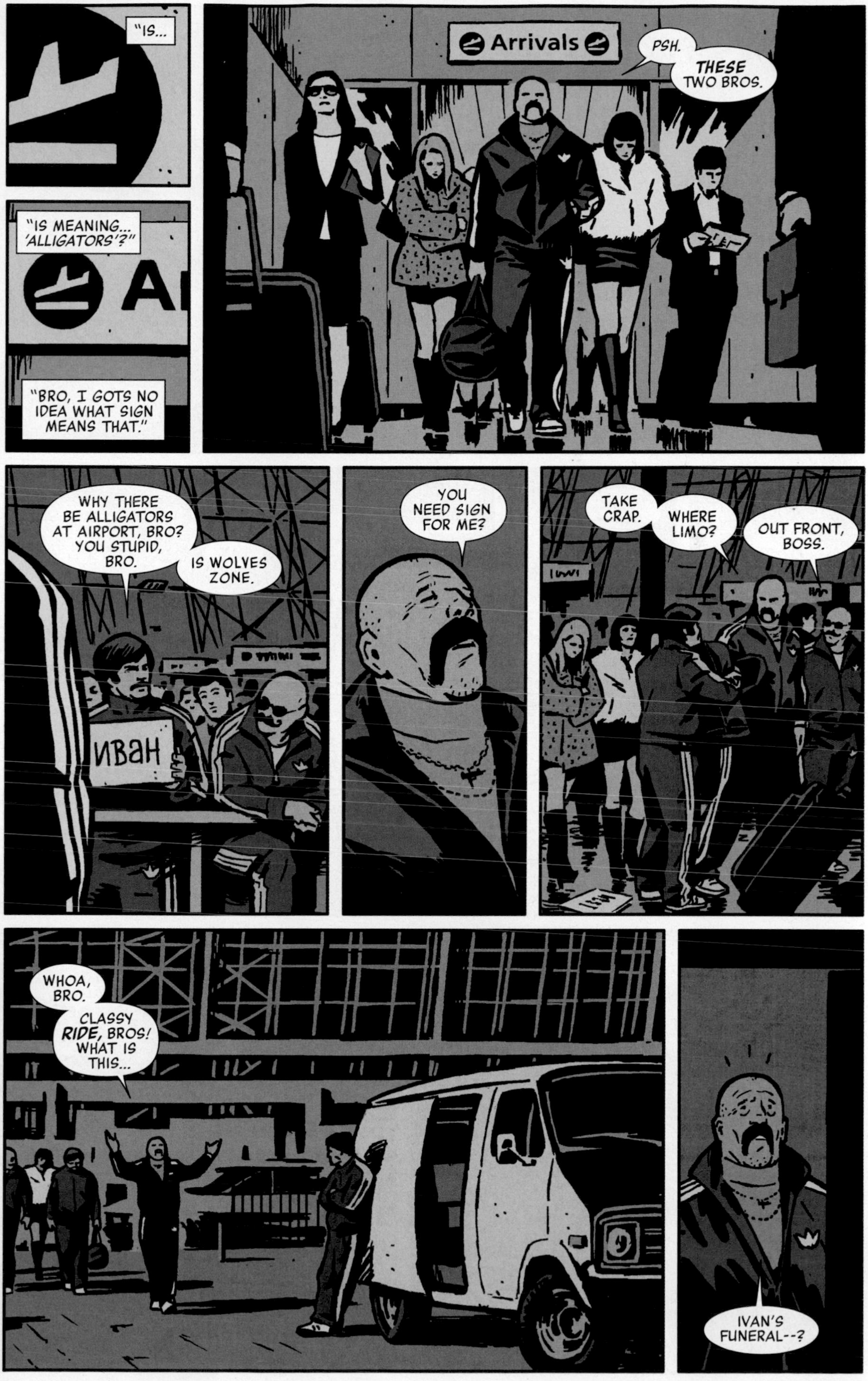
"IS...
"IS MEANING... 'ALLIGATORS'?"
"BRO, I GOTS NO IDEA WHAT SIGN MEANS THAT."
Arrivals
PSH. THESE TWO BROS.
WHY THERE BE ALLIGATORS AT AIRPORT, BRO? YOU STUPID, BRO.
IS WOLVES ZONE.
ИВАН
YOU NEED SIGN FOR ME?
TAKE CRAP.
WHERE LIMO?
OUT FRONT, BOSS.
WHOA, BRO.
CLASSY RIDE, BROS! WHAT IS THIS...
IVAN'S FUNERAL--?

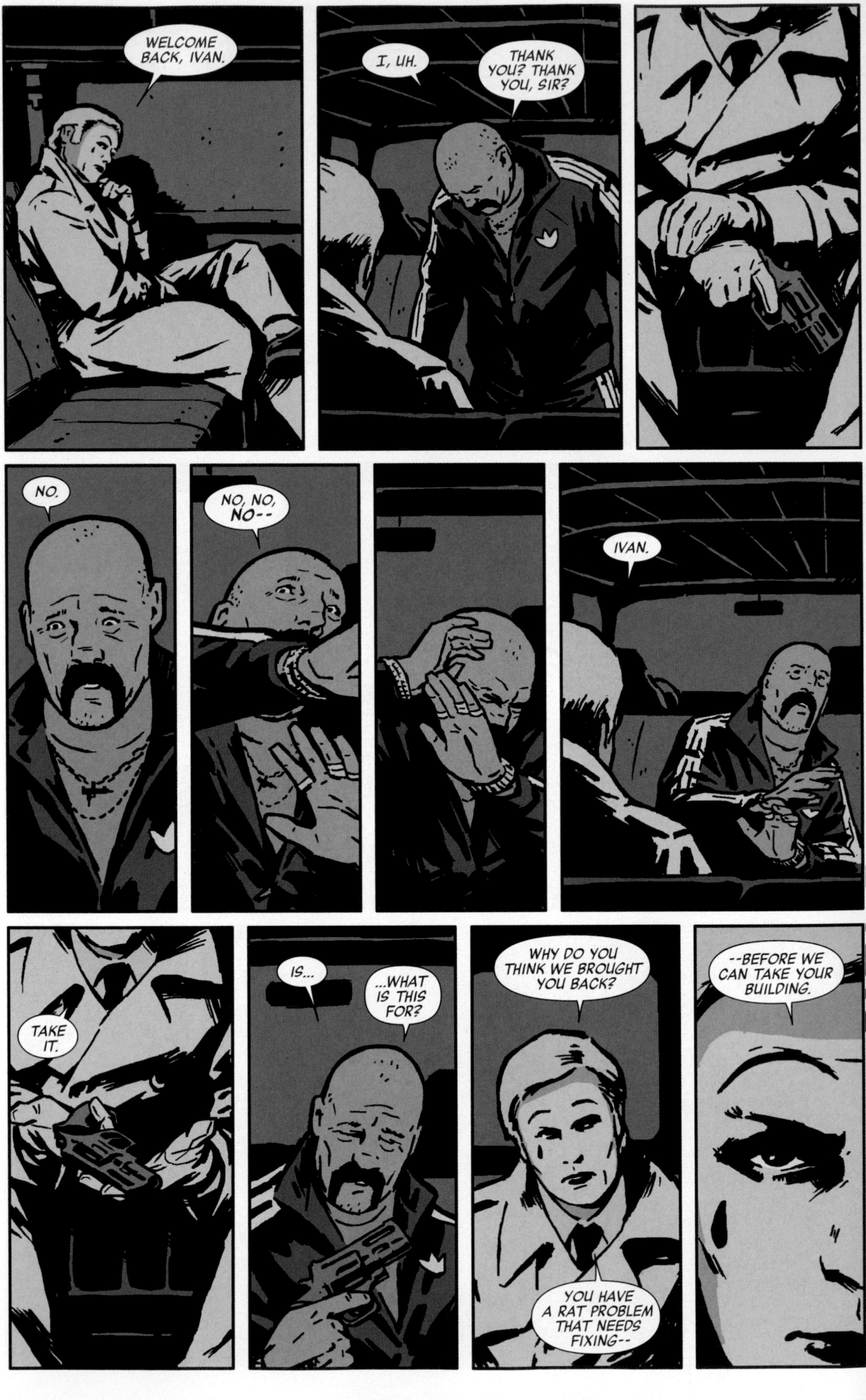
WELCOME BACK, IVAN.
I, UH.
THANK YOU? THANK YOU, SIR?
NO.
NO, NO, NO--
IVAN.
TAKE IT.
IS...
...WHAT IS THIS FOR?
WHY DO YOU THINK WE BROUGHT YOU BACK?
YOU HAVE A RAT PROBLEM THAT NEEDS FIXING--
--BEFORE WE CAN TAKE YOUR BUILDING.

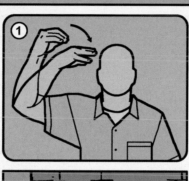

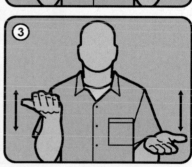

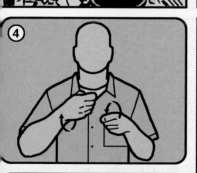

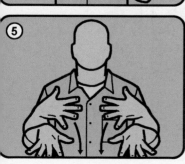

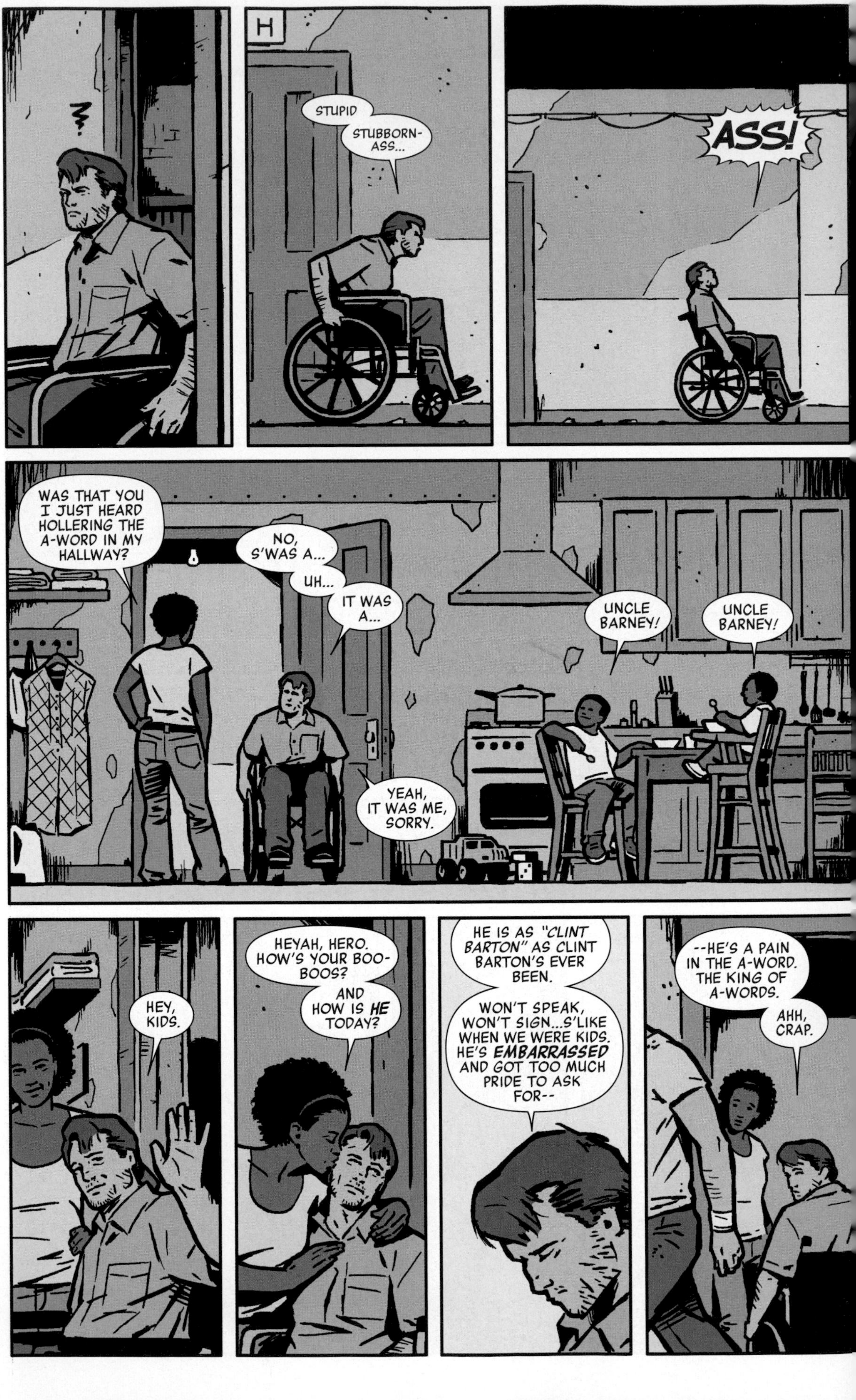
H
STUPID
STUBBORN-ASS...
ASS!
WAS THAT YOU I JUST HEARD HOLLERING THE A-WORD IN MY HALLWAY?
NO, S'WAS A...
UH...
IT WAS A...
YEAH, IT WAS ME, SORRY.
UNCLE BARNEY!
UNCLE BARNEY!
HEY, KIDS.
HEYAH, HERO. HOW'S YOUR BOO-BOOS?
AND HOW IS HE TODAY?
HE IS AS "CLINT BARTON" AS CLINT BARTON'S EVER BEEN.
WON'T SPEAK, WON'T SIGN...S'LIKE WHEN WE WERE KIDS. HE'S EMBARRASSED AND GOT TOO MUCH PRIDE TO ASK FOR--
--HE'S A PAIN IN THE A-WORD. THE KING OF A-WORDS.
AHH, CRAP.

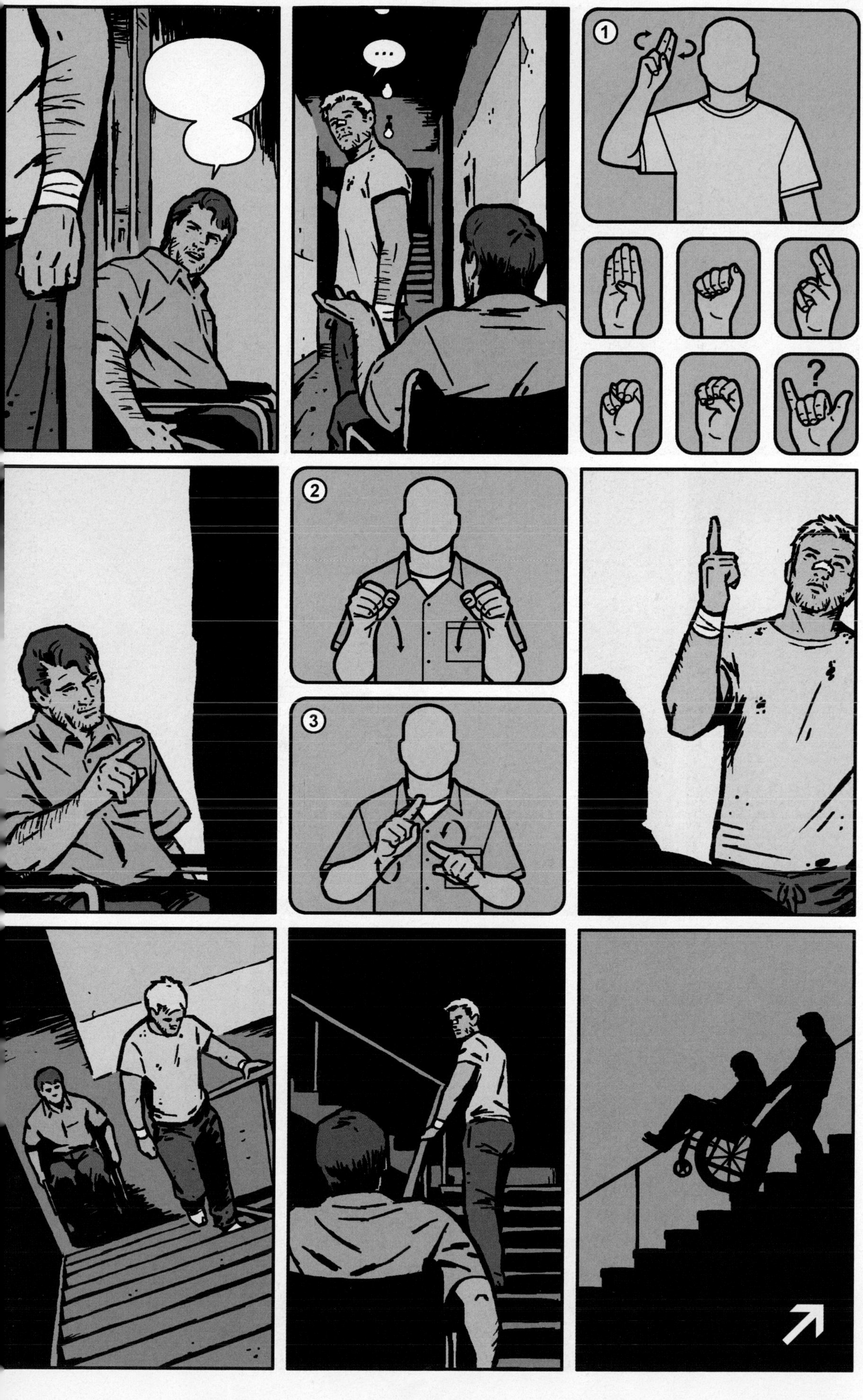
...
1
?
2
3

(something)
NOT MUTE.
YOU'RE
DEA(F)(?)

(YOU
CAN
STILL
MAKE
S --)

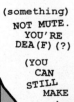

THEY TOOK EVERYTHING, BARNEY!

(NOT YE(T)(?).)

(Clint...)

(...Okay?)

(that son of a b(ench)?)
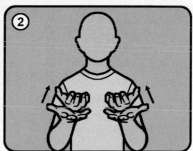
②

①

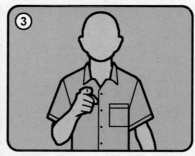
③
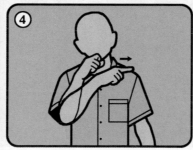
④

(something
get(?) up
Clint)

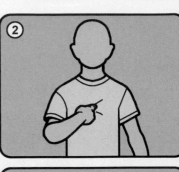

①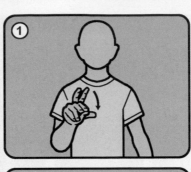

②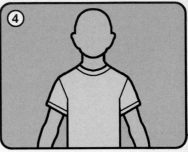

③

④

I CAN'T.

(GET
UP!)

RRAAAAA

(LOOK AT ME.)
(Make everything something to HIT WITH.)
(AND HIT THEM UNTIL THEY STOP.)
1
2
3
4
5
6
(Then we OUTLAST him)
(UNDERSTAND?)

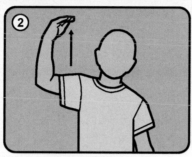

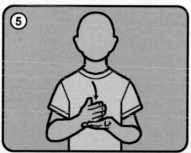

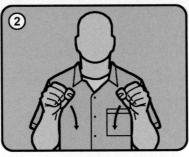

(1)
(2)
(3)
(4)
(5)

(I know you('re?)
    lip reading)

(you can get it back)

(look at ME)

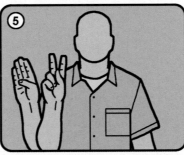

(you can get it ALL back)

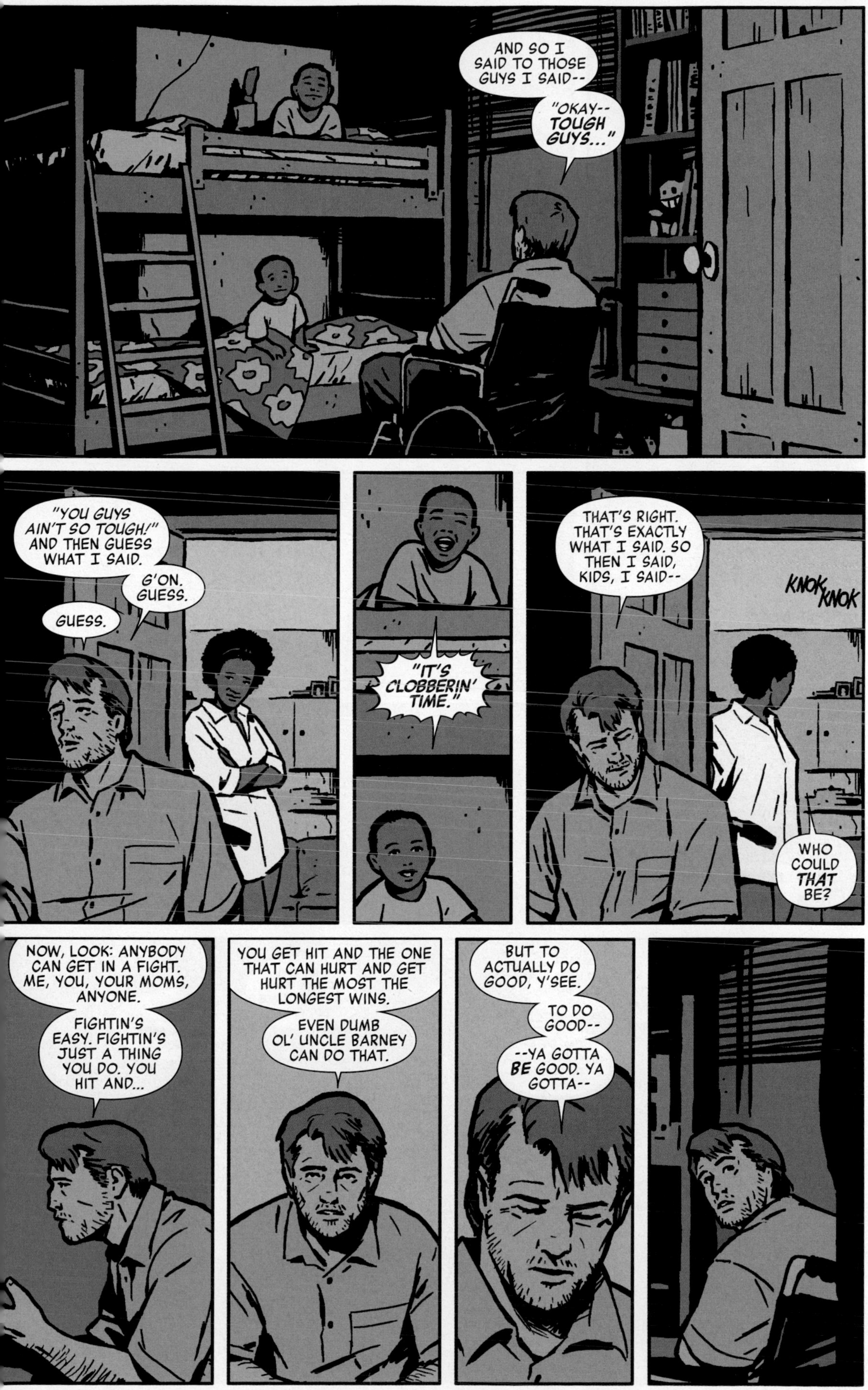
AND SO I SAID TO THOSE GUYS I SAID--
"OKAY-- TOUGH GUYS..."
"YOU GUYS AIN'T SO TOUGH!" AND THEN GUESS WHAT I SAID.
G'ON. GUESS.
GUESS.
"IT'S CLOBBERIN' TIME."
THAT'S RIGHT. THAT'S EXACTLY WHAT I SAID. SO THEN I SAID, KIDS, I SAID--
KNOK KNOK
WHO COULD THAT BE?
NOW, LOOK: ANYBODY CAN GET IN A FIGHT. ME, YOU, YOUR MOMS, ANYONE.
FIGHTIN'S EASY. FIGHTIN'S JUST A THING YOU DO. YOU HIT AND...
YOU GET HIT AND THE ONE THAT CAN HURT AND GET HURT THE MOST THE LONGEST WINS.
EVEN DUMB OL' UNCLE BARNEY CAN DO THAT.
BUT TO ACTUALLY DO GOOD, Y'SEE.
TO DO GOOD--
--YA GOTTA BE GOOD. YA GOTTA--

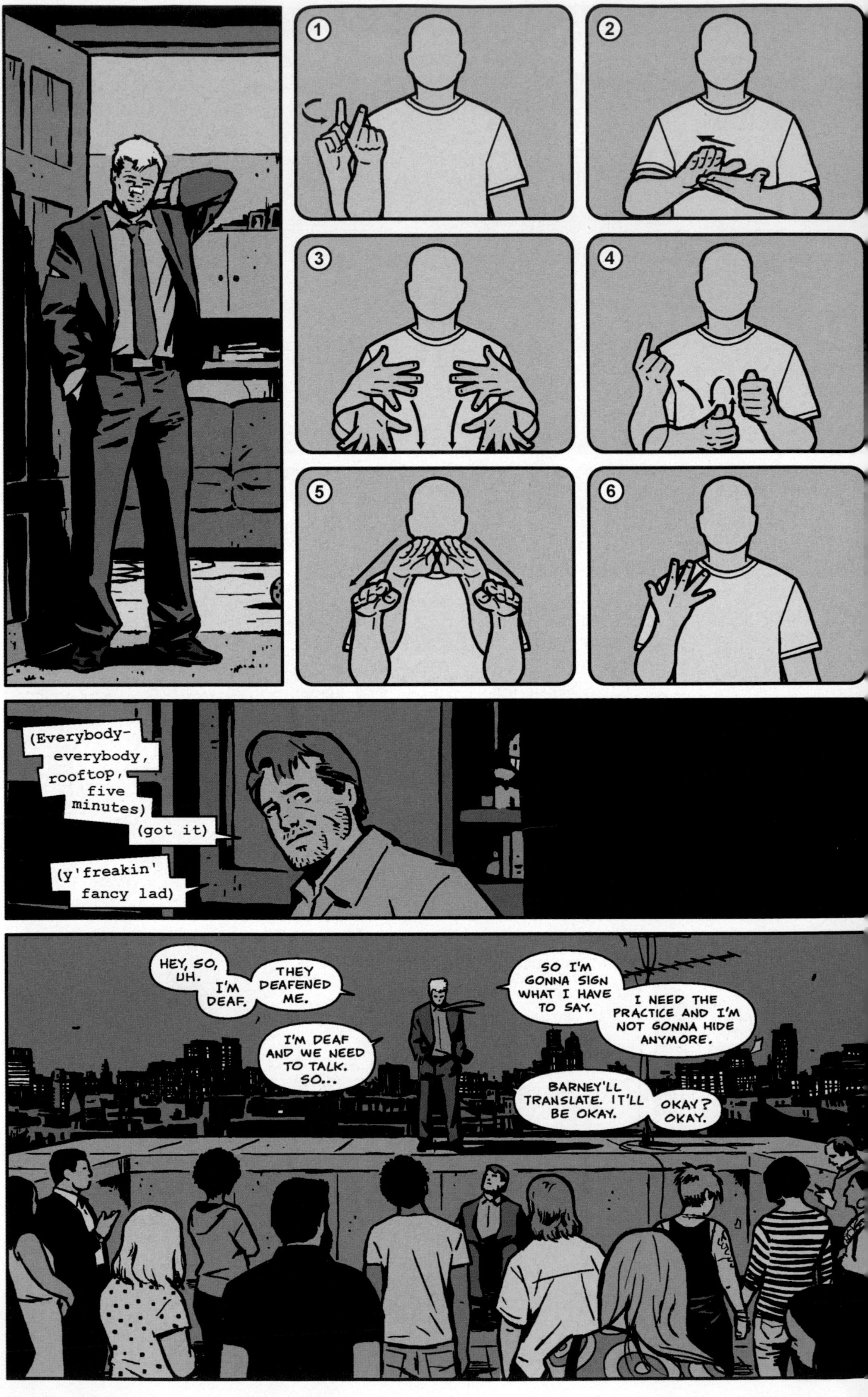

1
2
3
4
5
6
(Everybody-everybody, rooftop, five minutes)
(got it)
(y'freakin' fancy lad)
HEY, SO, UH.
I'M DEAF.
THEY DEAFENED ME.
I'M DEAF AND WE NEED TO TALK. SO...
SO I'M GONNA SIGN WHAT I HAVE TO SAY.
I NEED THE PRACTICE AND I'M NOT GONNA HIDE ANYMORE.
BARNEY'LL TRANSLATE. IT'LL BE OKAY.
OKAY? OKAY.

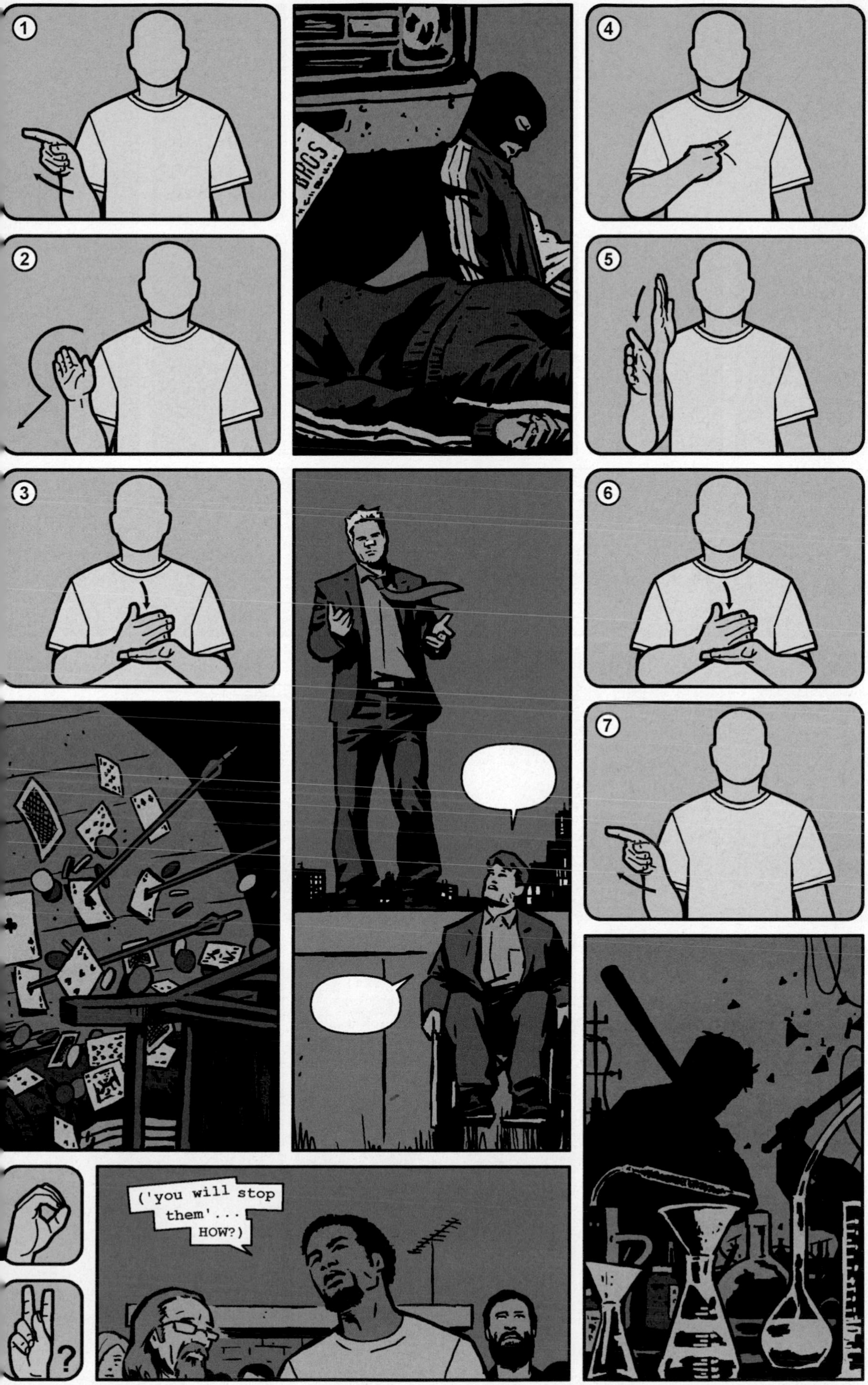
1
2
3
4
5
6
7
BROS
('you will stop them'... HOW?)

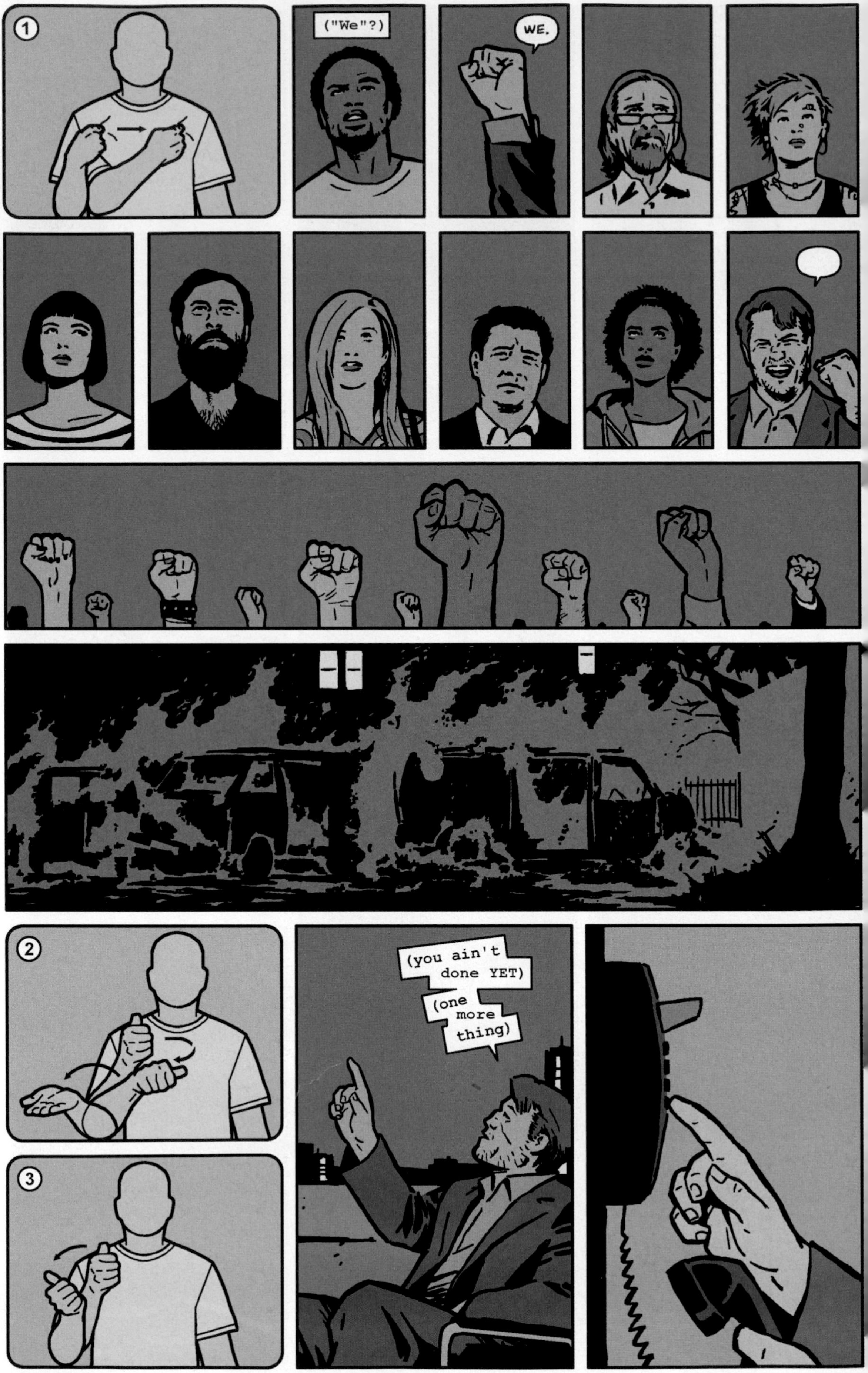
1
("We"?)
WE.
2
(you ain't done YET)
(one more thing)
3

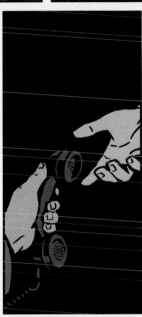

БОЛВАНЫ TOWN

JESS?

I'M SORRY AND I NEED YOUR HELP.

I NEED EVERYBODY'S HELP.

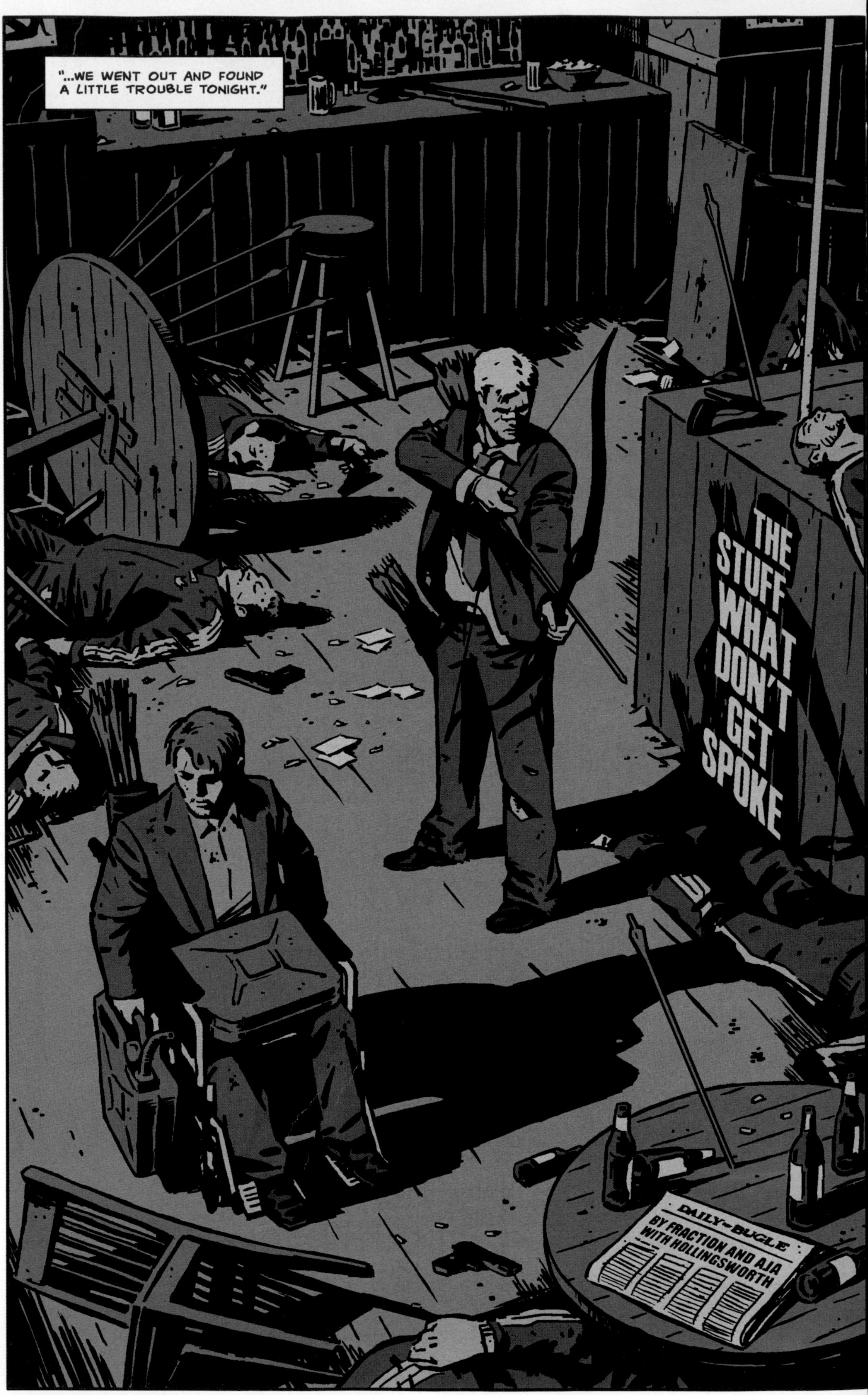
"...WE WENT OUT AND FOUND A LITTLE TROUBLE TONIGHT."
THE STUFF WHAT DON'T GET SPOKE
DAILY BUGLE
BY FRACTION AND AJA WITH HOLLINGSWORTH

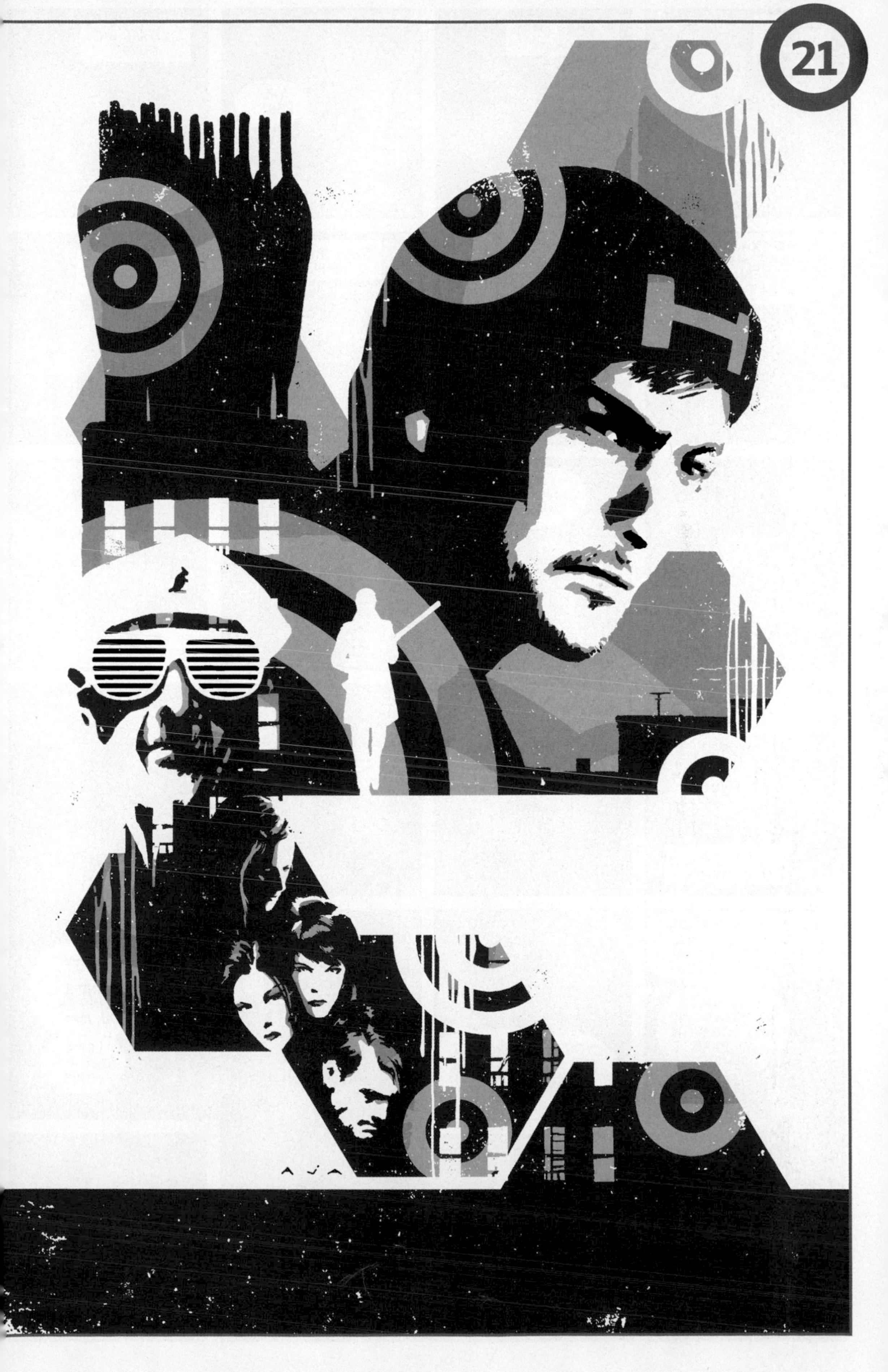
21

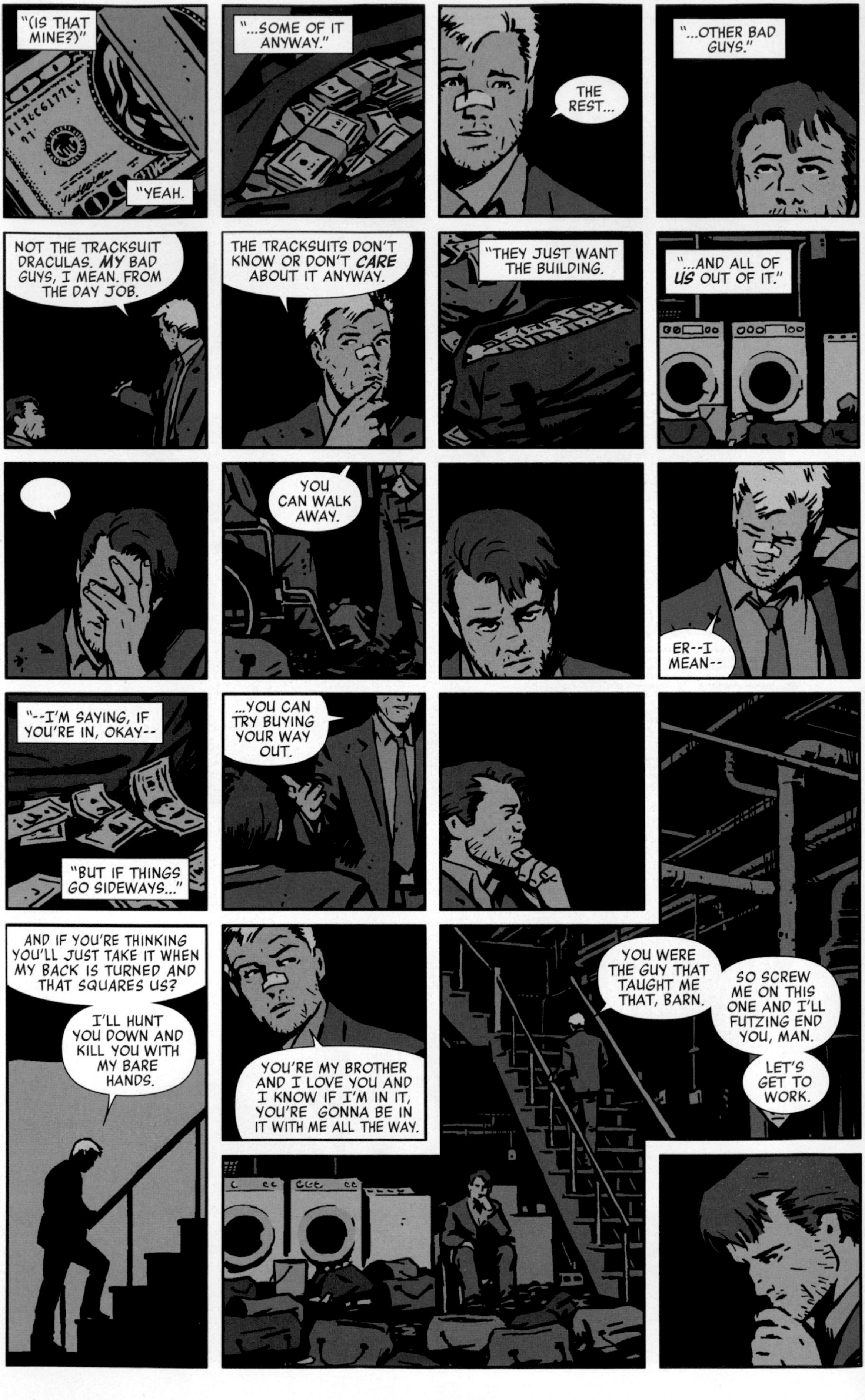
"(IS THAT MINE?)"
"YEAH.
"...SOME OF IT ANYWAY."
THE REST...
"...OTHER BAD GUYS."
NOT THE TRACKSUIT DRACULAS. MY BAD GUYS, I MEAN. FROM THE DAY JOB.
THE TRACKSUITS DON'T KNOW OR DON'T CARE ABOUT IT ANYWAY.
"THEY JUST WANT THE BUILDING.
"...AND ALL OF US OUT OF IT."
YOU CAN WALK AWAY.
ER--I MEAN--
"--I'M SAYING, IF YOU'RE IN, OKAY--
"BUT IF THINGS GO SIDEWAYS..."
...YOU CAN TRY BUYING YOUR WAY OUT.
AND IF YOU'RE THINKING YOU'LL JUST TAKE IT WHEN MY BACK IS TURNED AND THAT SQUARES US?
I'LL HUNT YOU DOWN AND KILL YOU WITH MY BARE HANDS.
YOU'RE MY BROTHER AND I LOVE YOU AND I KNOW IF I'M IN IT, YOU'RE GONNA BE IN IT WITH ME ALL THE WAY.
YOU WERE THE GUY THAT TAUGHT ME THAT, BARN.
SO SCREW ME ON THIS ONE AND I'LL FUTZING END YOU, MAN.
LET'S GET TO WORK.

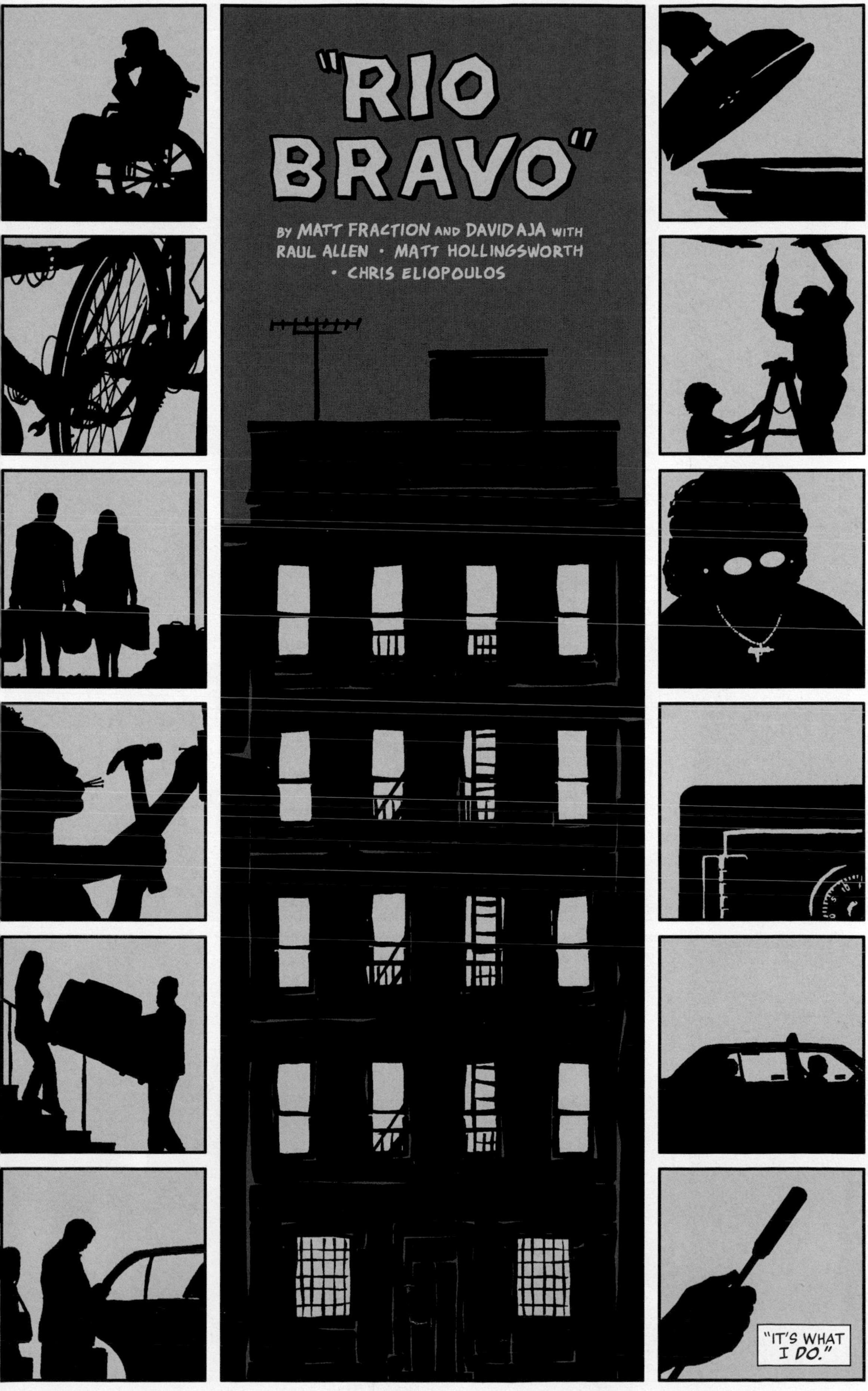
"RIO BRAVO"
BY MATT FRACTION AND DAVID AJA WITH
RAUL ALLEN • MATT HOLLINGSWORTH
• CHRIS ELIOPOULOS
"IT'S WHAT I DO."

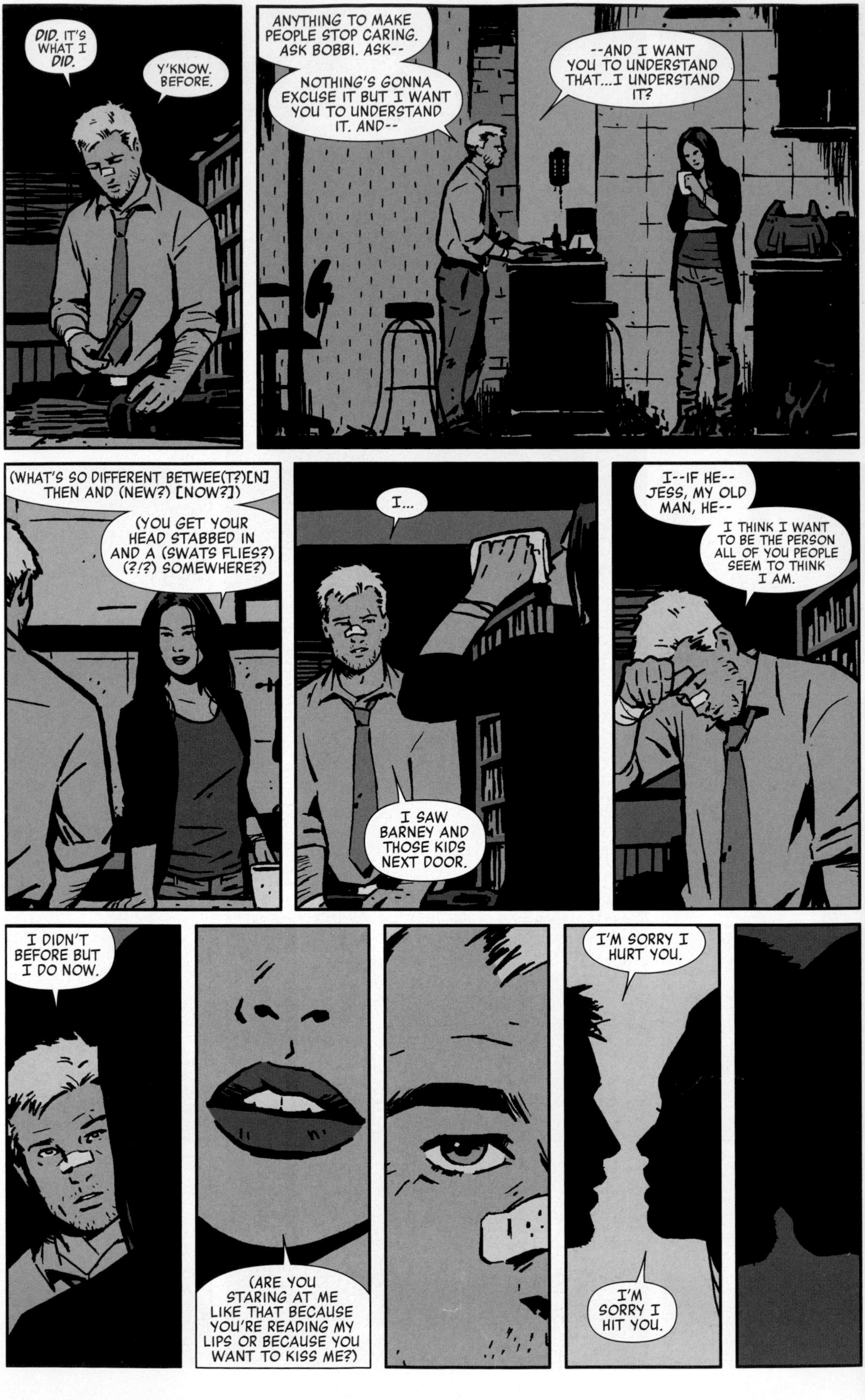
DID. IT'S WHAT I DID.
Y'KNOW. BEFORE.
ANYTHING TO MAKE PEOPLE STOP CARING. ASK BOBBI. ASK--
NOTHING'S GONNA EXCUSE IT BUT I WANT YOU TO UNDERSTAND IT. AND--
--AND I WANT YOU TO UNDERSTAND THAT...I UNDERSTAND IT?
(WHAT'S SO DIFFERENT BETWEE(T?)[N] THEN AND (NEW?) [NOW?])
(YOU GET YOUR HEAD STABBED IN AND A (SWATS FLIES?) (?!?) SOMEWHERE?)
I...
I SAW BARNEY AND THOSE KIDS NEXT DOOR.
I--IF HE-- JESS, MY OLD MAN, HE--
I THINK I WANT TO BE THE PERSON ALL OF YOU PEOPLE SEEM TO THINK I AM.
I DIDN'T BEFORE BUT I DO NOW.
(ARE YOU STARING AT ME LIKE THAT BECAUSE YOU'RE READING MY LIPS OR BECAUSE YOU WANT TO KISS ME?)
I'M SORRY I HURT YOU.
I'M SORRY I HIT YOU.

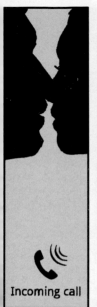

Incoming call

(WORK.)

"YOU GO.

"THEY DON'T NEED ME."

(CLINT...)

(YOU ARE SO WRONG ABOUT THAT.)

JUST GOTTA WRAP STUFF UP HERE, S'ALL.

WE'LL BE FINE.

Besides...

HOW MUCH WORSE can it get?

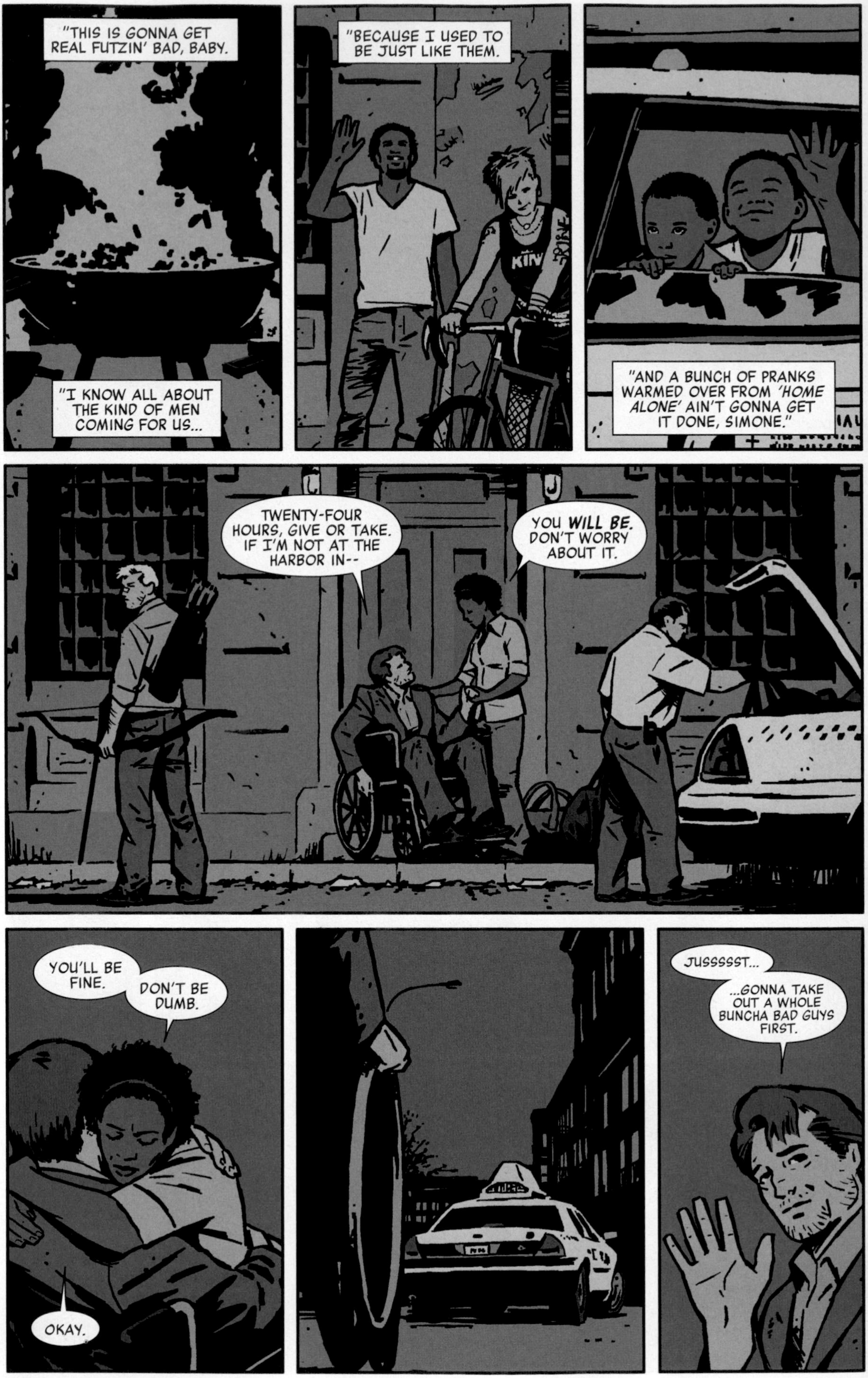
"THIS IS GONNA GET REAL FUTZIN' BAD, BABY.
"I KNOW ALL ABOUT THE KIND OF MEN COMING FOR US...
"BECAUSE I USED TO BE JUST LIKE THEM.
"AND A BUNCH OF PRANKS WARMED OVER FROM *'HOME ALONE'* AIN'T GONNA GET IT DONE, SIMONE."
TWENTY-FOUR HOURS, GIVE OR TAKE. IF I'M NOT AT THE HARBOR IN--
YOU **WILL BE.** DON'T WORRY ABOUT IT.
YOU'LL BE FINE.
DON'T BE DUMB.
OKAY.
JUSSSSST...
...GONNA TAKE OUT A WHOLE BUNCHA BAD GUYS FIRST.

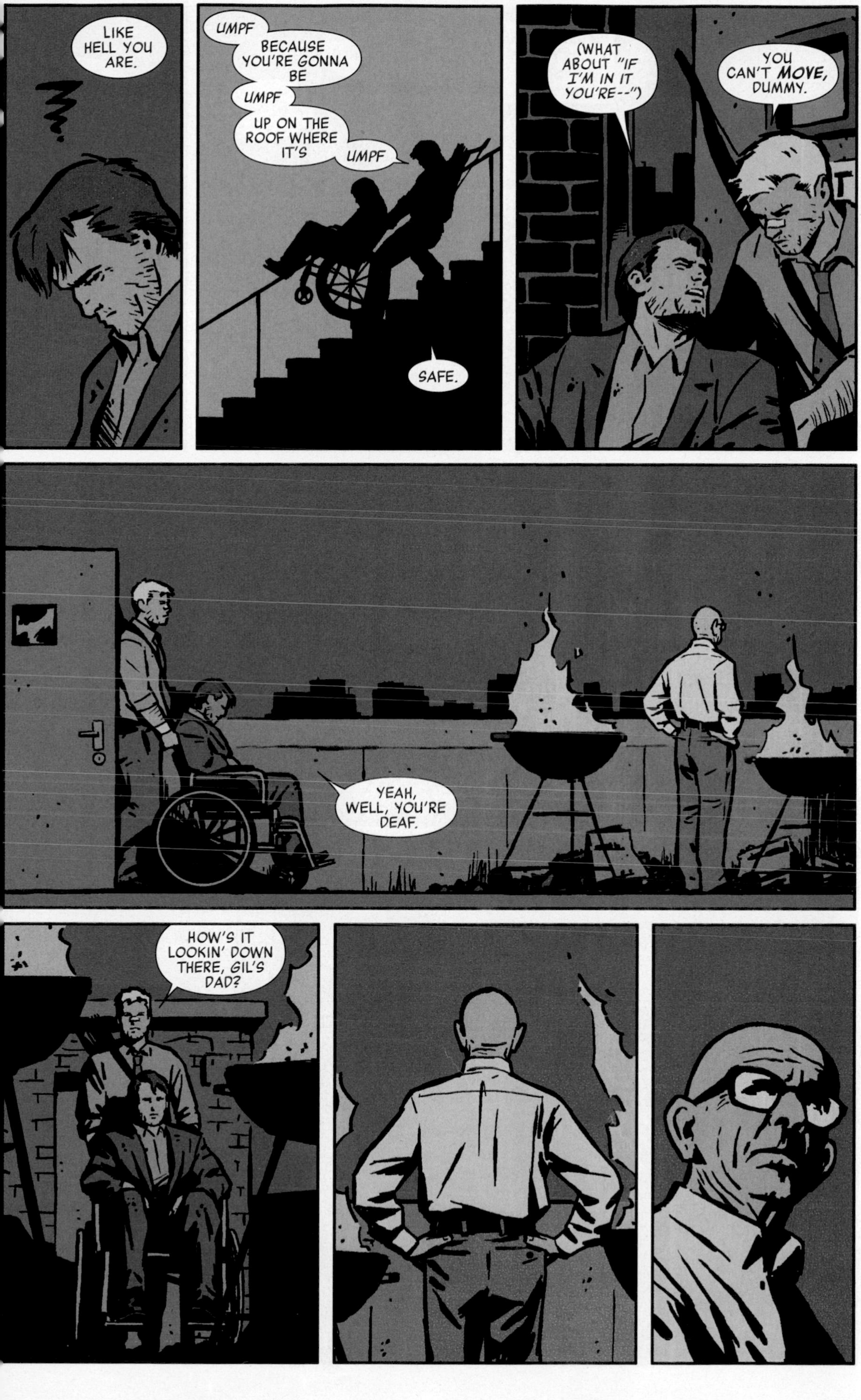

LIKE HELL YOU ARE.
UMPF
BECAUSE YOU'RE GONNA BE
UMPF
UP ON THE ROOF WHERE IT'S
UMPF
SAFE.
(WHAT ABOUT "IF I'M IN IT YOU'RE--")
YOU CAN'T MOVE, DUMMY.
YEAH, WELL, YOU'RE DEAF.
HOW'S IT LOOKIN' DOWN THERE, GIL'S DAD?

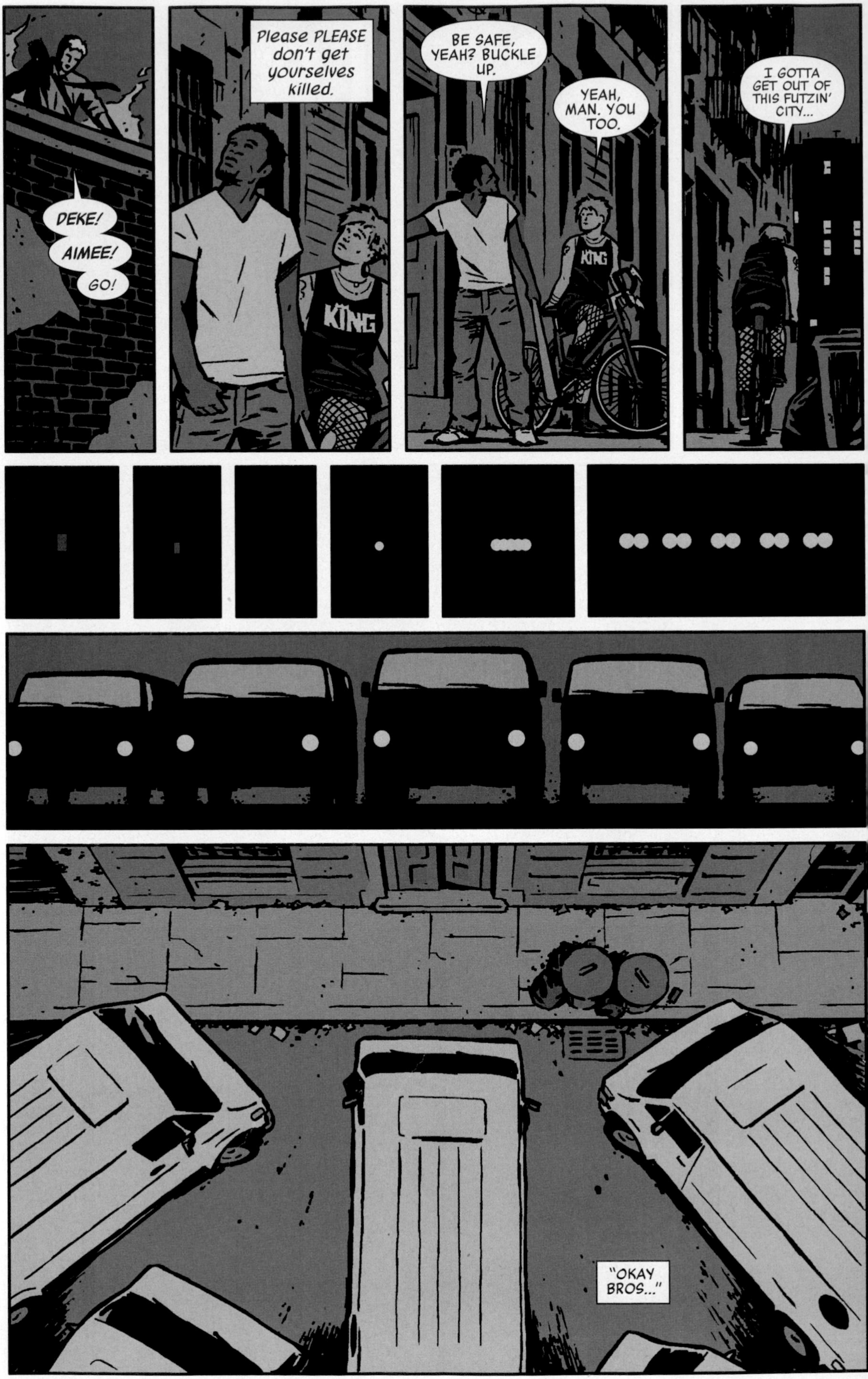

DEKE!
AIMEE!
GO!
Please PLEASE don't get yourselves killed.
BE SAFE, YEAH? BUCKLE UP.
YEAH, MAN. YOU TOO.
I GOTTA GET OUT OF THIS FUTZIN' CITY...
KING
"OKAY BROS..."

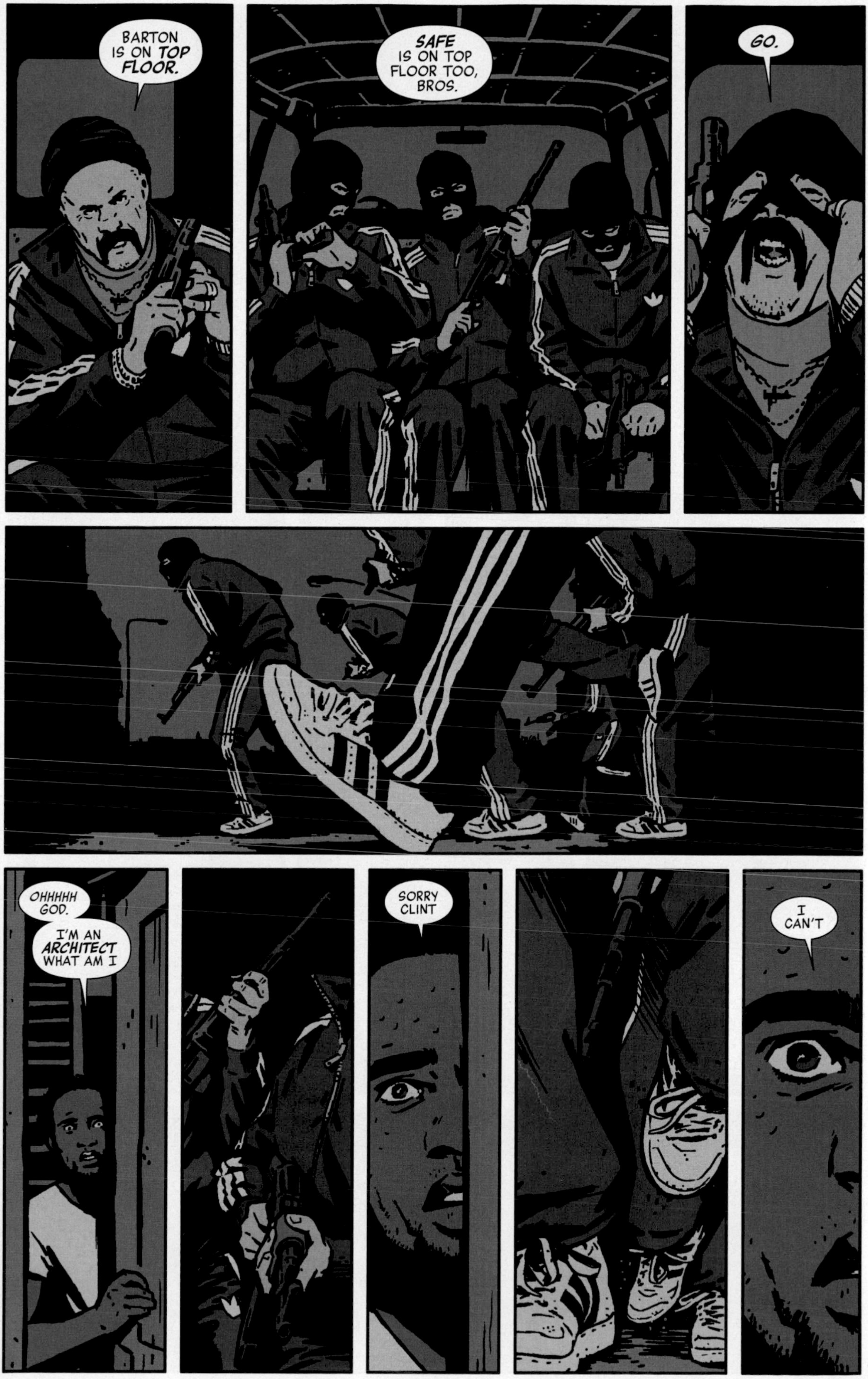
BARTON IS ON TOP FLOOR.
SAFE IS ON TOP FLOOR TOO, BROS.
GO.
OHHHHH GOD.
I'M AN ARCHITECT WHAT AM I
SORRY CLINT
I CAN'T

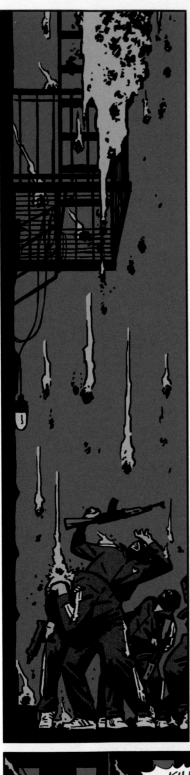

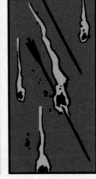

KILL THEM BROS NOW!!!

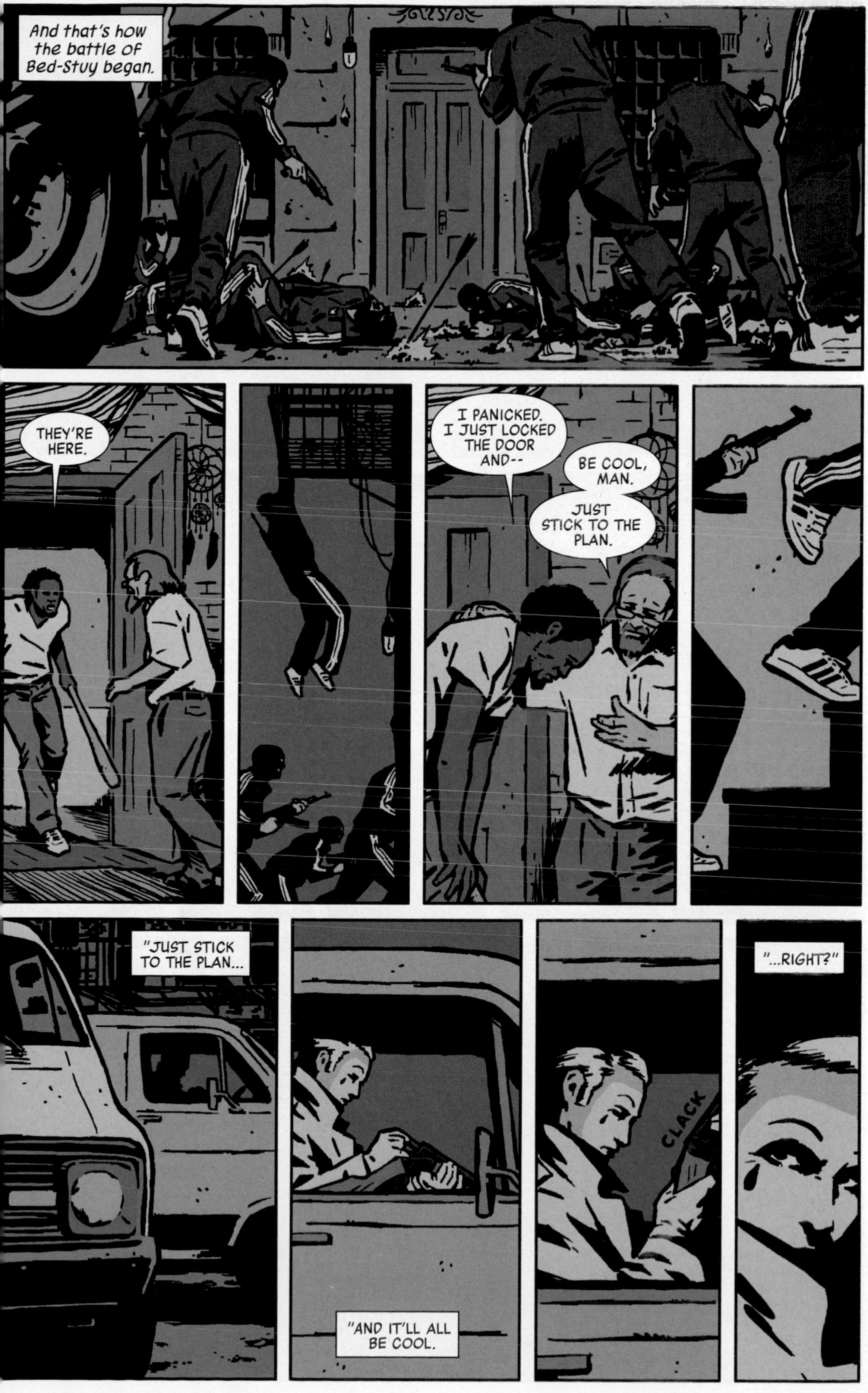
And that's how the battle of Bed-Stuy began.
THEY'RE HERE.
I PANICKED. I JUST LOCKED THE DOOR AND--
BE COOL, MAN.
JUST STICK TO THE PLAN.
"JUST STICK TO THE PLAN...
"AND IT'LL ALL BE COOL.
CLACK
"...RIGHT?"

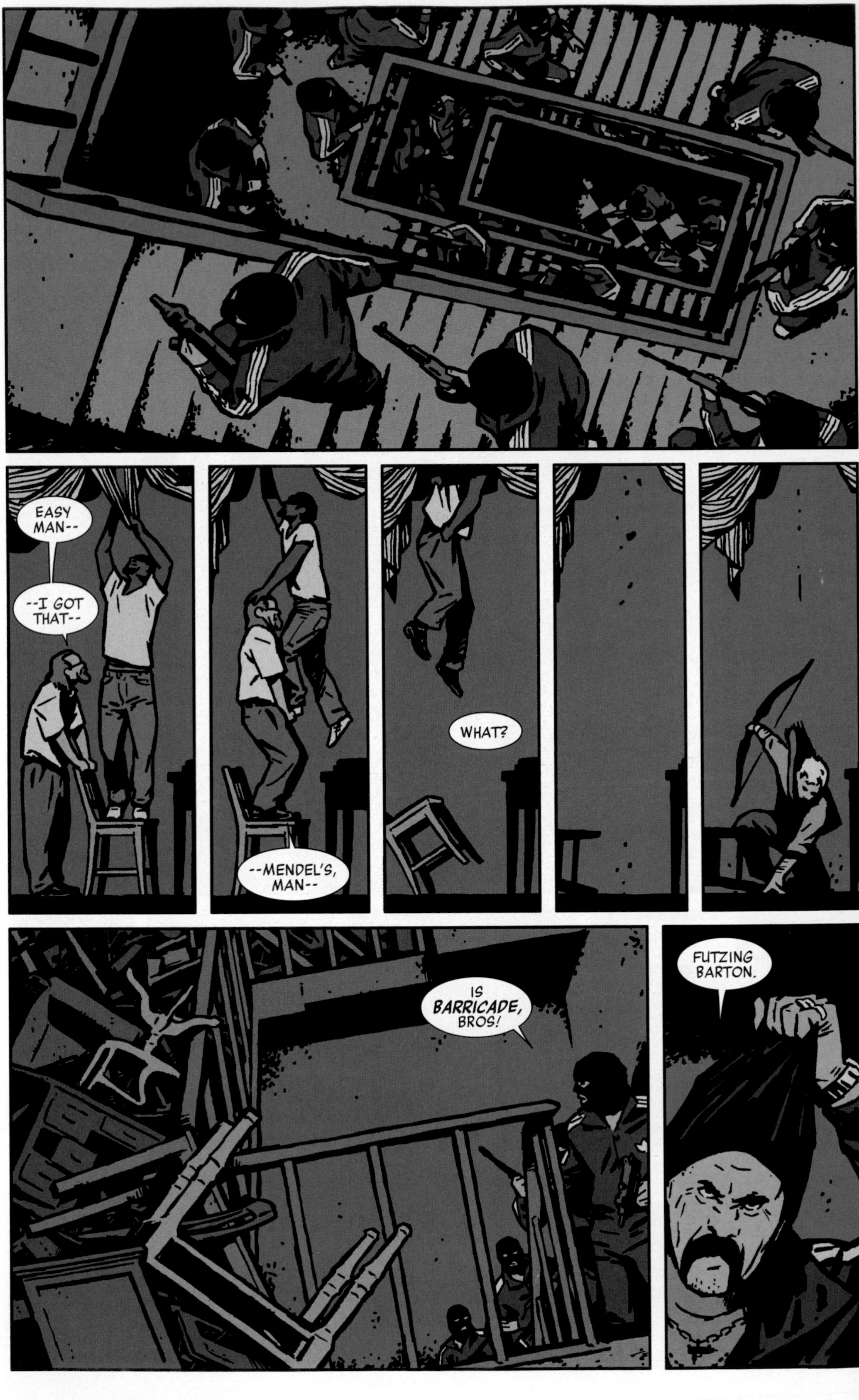
EASY MAN--
--I GOT THAT--
--MENDEL'S, MAN--
WHAT?
IS BARRICADE, BROS!
FUTZING BARTON.

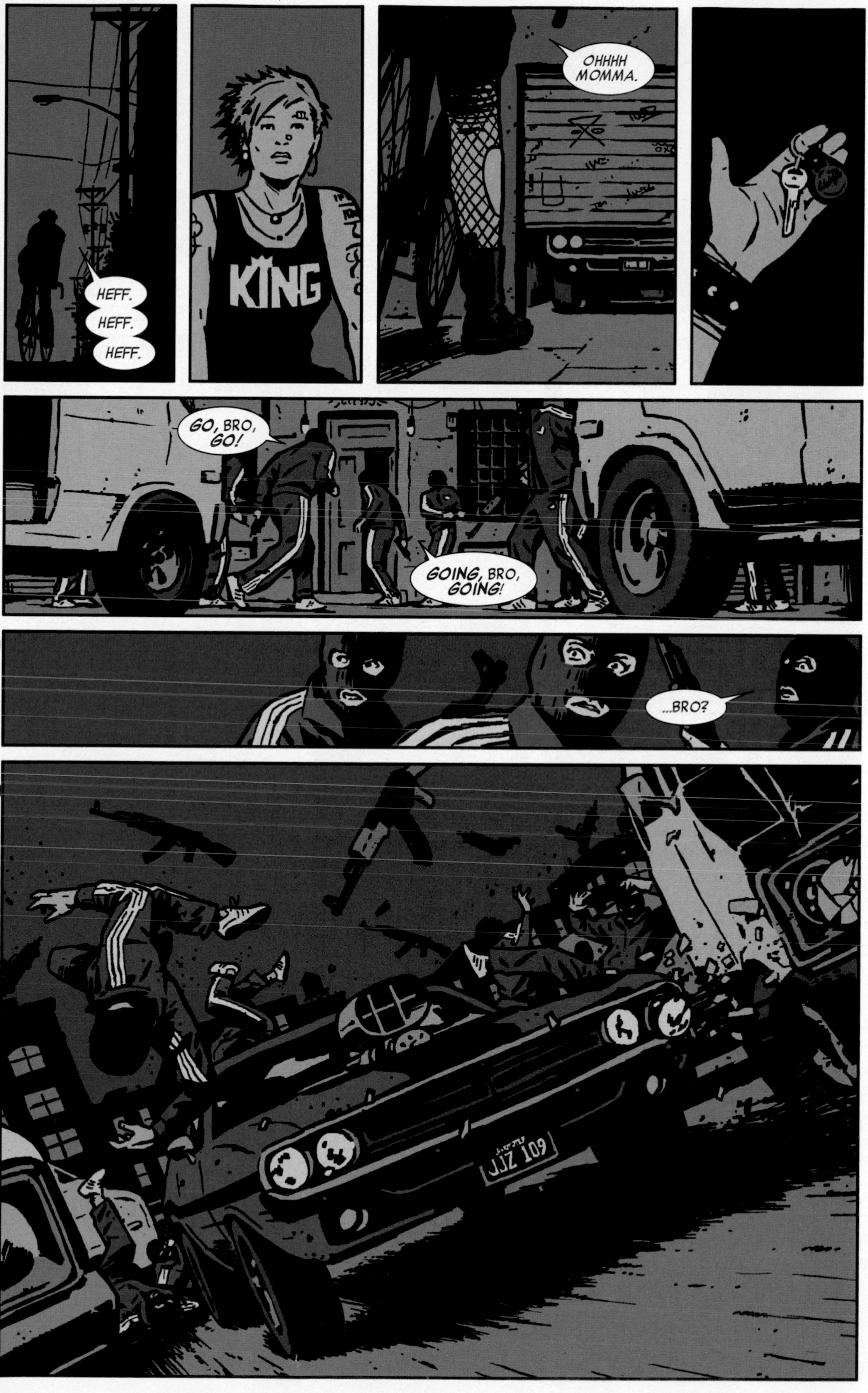
HEFF.
HEFF.
HEFF.
OHHHH MOMMA.
GO, BRO, GO!
GOING, BRO, GOING!
...BRO?
JJZ 109

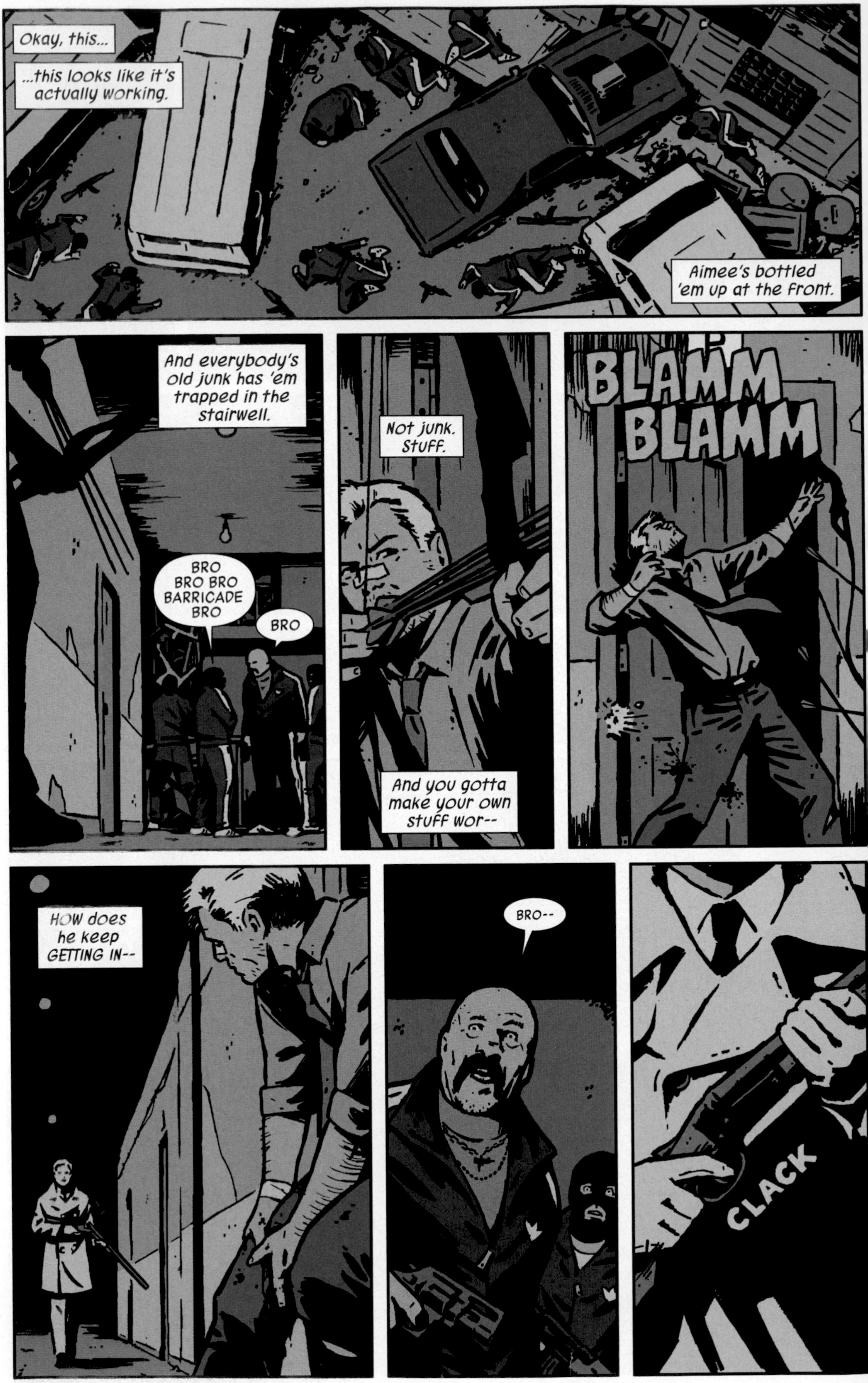

Okay, this...
...this looks like it's actually working.
Aimee's bottled 'em up at the front.
And everybody's old junk has 'em trapped in the stairwell.
BRO BRO BRO BARRICADE BRO
BRO
Not junk. Stuff.
And you gotta make your own stuff wor--
BLAMM BLAMM
HOW does he keep GETTING IN--
BRO--
CLACK

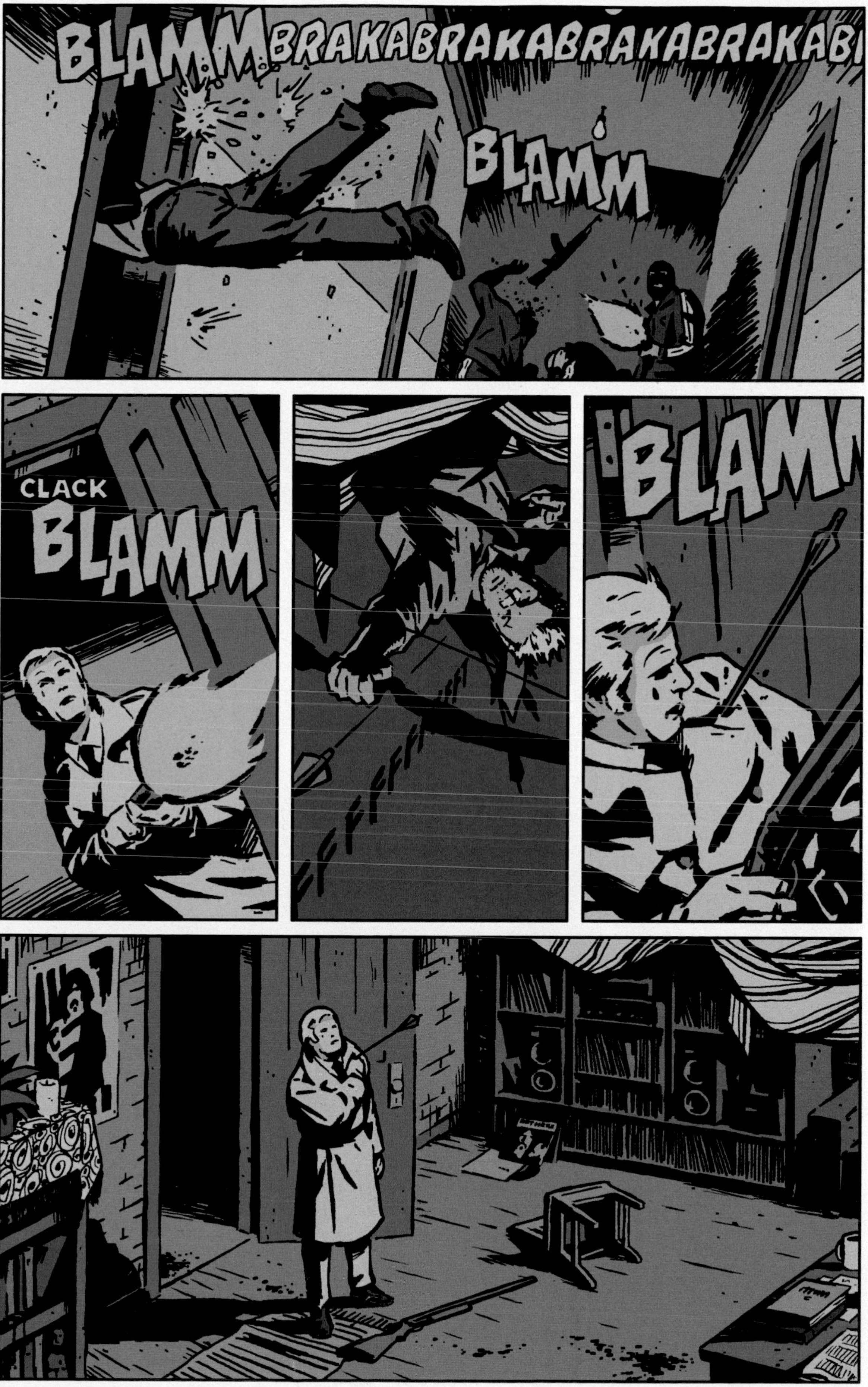
BLAMM
BRAKABRAKABRAKABRAKAB
BLAMM
CLACK
BLAMM
BLAMM

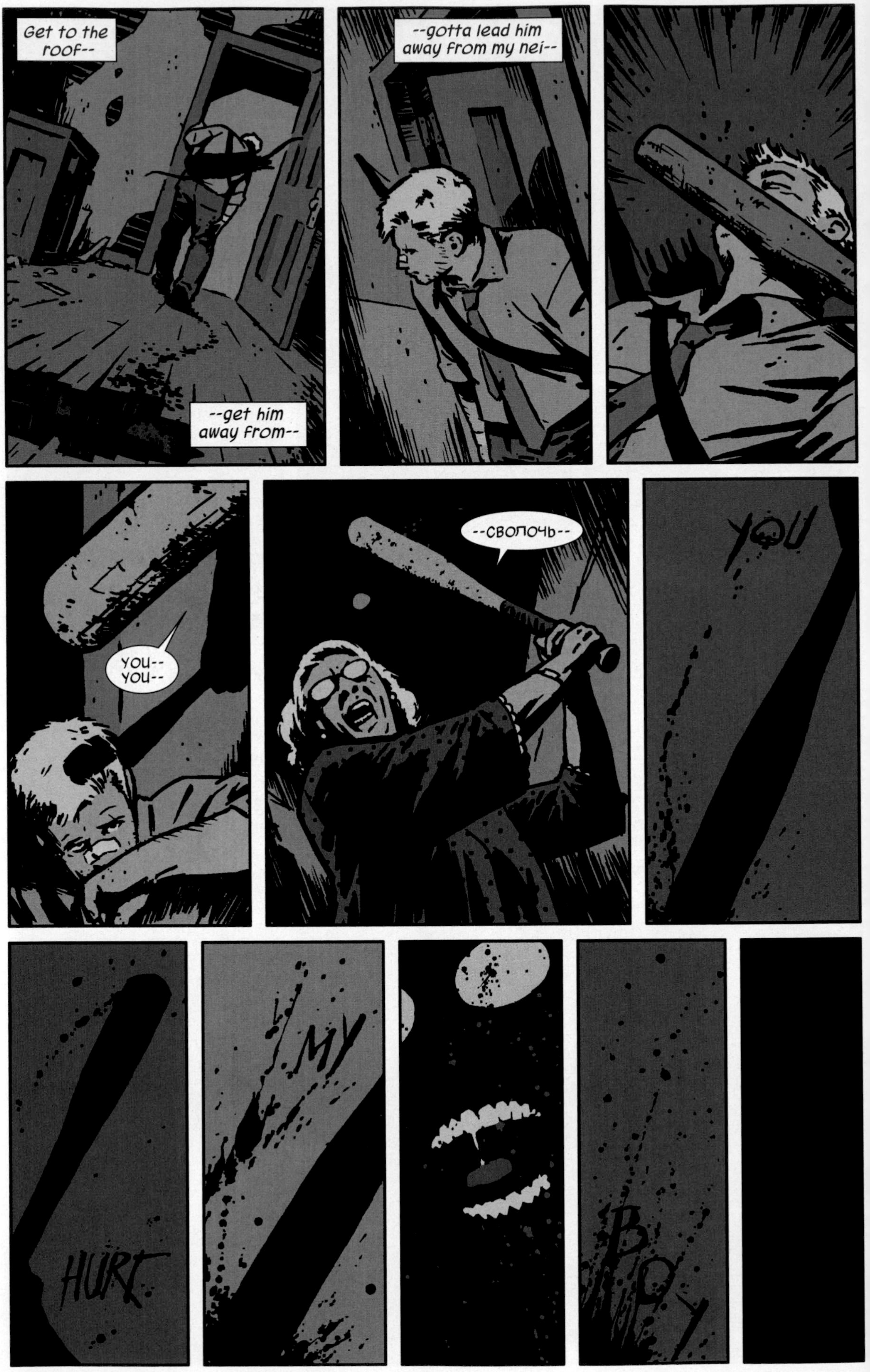
Get to the roof--
--get him away from--
--gotta lead him away from my nei--
YOU--
YOU--
--СВОЛОЧЬ--
YOU
HURT
MY
BOY

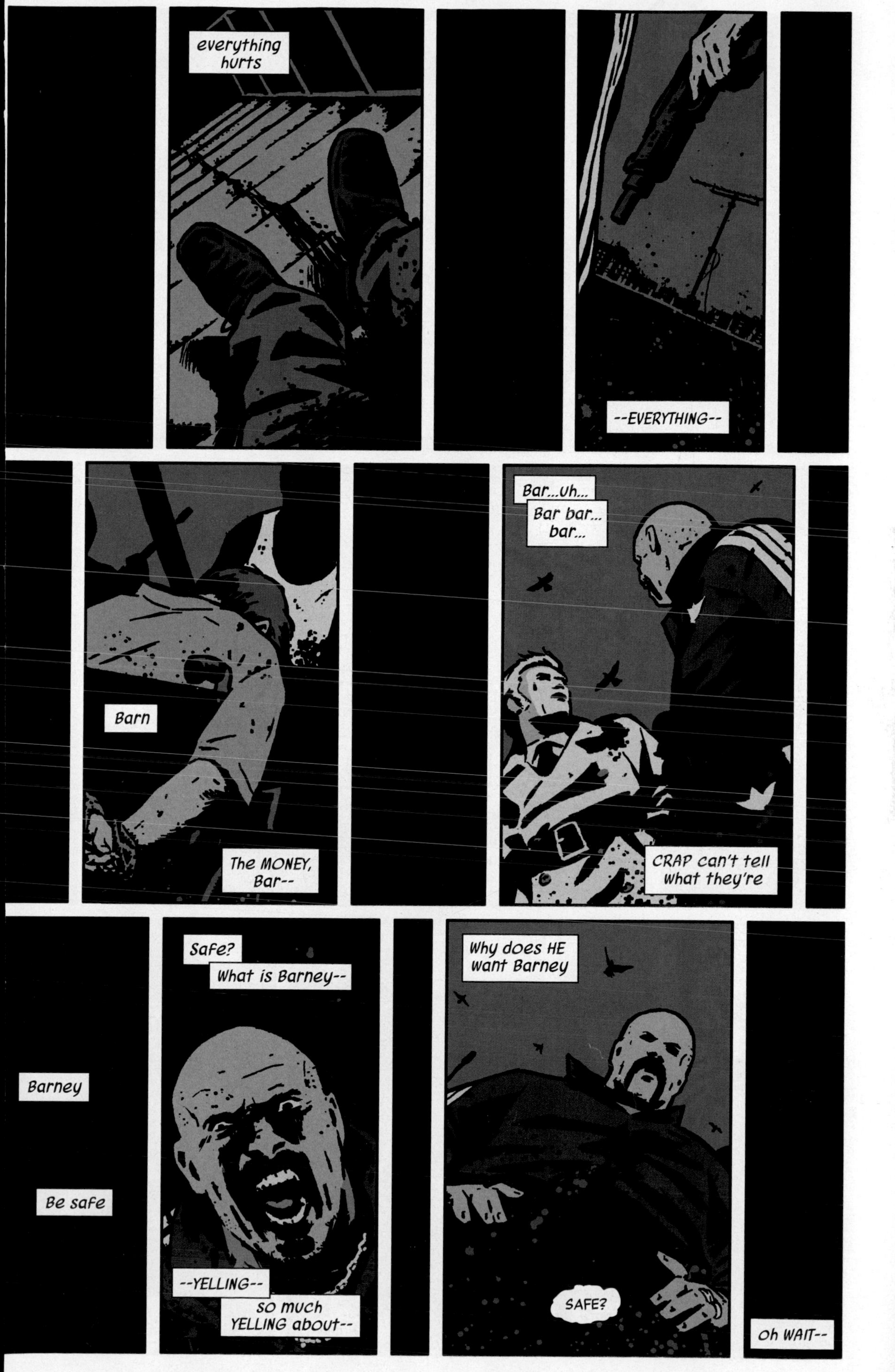
everything hurts
--EVERYTHING--
Barn
The MONEY, Bar--
Bar...uh...
Bar bar... bar...
CRAP can't tell what they're
Barney
Be safe
Safe?
What is Barney--
--YELLING--
so much YELLING about--
Why does HE want Barney
SAFE?
Oh WAIT--

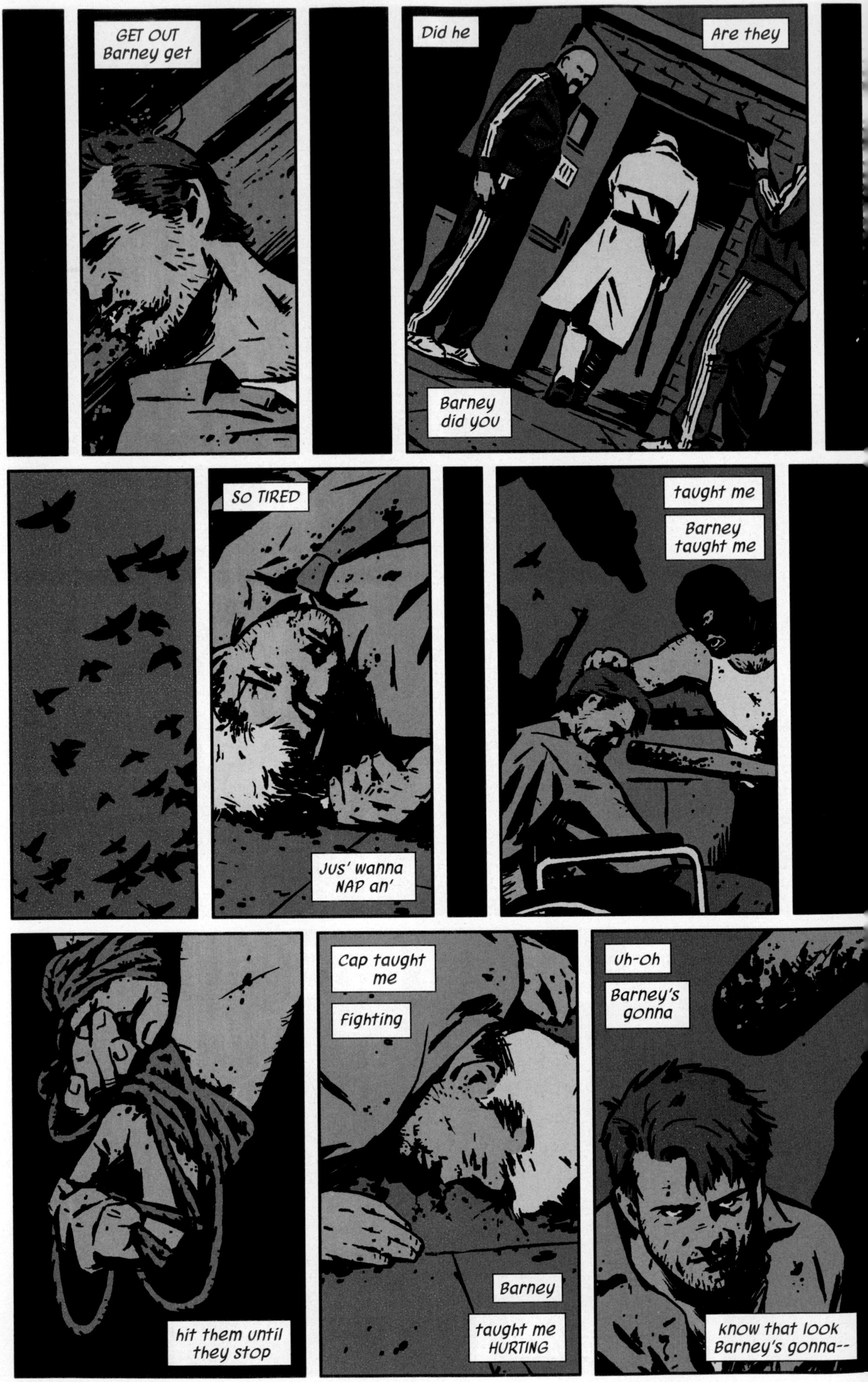
GET OUT
Barney get
Did he
Are they
Barney did you
SO TIRED
Jus' wanna NAP an'
taught me
Barney taught me
Cap taught me
Fighting
Barney
taught me HURTING
hit them until they stop
Uh-oh
Barney's gonna
know that look Barney's gonna--

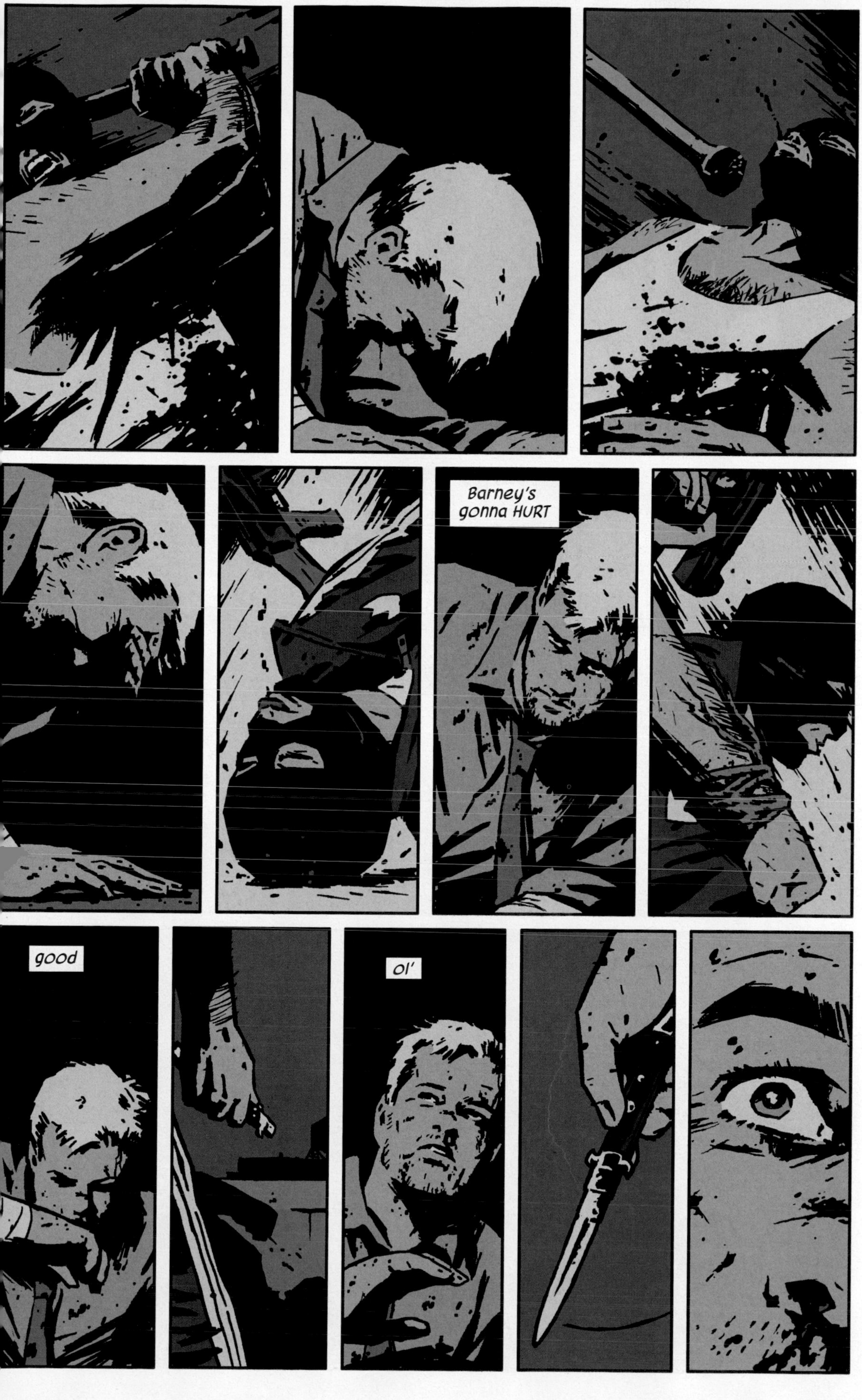
Barney's gonna HURT
good
ol'

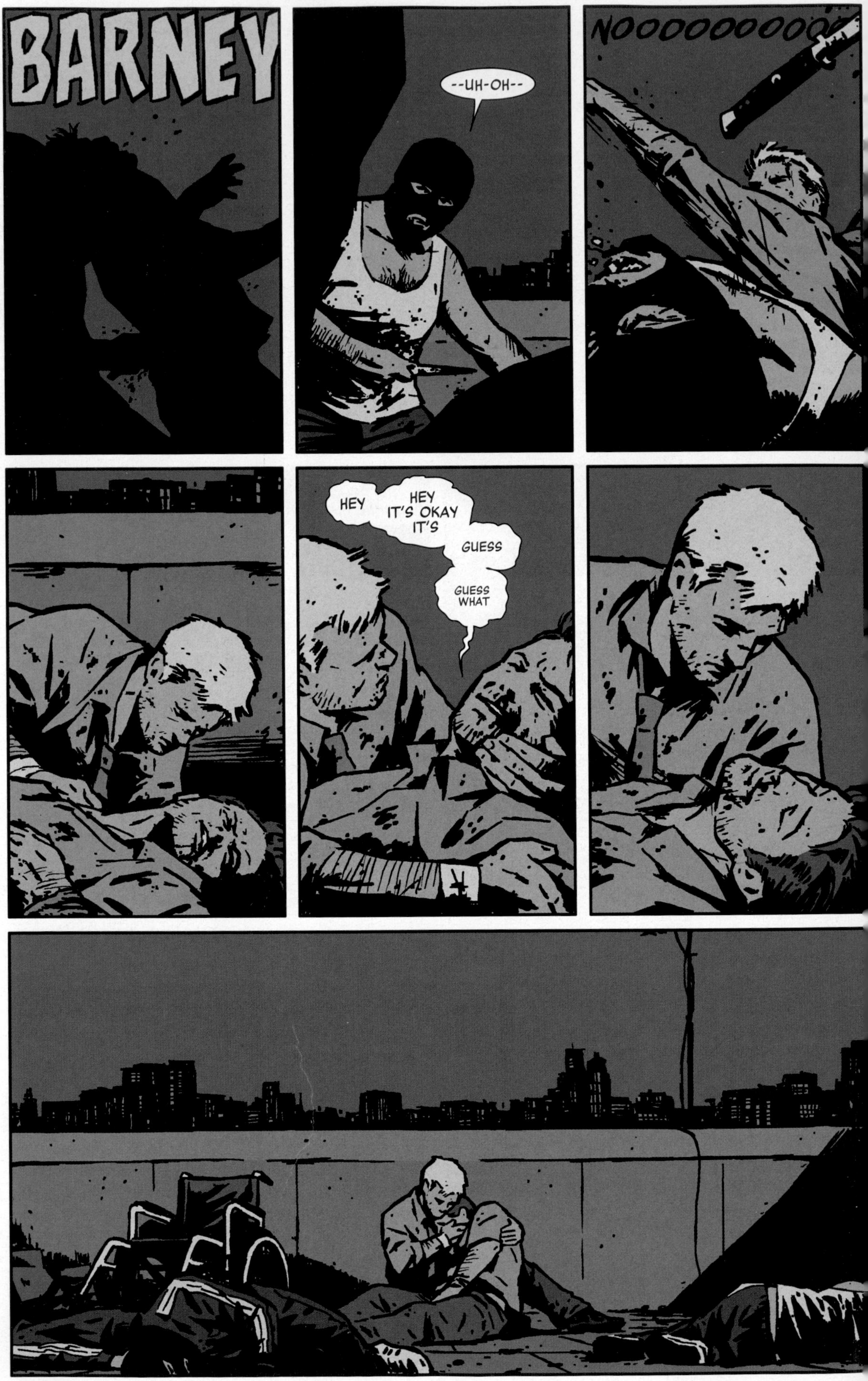
BARNEY
--UH-OH--
NOOOOOOOOOO
HEY
HEY
IT'S OKAY
IT'S
GUESS
GUESS
WHAT

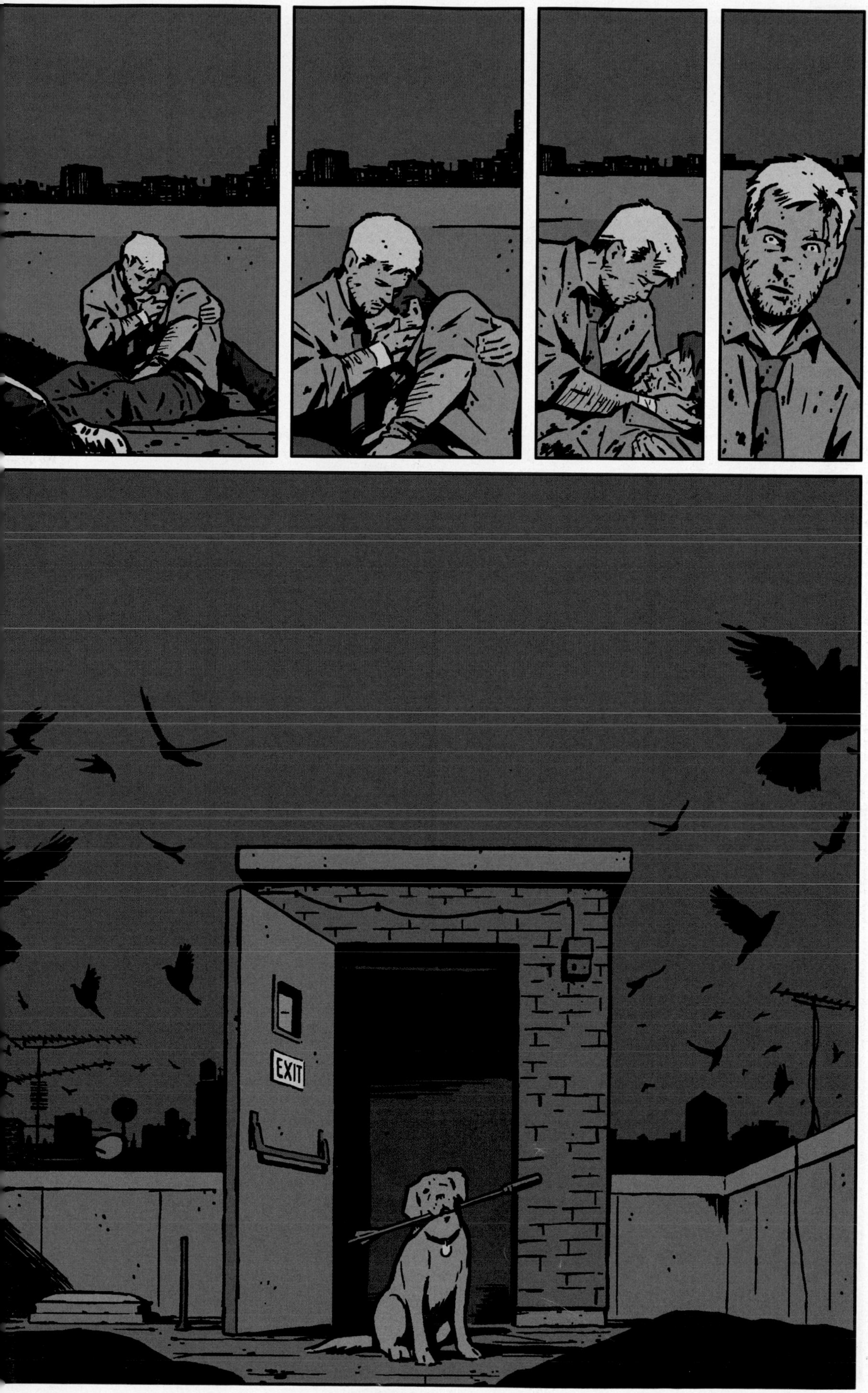
EXIT

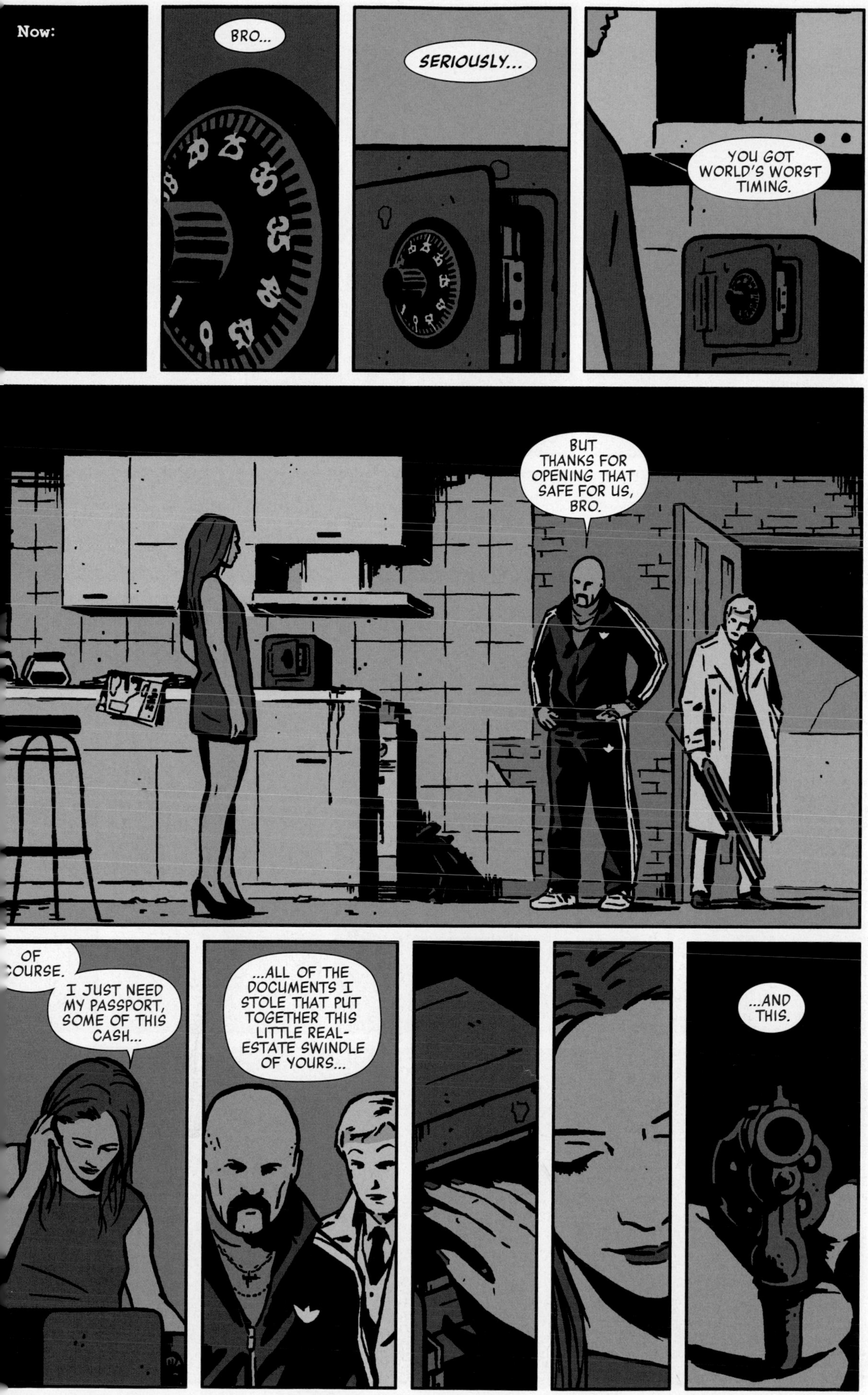
Now:
BRO...
SERIOUSLY...
YOU GOT WORLD'S WORST TIMING.
BUT THANKS FOR OPENING THAT SAFE FOR US, BRO.
OF COURSE.
I JUST NEED MY PASSPORT, SOME OF THIS CASH...
...ALL OF THE DOCUMENTS I STOLE THAT PUT TOGETHER THIS LITTLE REAL-ESTATE SWINDLE OF YOURS...
...AND THIS.

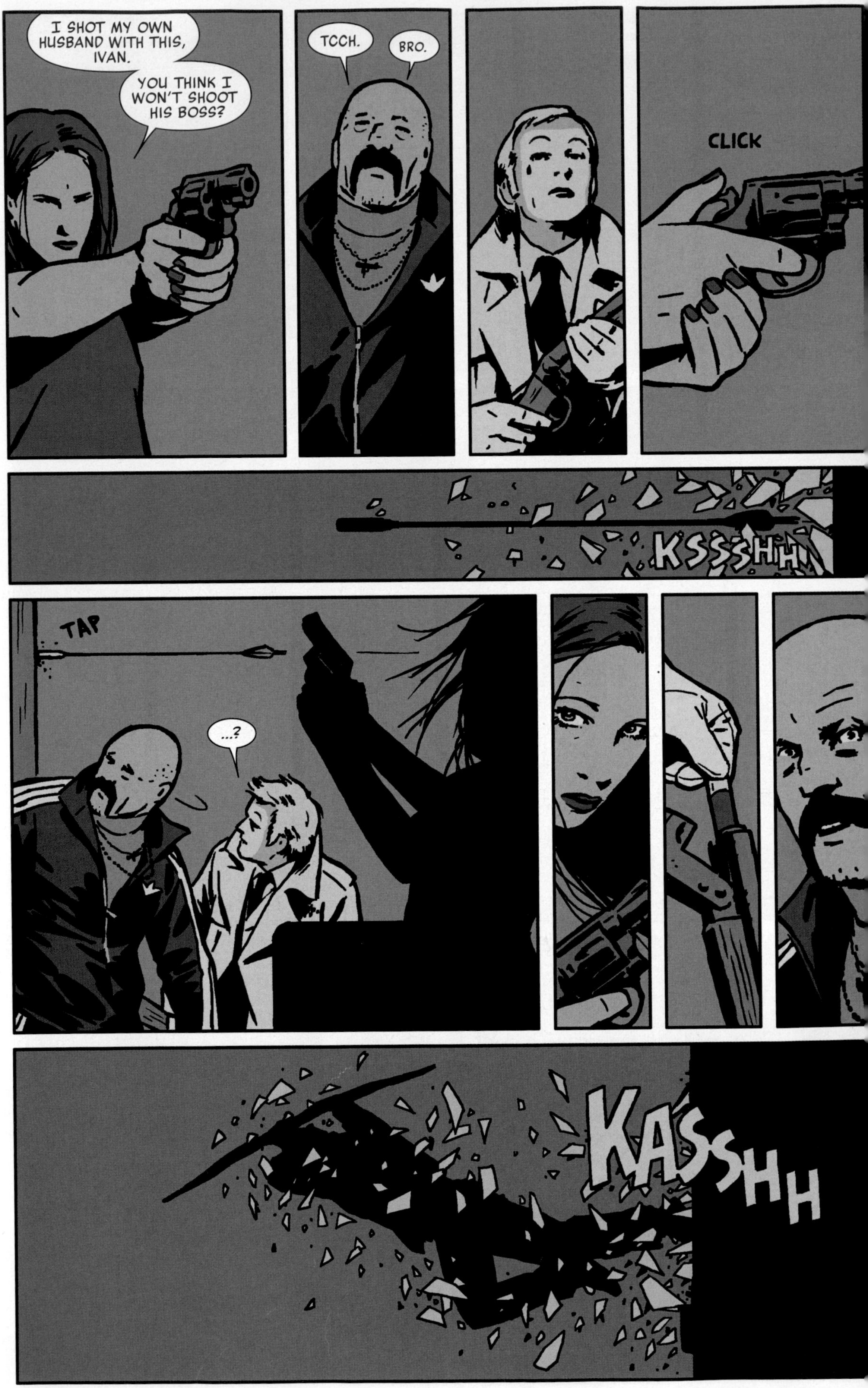
I SHOT MY OWN HUSBAND WITH THIS, IVAN.
YOU THINK I WON'T SHOOT HIS BOSS?
TCCH.
BRO.
CLICK
KSSSHH
TAP
...?
KASSHH

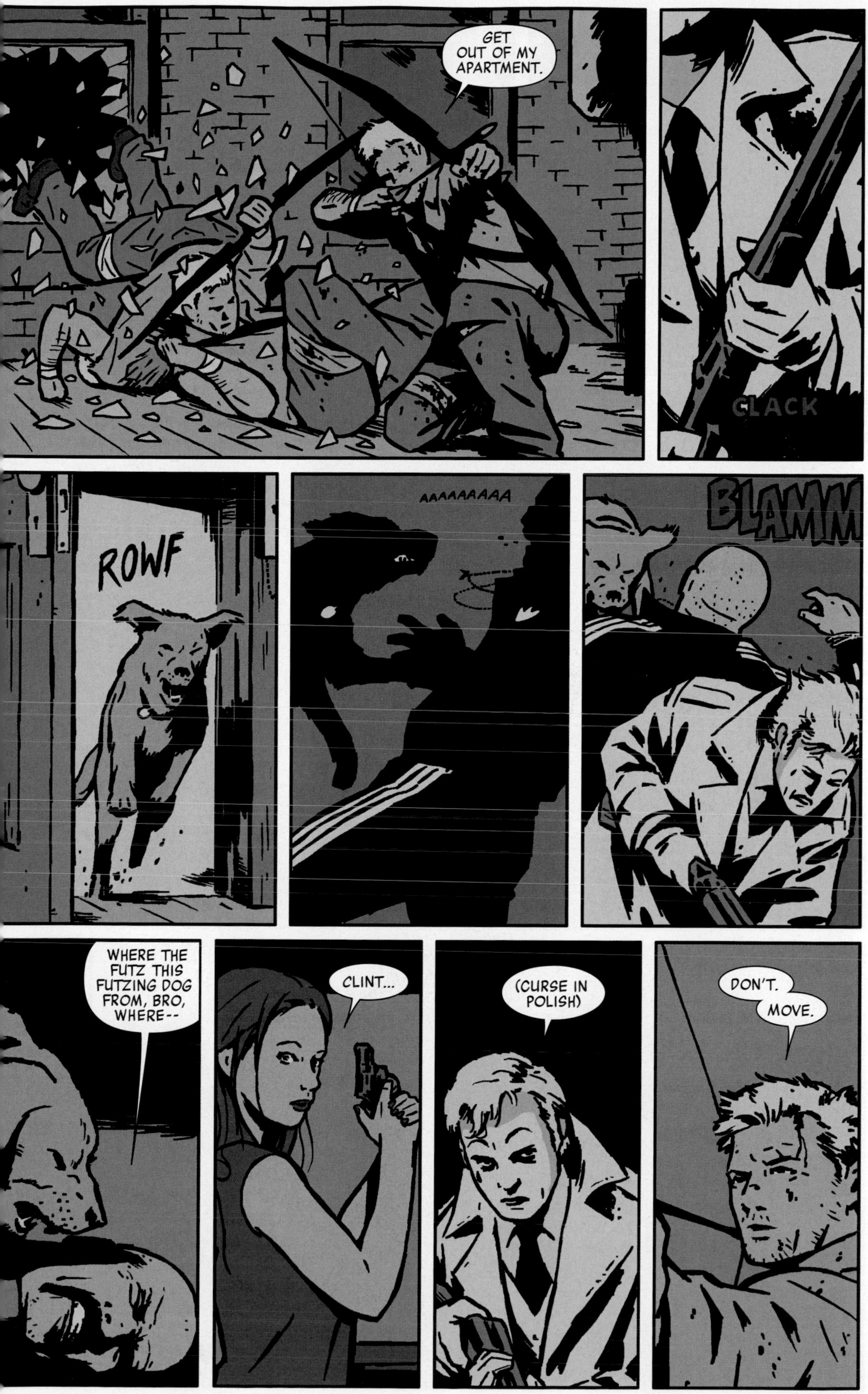
GET OUT OF MY APARTMENT.
CLACK
ROWF
AAAAAAAAA
BLAMM
WHERE THE FUTZ THIS FUTZING DOG FROM, BRO, WHERE--
CLINT...
(CURSE IN POLISH)
DON'T.
MOVE.

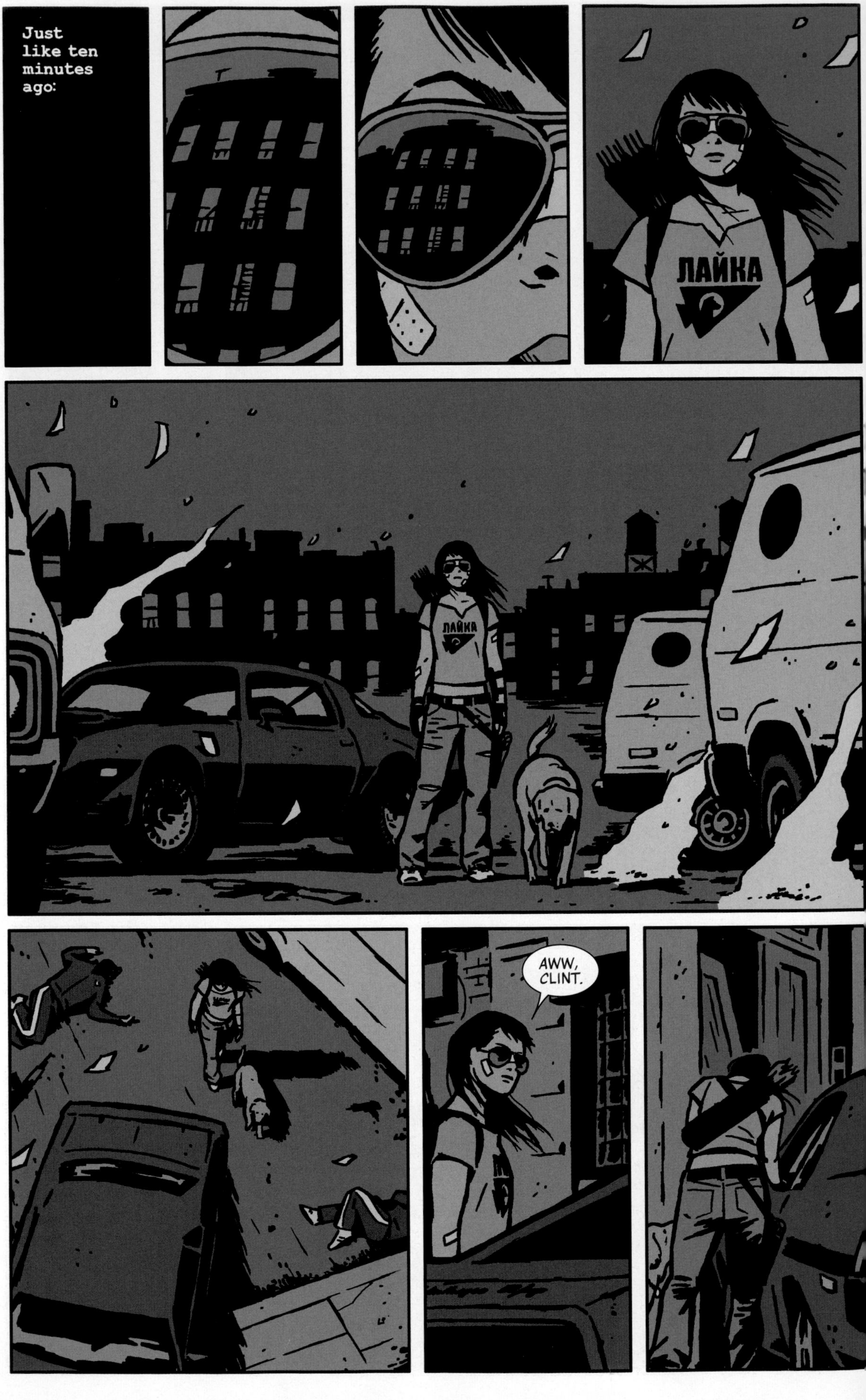
Just like ten minutes ago:
ЛАЙКА
ЛАЙКА
AWW, CLINT.

AIMEE?

STILL WITH US, KID?

UHN. HEYYYY, HAWKEYE. WELCOME HOME.

WE BEAT THE BAD GUYS YET?

FIXIN' TO.

OOF.

LIFT WITH *BACK*, BRO.

BRO, LOOK AT ALL THIS CRAP, BRO.

NEED DANG *DYNAMITE*--

TAP

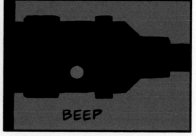

BEEP

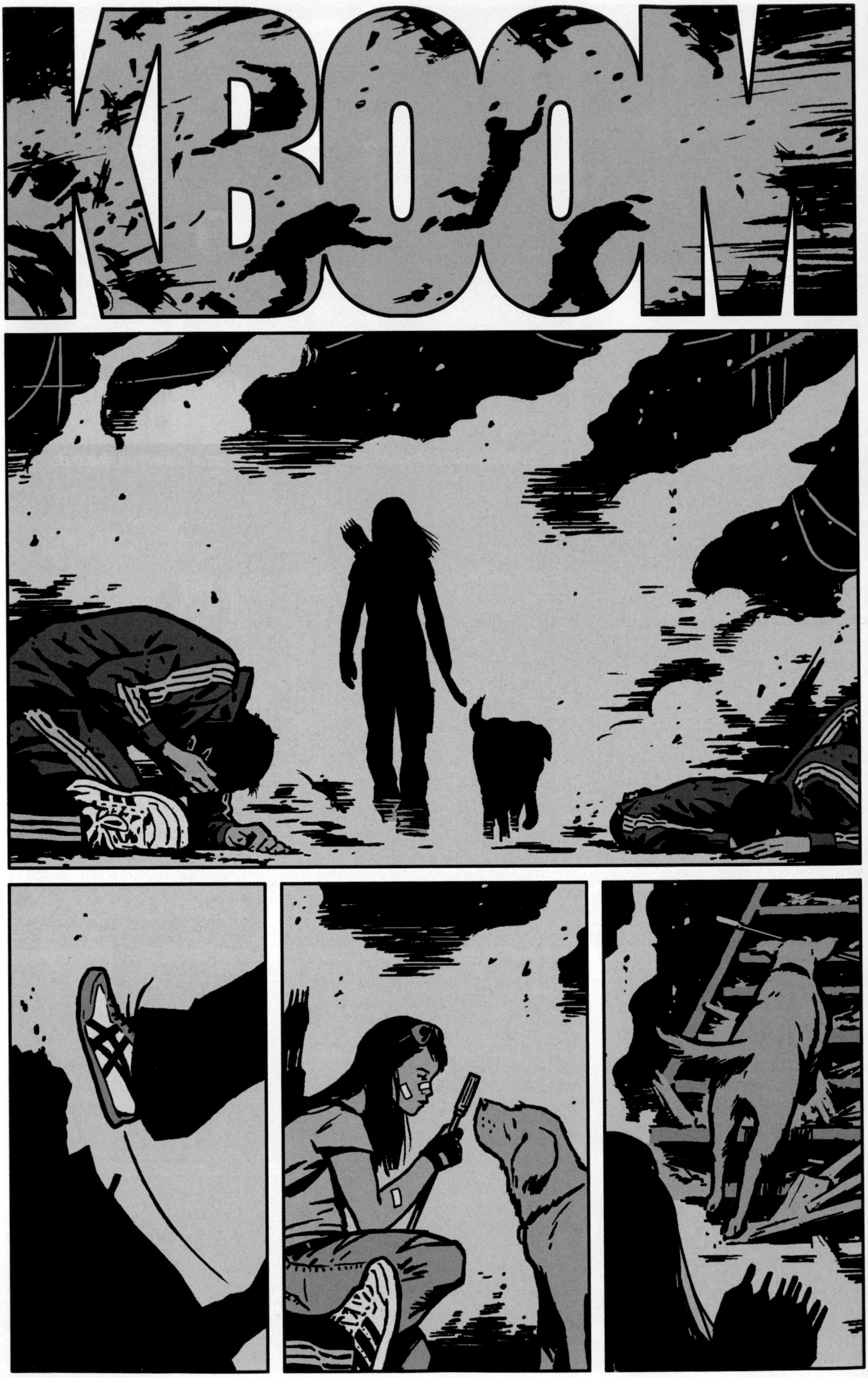
KBOOM

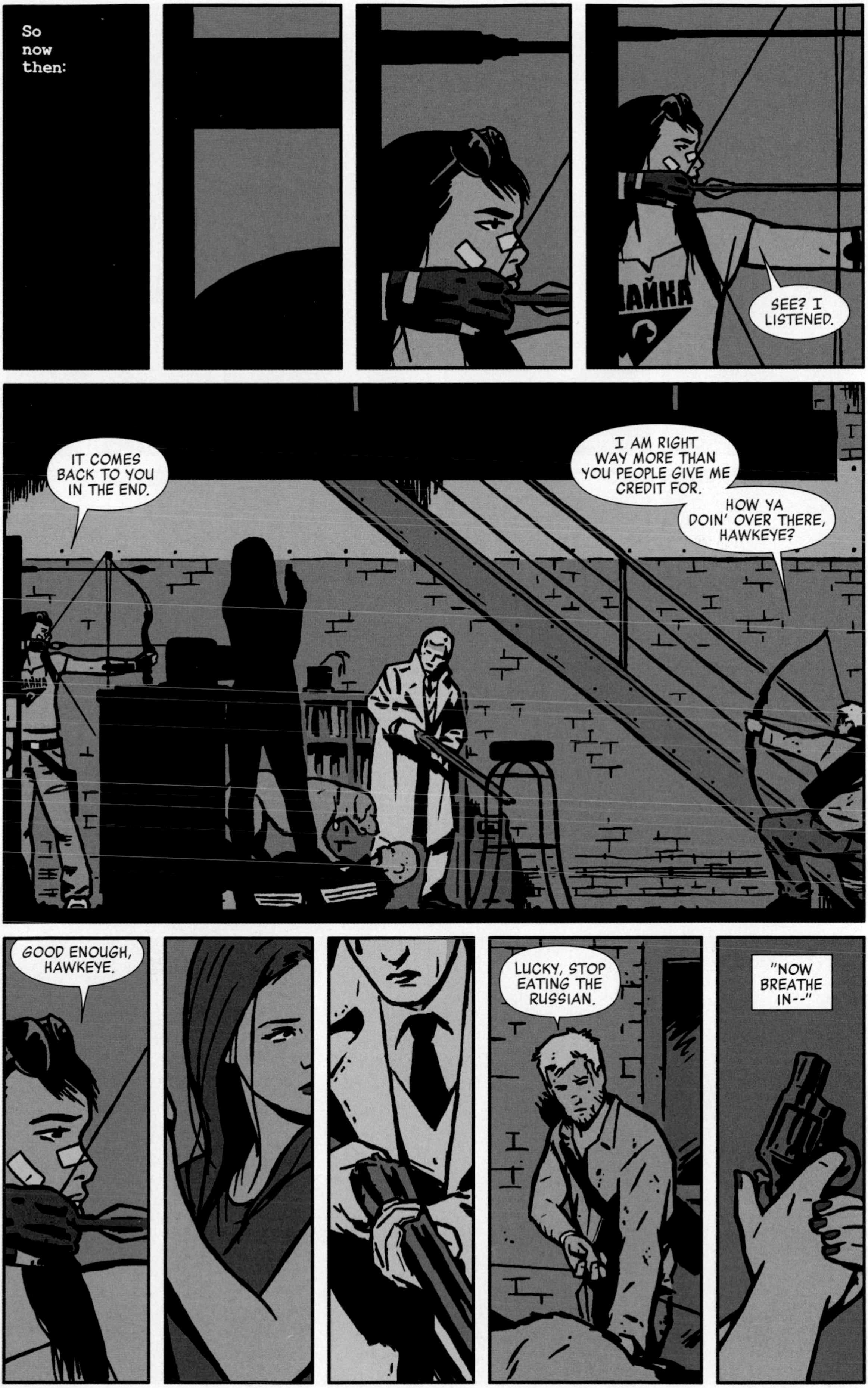
So now then:
SEE? I LISTENED.
IT COMES BACK TO YOU IN THE END.
I AM RIGHT WAY MORE THAN YOU PEOPLE GIVE ME CREDIT FOR.
HOW YA DOIN' OVER THERE, HAWKEYE?
GOOD ENOUGH, HAWKEYE.
LUCKY, STOP EATING THE RUSSIAN.
"NOW BREATHE IN--"

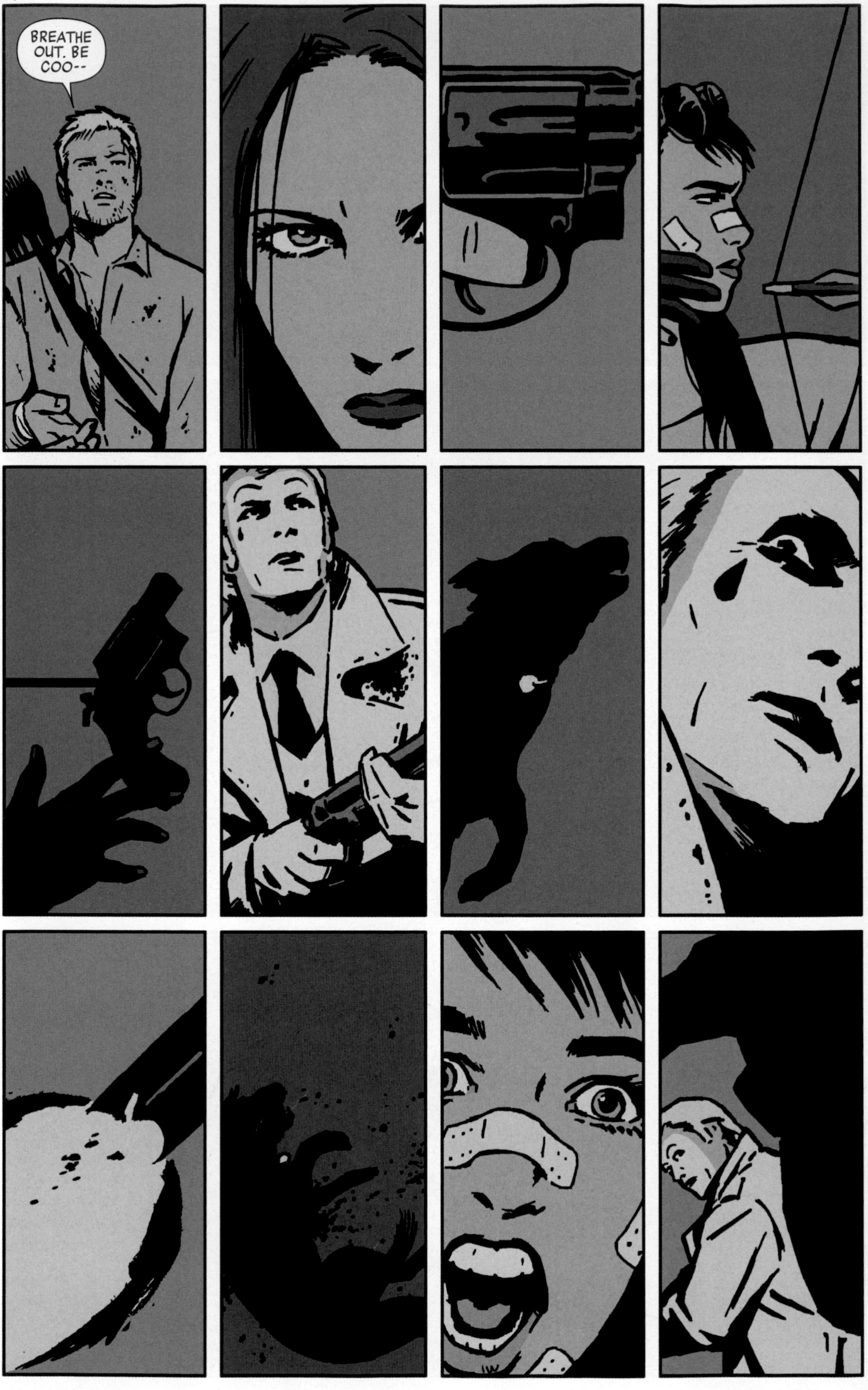
BREATHE OUT. BE COO--

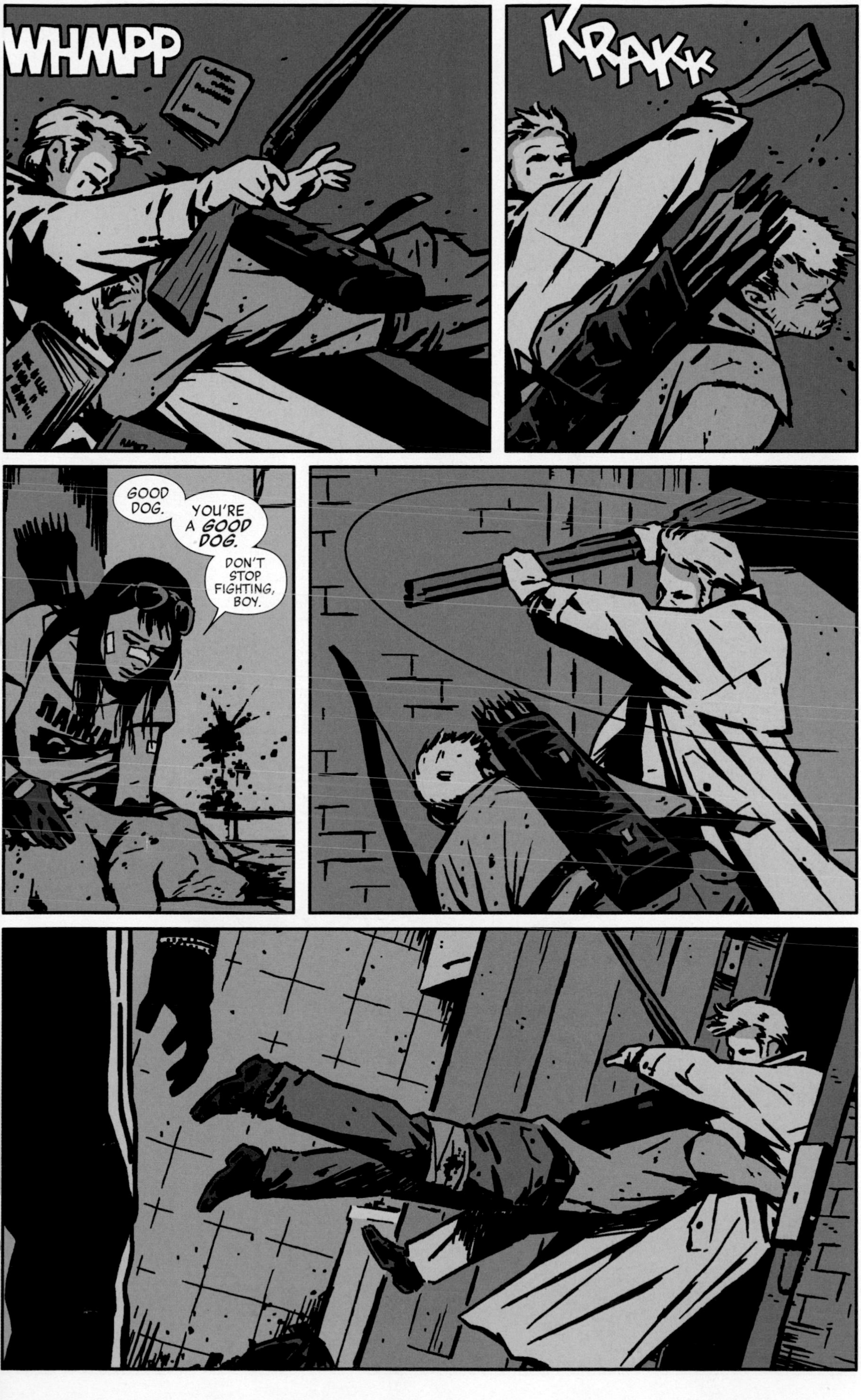
WHMPP
KRAKK
GOOD DOG.
YOU'RE A GOOD DOG.
DON'T STOP FIGHTING, BOY.

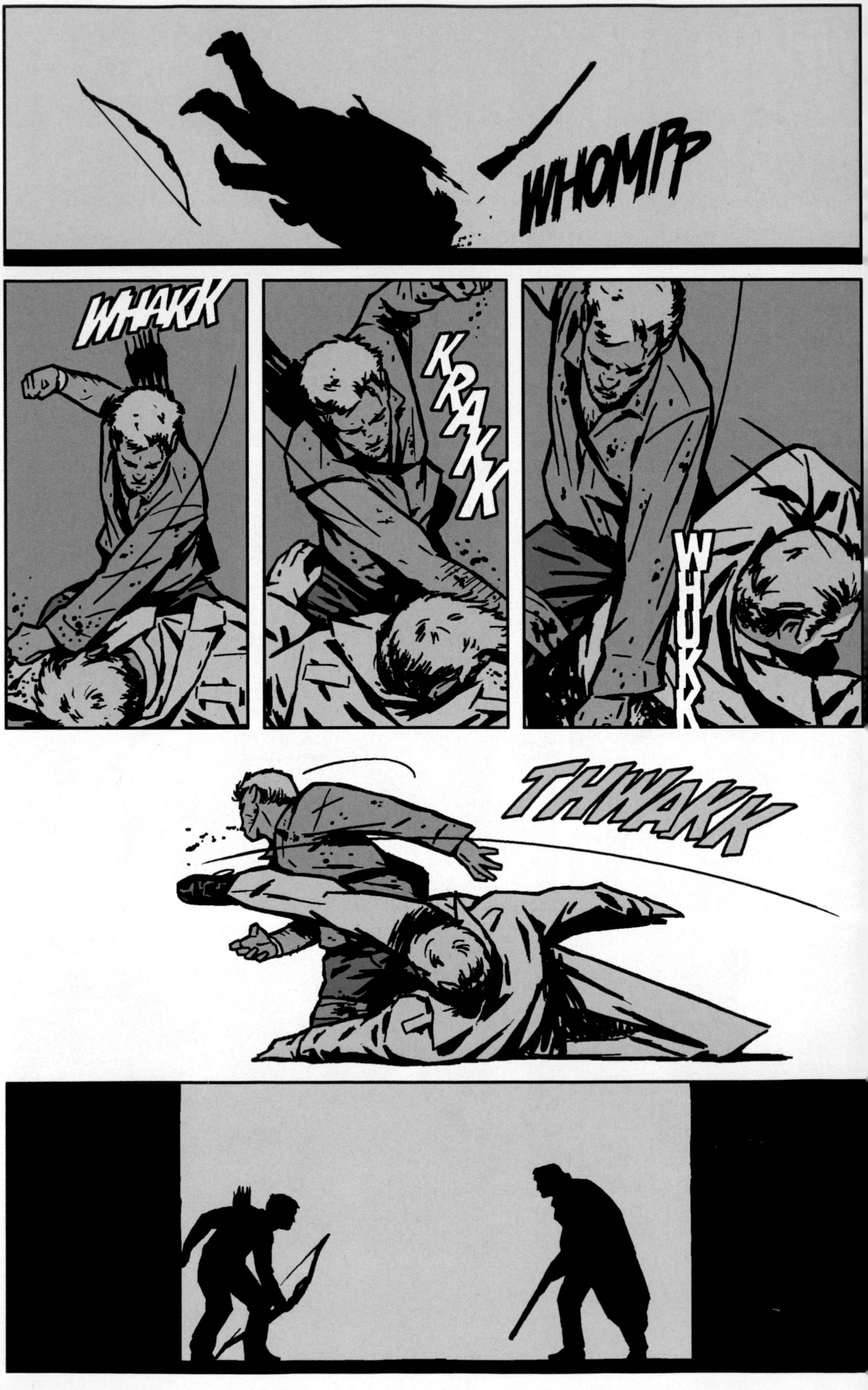
WHOMPP
WHAKK
KRAKK
WHUKK
THWAKK

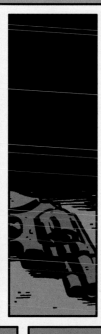

BLINK. AND I SHOOT.

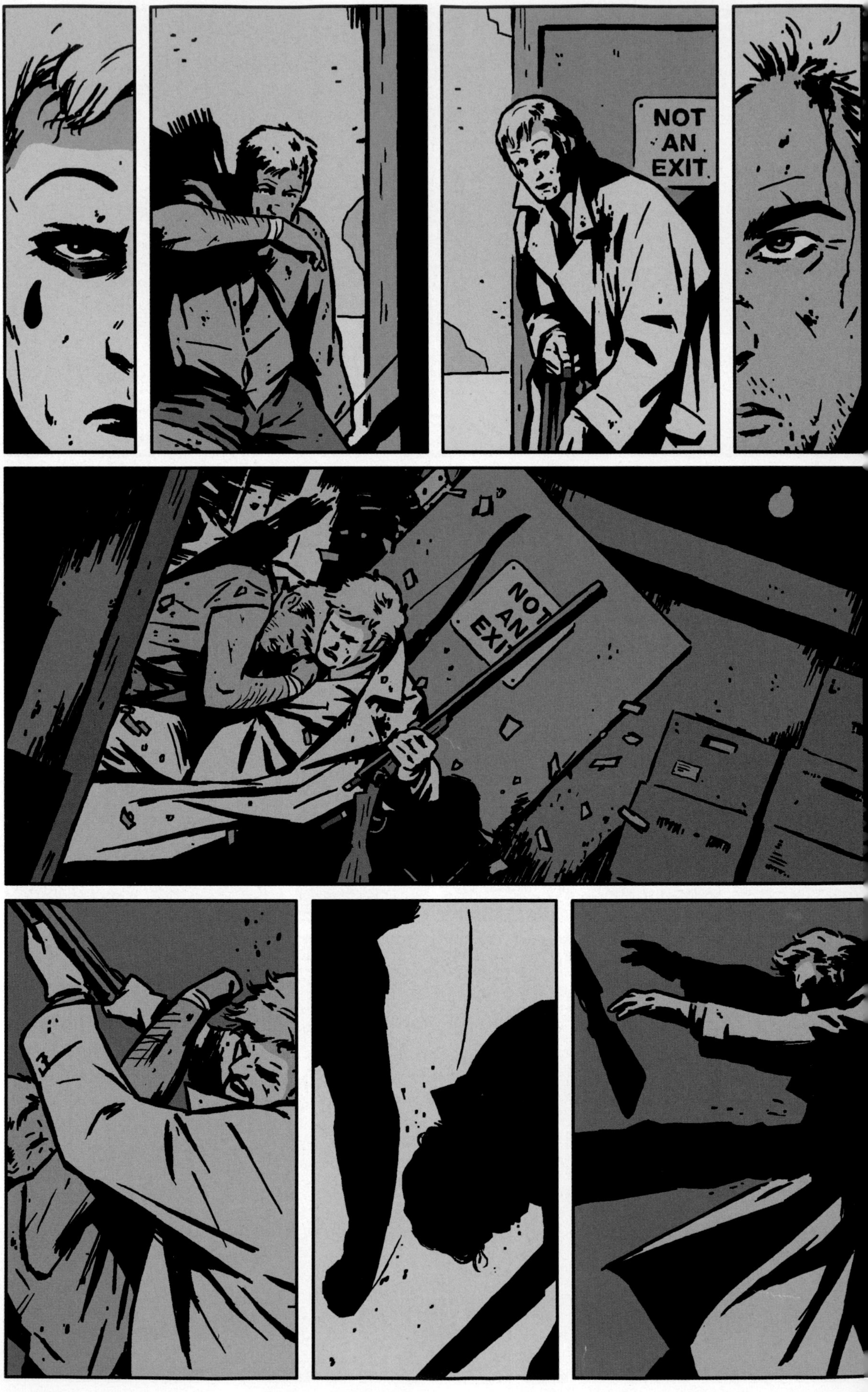
NOT
AN
EXIT

KEEP TRYING TO THINK WHY I SHOULDN'T DO IT.
AND?
AND I'M NOT LIKE YOU.
1
2
TOO BAD.
BLAM

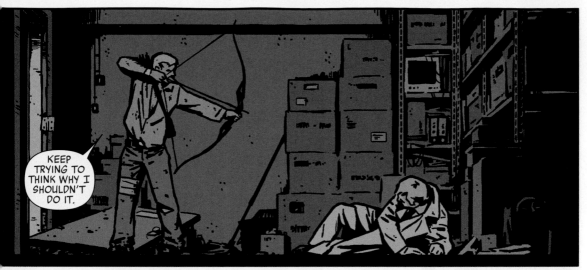

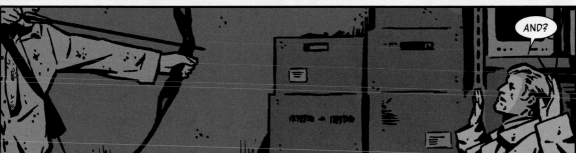

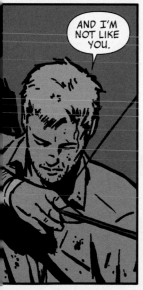

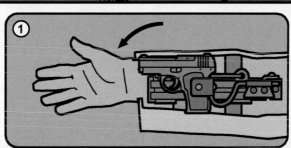

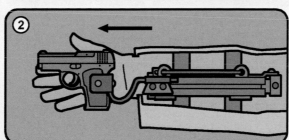

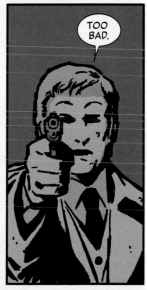

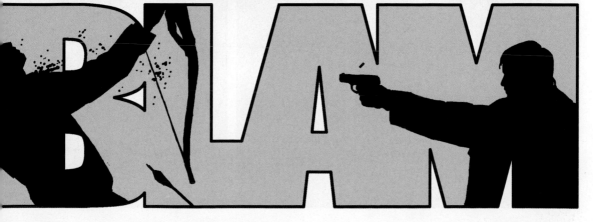

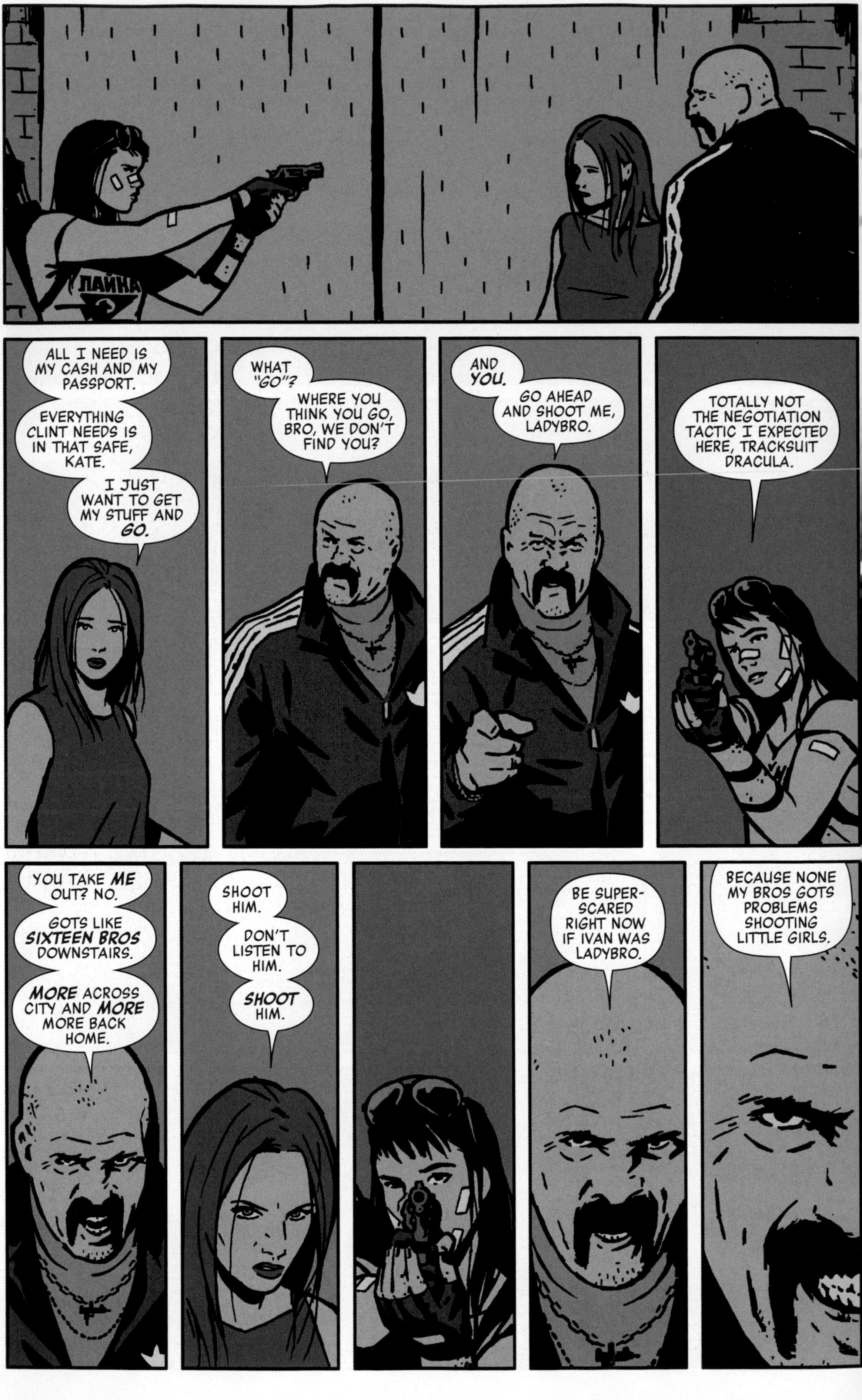
ЛАЙКА
ALL I NEED IS MY CASH AND MY PASSPORT.
EVERYTHING CLINT NEEDS IS IN THAT SAFE, KATE.
I JUST WANT TO GET MY STUFF AND *GO.*
WHAT *"GO"?*
WHERE YOU THINK YOU GO, BRO, WE DON'T FIND YOU?
AND *YOU.*
GO AHEAD AND SHOOT ME, LADYBRO.
TOTALLY NOT THE NEGOTIATION TACTIC I EXPECTED HERE, TRACKSUIT DRACULA.
YOU TAKE *ME* OUT? NO.
GOTS LIKE ***SIXTEEN BROS*** DOWNSTAIRS.
MORE ACROSS CITY AND ***MORE*** MORE BACK HOME.
SHOOT HIM.
DON'T LISTEN TO HIM.
SHOOT HIM.
BE SUPER-SCARED RIGHT NOW IF IVAN WAS LADYBRO.
BECAUSE NONE MY BROS GOTS PROBLEMS SHOOTING LITTLE GIRLS.

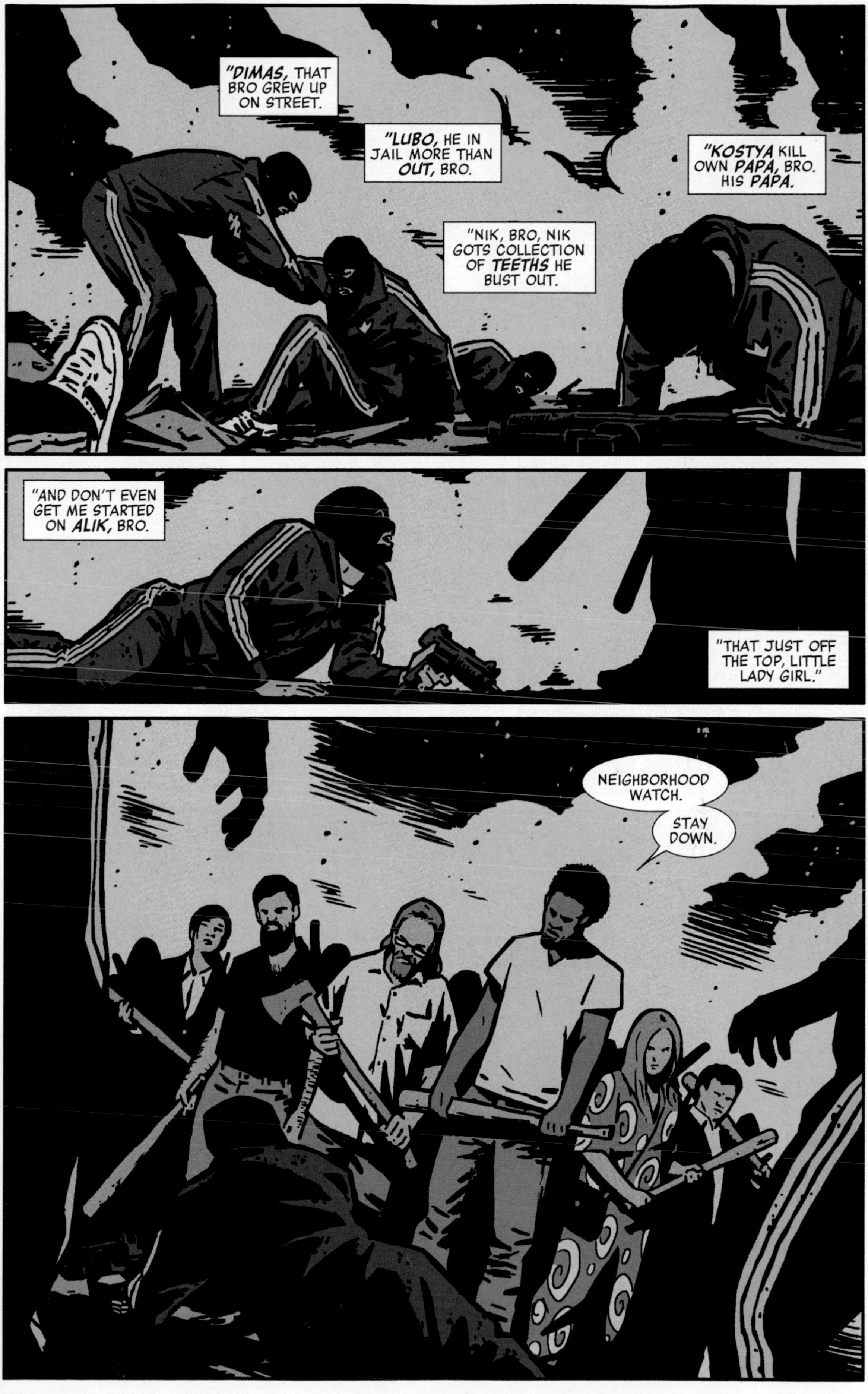
"DIMAS, THAT BRO GREW UP ON STREET.
"LUBO, HE IN JAIL MORE THAN OUT, BRO.
"KOSTYA KILL OWN PAPA, BRO. HIS PAPA.
"NIK, BRO, NIK GOTS COLLECTION OF TEETHS HE BUST OUT.
"AND DON'T EVEN GET ME STARTED ON ALIK, BRO.
"THAT JUST OFF THE TOP, LITTLE LADY GIRL."
NEIGHBORHOOD WATCH.
STAY DOWN.

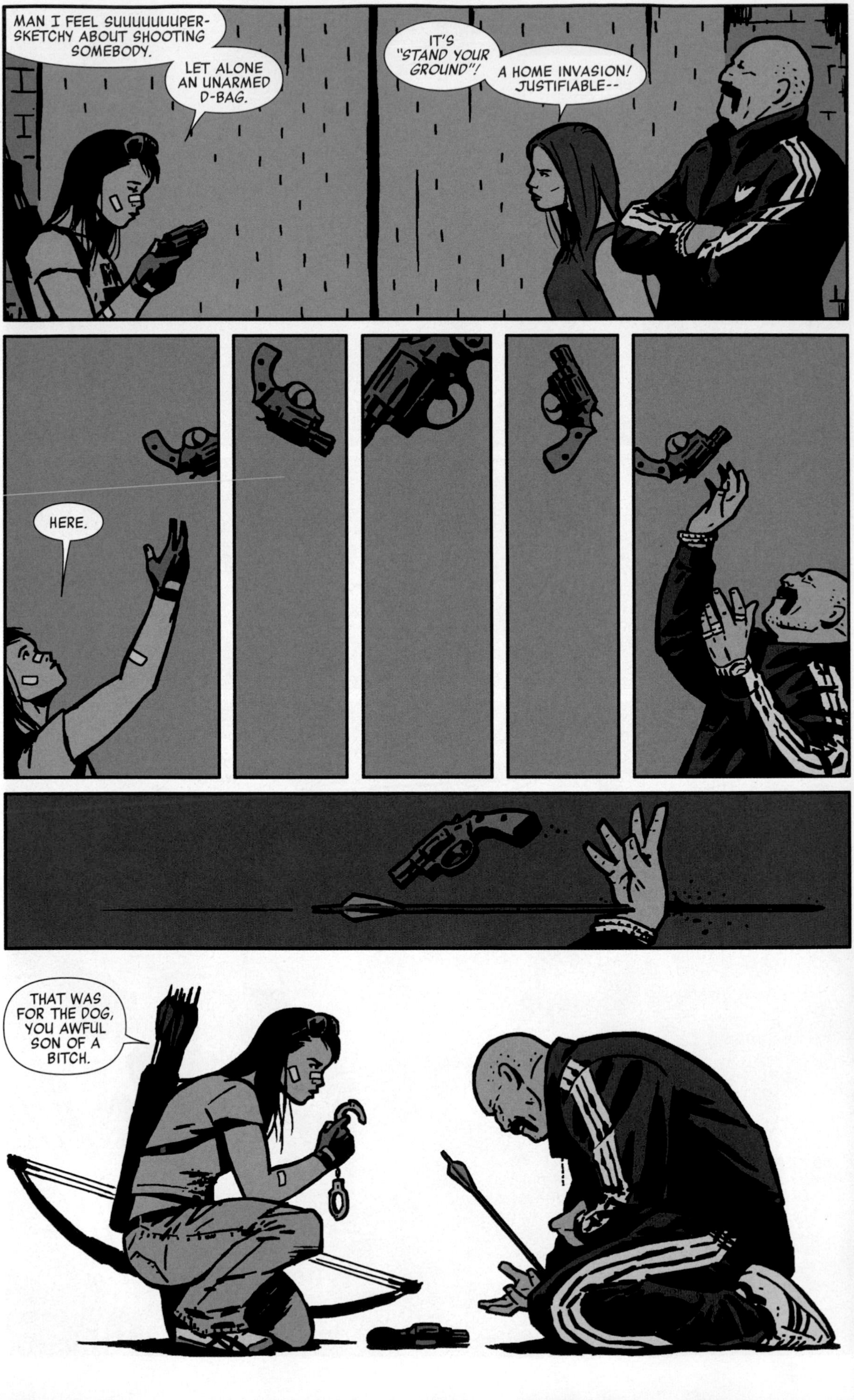
MAN I FEEL SUUUUUUUPER-SKETCHY ABOUT SHOOTING SOMEBODY.
LET ALONE AN UNARMED D-BAG.
IT'S "STAND YOUR GROUND"!
A HOME INVASION! JUSTIFIABLE--
HERE.
THAT WAS FOR THE DOG, YOU AWFUL SON OF A BITCH.

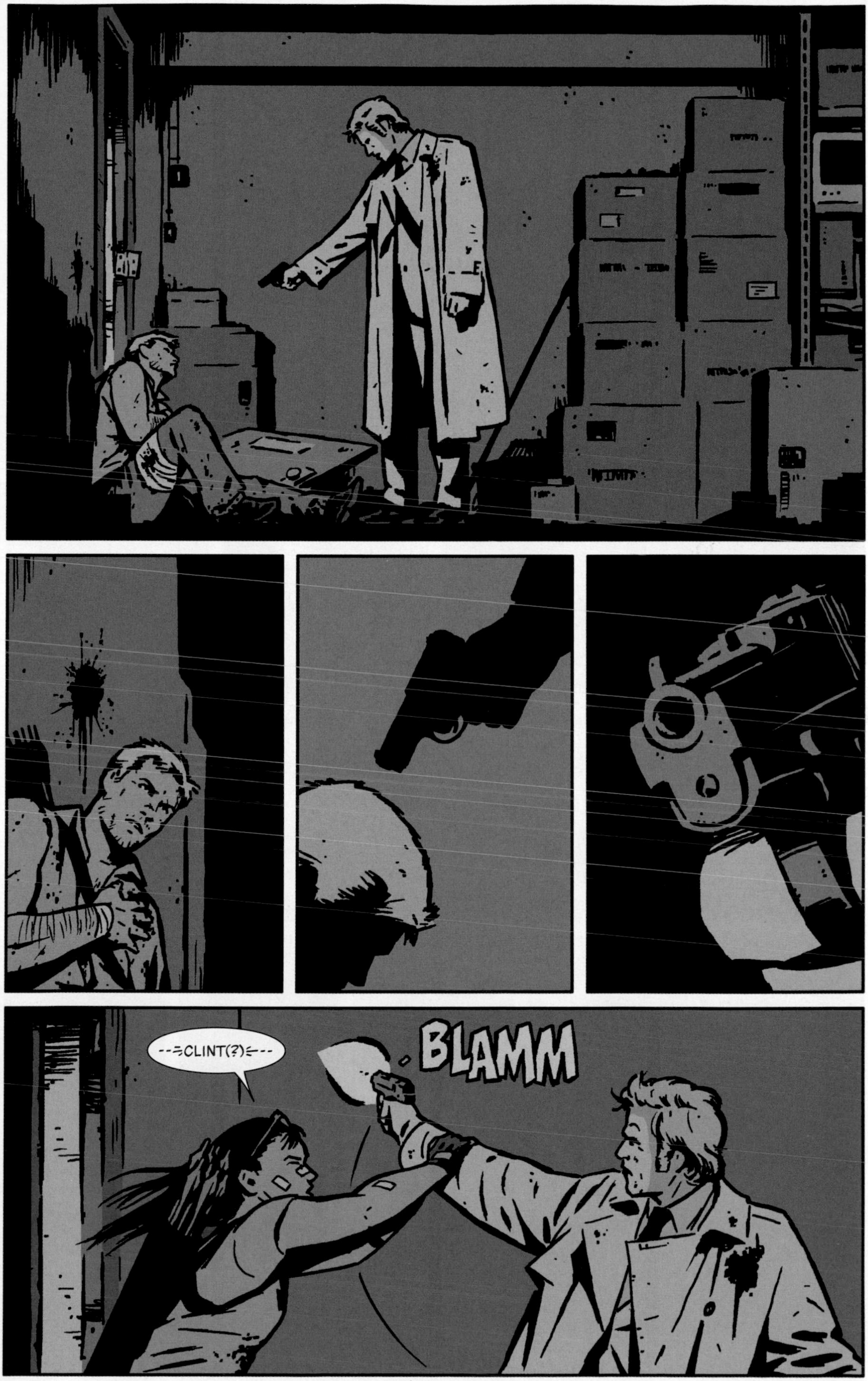
--CLINT(?)---
BLAMM

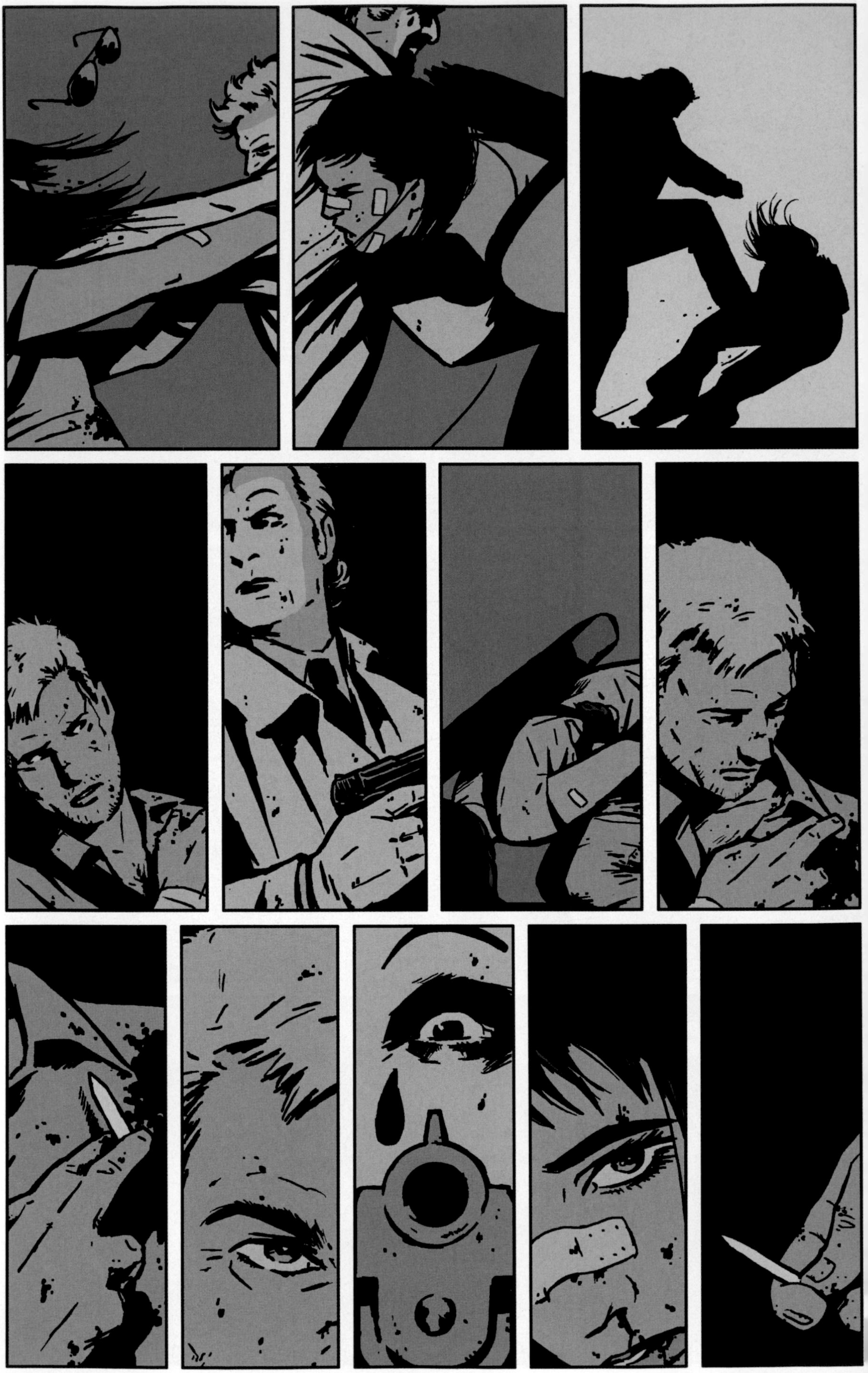

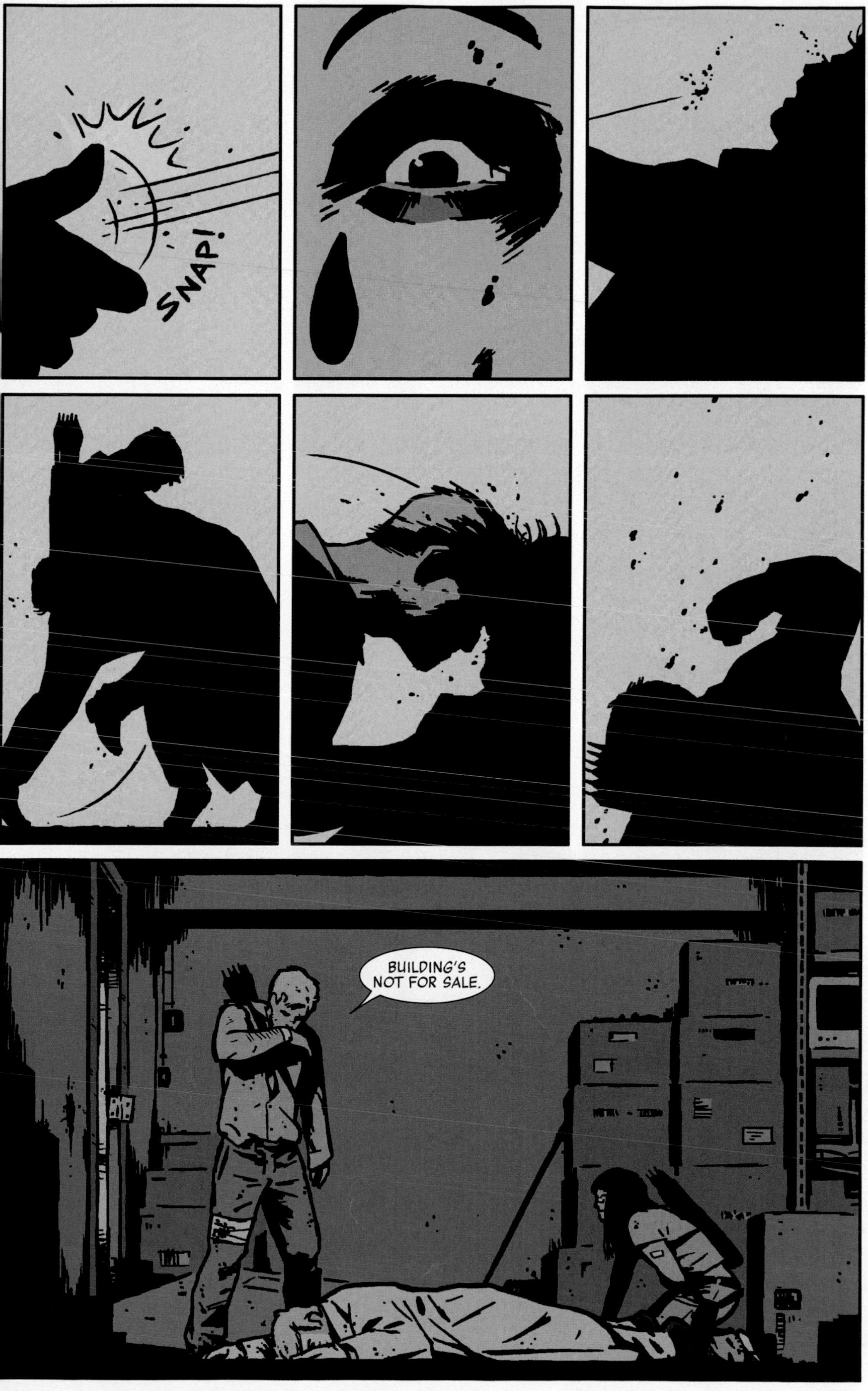
SNAP!
BUILDING'S NOT FOR SALE.

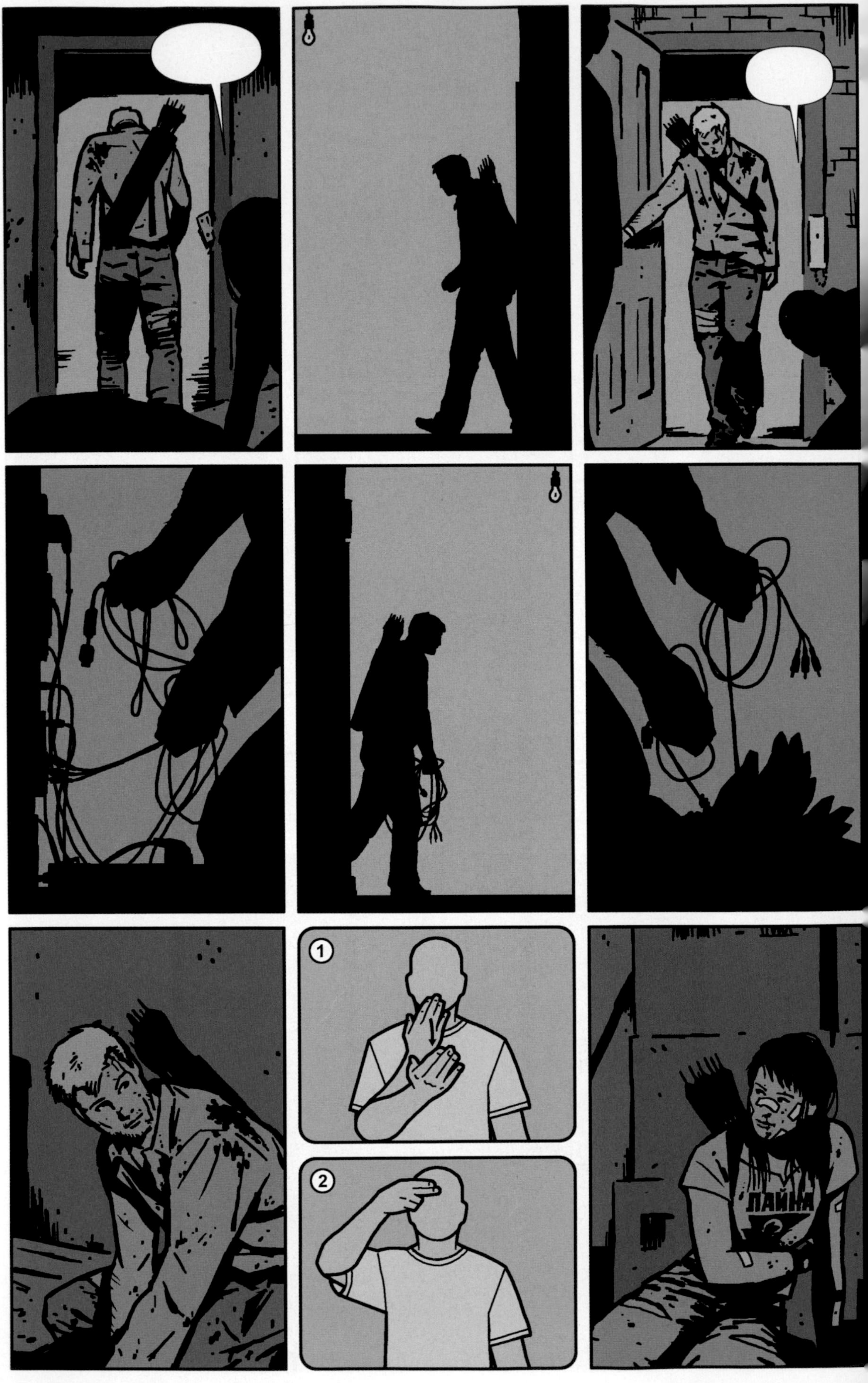
1
2
ЛАЙКА

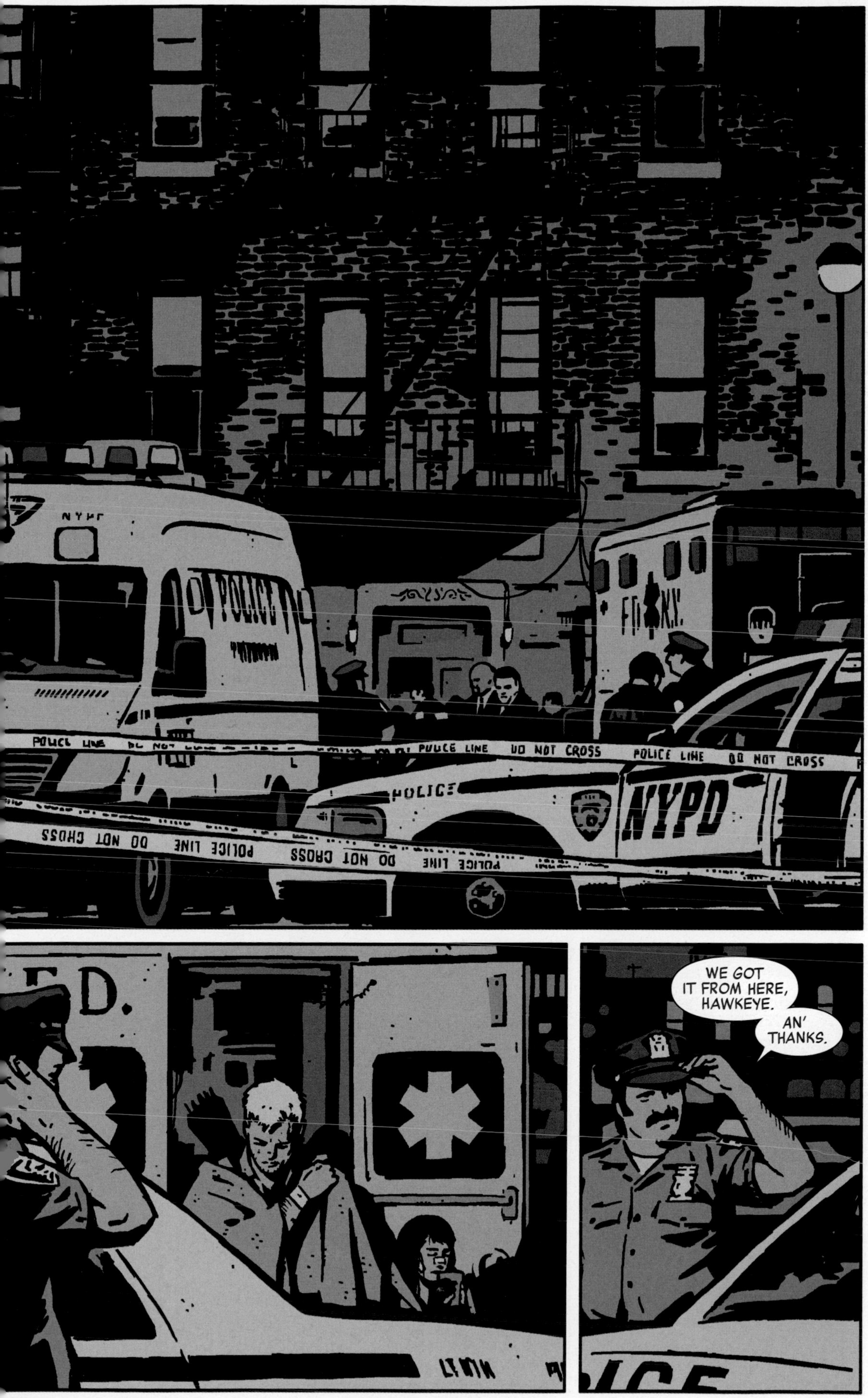
POLICE LINE DO NOT CROSS
NYPD
POLICE
WE GOT IT FROM HERE, HAWKEYE.
AN' THANKS.

But then:

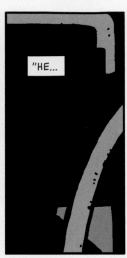

"HE...

"...HE WAS--

"--I SWEAR HE WAS RIGHT HERE."

AFTER YOU WENT BACK DOWN, HE STARTED MOVIN' AGAIN.

HE UNTIED ME.

SO THEN WHAT HAPPENED?

WELL I FIGURED HE WAS OFF TO HELP YOU.

I'DA BET ALL MY MONEY HE--

--MONEY.

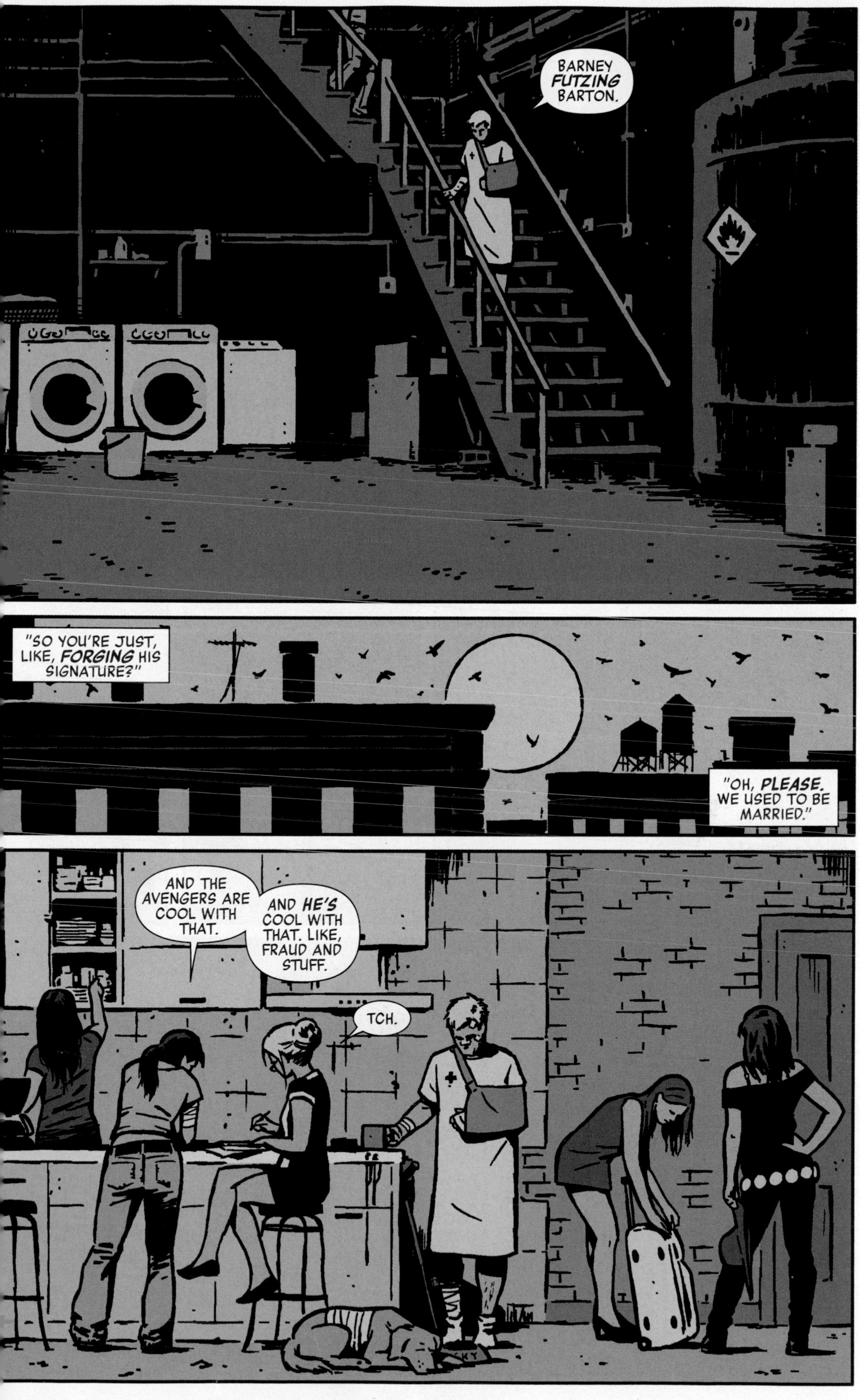
BARNEY FUTZING BARTON.
"SO YOU'RE JUST, LIKE, FORGING HIS SIGNATURE?"
"OH, PLEASE. WE USED TO BE MARRIED."
AND THE AVENGERS ARE COOL WITH THAT.
AND HE'S COOL WITH THAT. LIKE, FRAUD AND STUFF.
TCH.

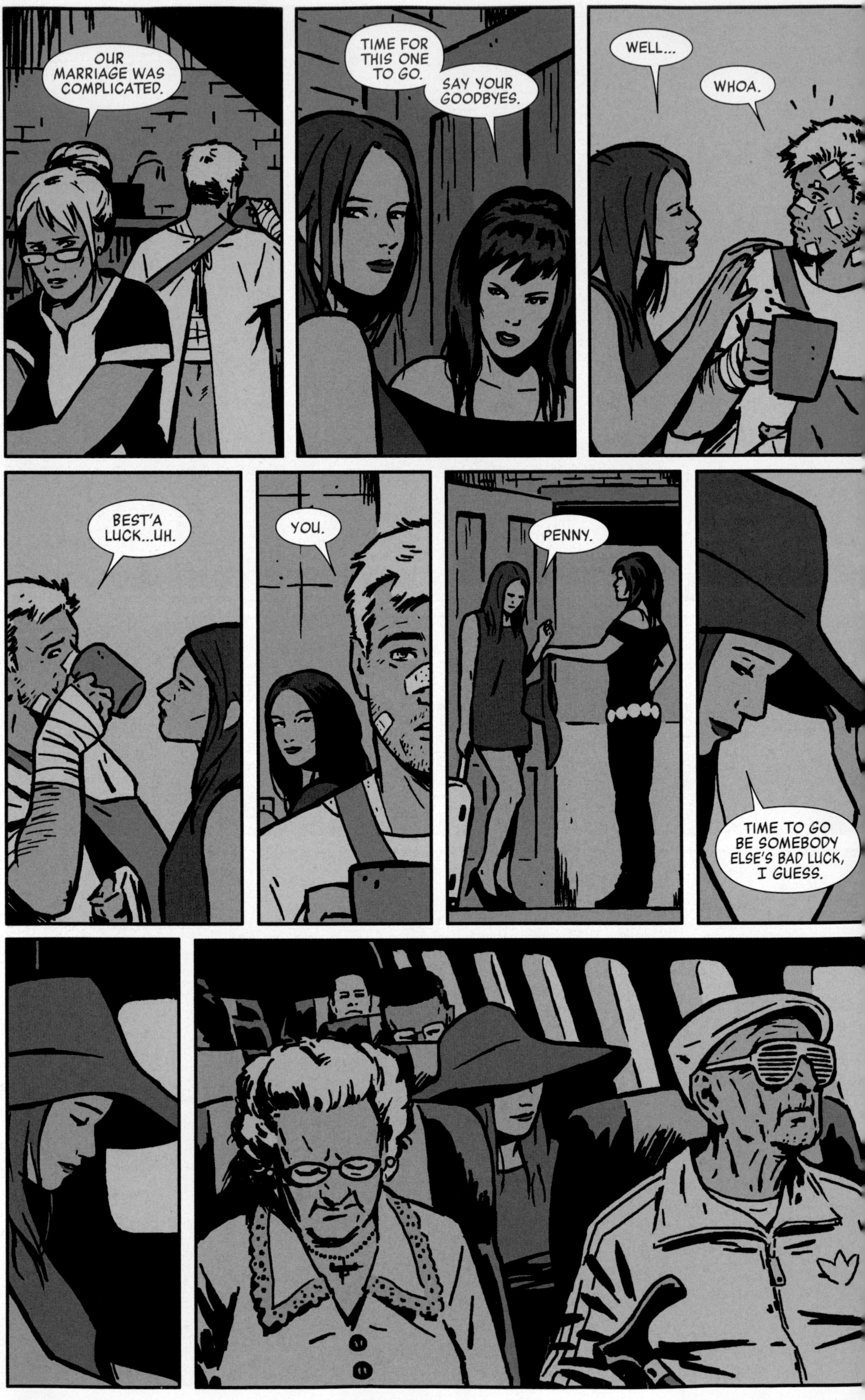
OUR MARRIAGE WAS COMPLICATED.
TIME FOR THIS ONE TO GO.
SAY YOUR GOODBYES.
WELL...
WHOA.
BEST'A LUCK...UH.
YOU.
PENNY.
TIME TO GO BE SOMEBODY ELSE'S BAD LUCK, I GUESS.

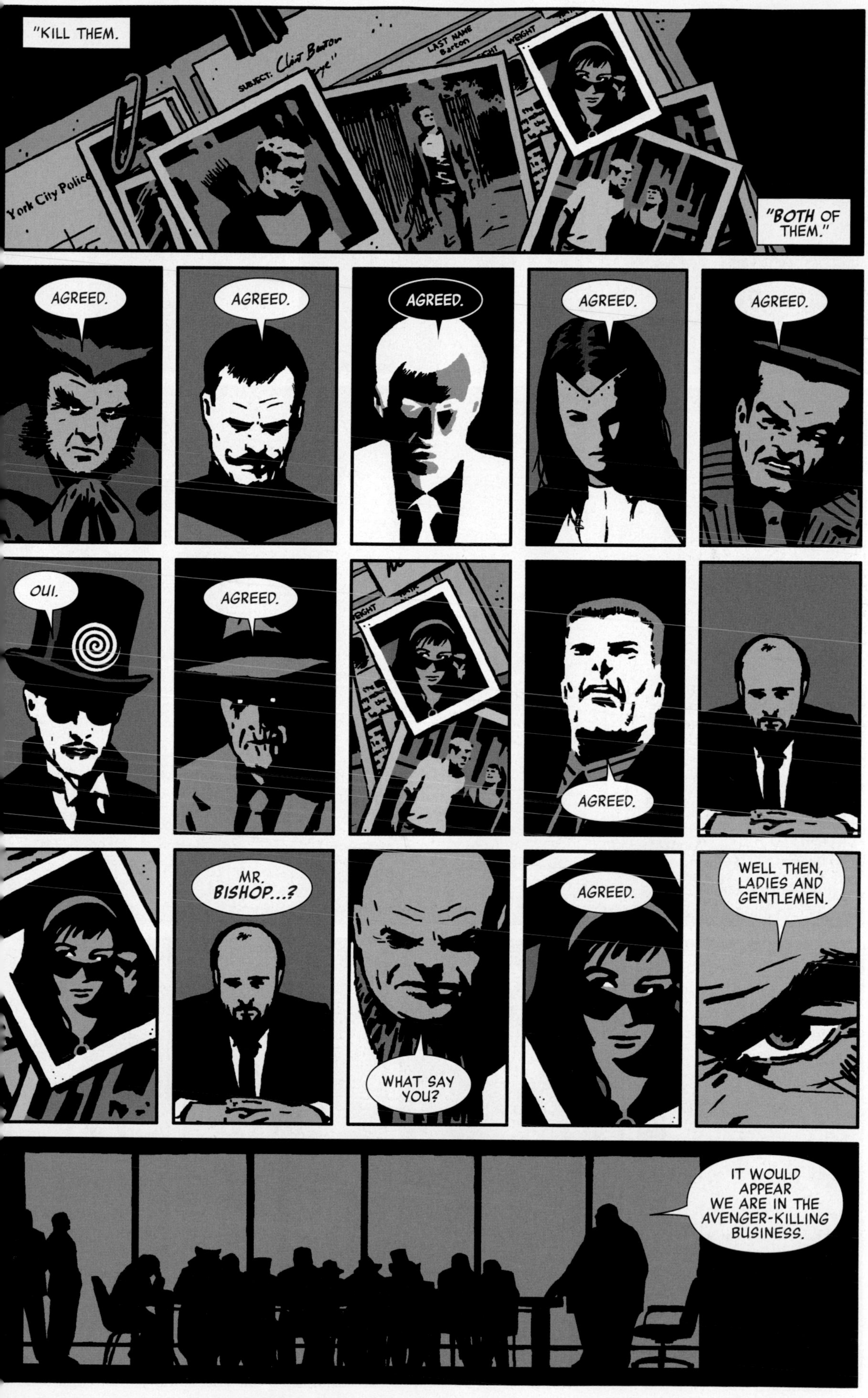
"KILL THEM.
LAST NAME
Barton
WEIGHT
York City Police
"BOTH OF THEM."
AGREED.
AGREED.
AGREED.
AGREED.
AGREED.
OUI.
AGREED.
AGREED.
MR. BISHOP...?
WHAT SAY YOU?
AGREED.
WELL THEN, LADIES AND GENTLEMEN.
IT WOULD APPEAR WE ARE IN THE AVENGER-KILLING BUSINESS.

And THEN:

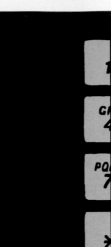 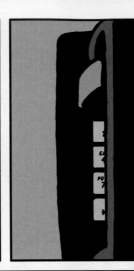 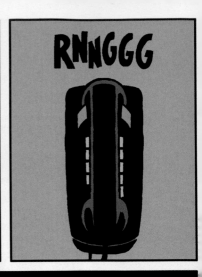

RNNGGG

RNNGGG

UH... CAP?

GUESS WHAT.

BARNEY.

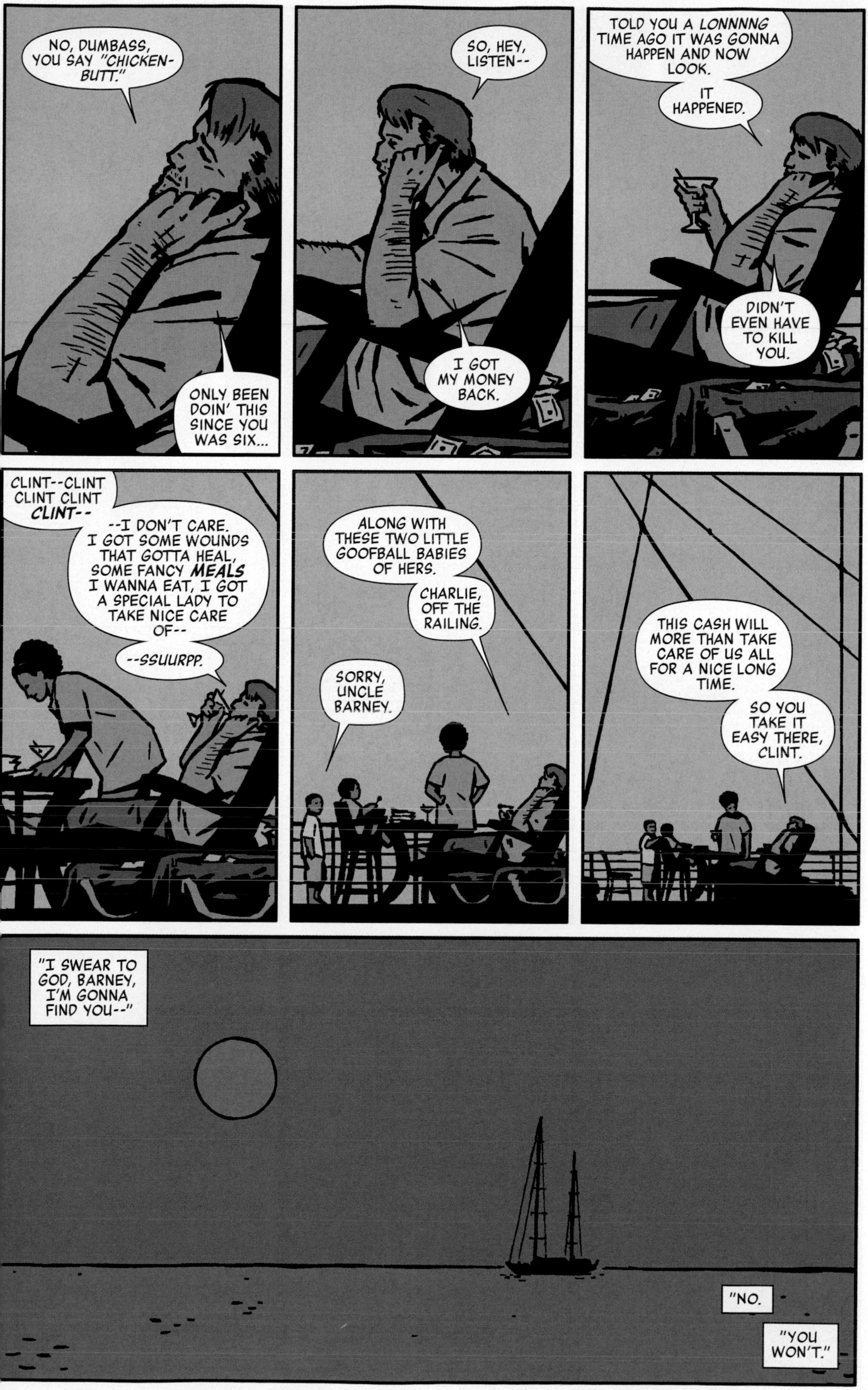
NO, DUMBASS, YOU SAY "CHICKEN-BUTT."
ONLY BEEN DOIN' THIS SINCE YOU WAS SIX...
SO, HEY, LISTEN--
I GOT MY MONEY BACK.
TOLD YOU A LONNNNG TIME AGO IT WAS GONNA HAPPEN AND NOW LOOK.
IT HAPPENED.
DIDN'T EVEN HAVE TO KILL YOU.
CLINT--CLINT CLINT CLINT CLINT--
--I DON'T CARE. I GOT SOME WOUNDS THAT GOTTA HEAL, SOME FANCY MEALS I WANNA EAT, I GOT A SPECIAL LADY TO TAKE NICE CARE OF--
--SSUURPP.
ALONG WITH THESE TWO LITTLE GOOFBALL BABIES OF HERS.
CHARLIE, OFF THE RAILING.
SORRY, UNCLE BARNEY.
THIS CASH WILL MORE THAN TAKE CARE OF US ALL FOR A NICE LONG TIME.
SO YOU TAKE IT EASY THERE, CLINT.
"I SWEAR TO GOD, BARNEY, I'M GONNA FIND YOU--"
"NO.
"YOU WON'T."

CLICK

...

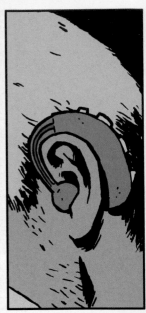

7
8
9
7 8 9 X 9 8 7
9
8
7

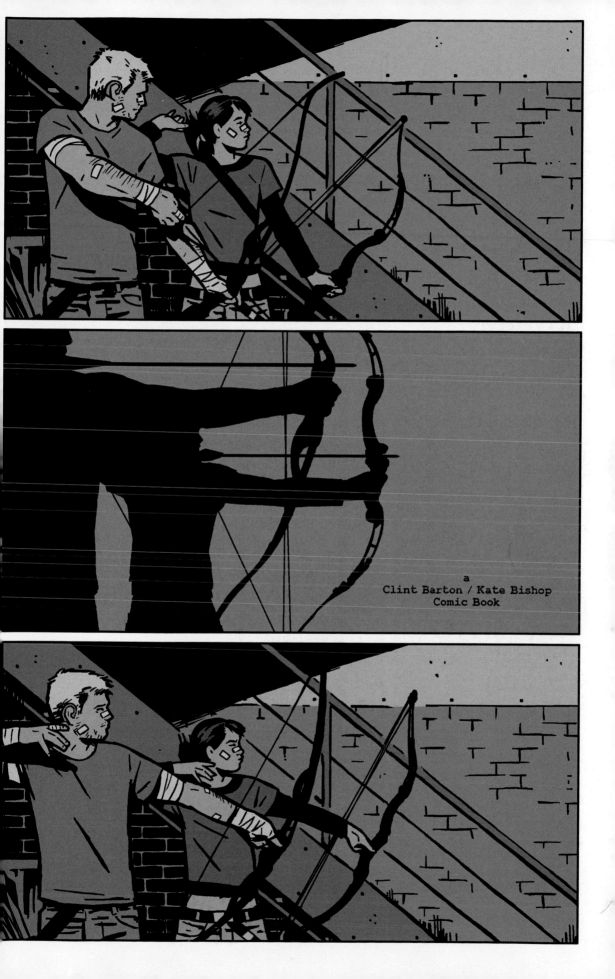

a
Clint Barton / Kate Bishop
Comic Book

by
Matt Fraction & David Aja

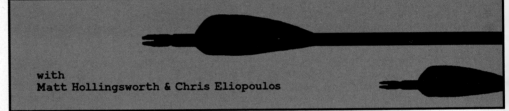

with
Matt Hollingsworth & Chris Eliopoulos

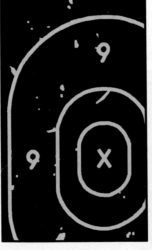

End.